(MY) LIFE'S OPERA

(MY) LIFE'S OPERA

Adrea Adams

Triple A Book Publishing
Oakland, California

(MY) LIFE'S OPERA

Published by:
Triple A Book Publishing
P. O. Box 20747
Oakland, CA 94620
(510) 206-9108
adreaadams@aol.com

Adrea Adams, Publisher
Yvonne Rose / www.QualityPress.Info, Book Packager

ALL RIGHTS RESERVED
This book or parts thereof may not be reproduced in any form, stored in a retrieval system, or transmitted in any form by any means – electronic, mechanical, photographic, (photocopying, recording, or otherwise) – without prior written permission by the publisher, except as provided by the United States of America copyright law.

Printed in the United States of America

Copyright © 2017 by Adrea A. Adams
ISBN #: 978-0-692-87929-0
Library of Congress Control Number: 2017908109

Dedication

My memoir, *Life's Opera* is dedicated to the memory of my composers and producers, *Melvin S. Adams, Sr. and *Carletha M. Adams, and my greatest source of inspiration, my dearest friend, mentor, and confidante, Henry A. Paige, my stone mountain, who sustains me constantly and consistently builds me up.

*September, 2008 brought honor and recognition of her composers and producers when Adrea Adams was inducted into The 2008 West Virginia All Black Schools Sports and Academic Hall Of Fame and received the Vanguard Legacy Honors Award, West Virginia State School for Deaf and Blind, Institute, WV.

"This is a story about life, mostly about my life and oh, people, I want to share it with you. If in some way, I can help someone, maybe someone is lost and needs to see the light. Listen people, about a story of *Life's Opera*."

Courtesy, Marvin Gaye –
Posthumously released on album
"Dream of a Lifetime"

My Life's Opera

Table of Contents

Presented in Three Acts, the Fourth Act is still in performance

Dedication i

Prelude: vi

The Why of (My) Life's Opera vi

ACT I 1

Dedication to My Father.. 2
Homestead Days 3
For Olin (My Stepfather) MY HERO MY JAZZ MAN 5
Mothers – Side A 6
Gifts 13
Bobby and Felicia on the Knoll 17
I am a Negro Soy Angelito Negro 22
Earliest Recollections 25
Some Childhood Memories 28
Bitten 32
HATTIE and the Puppy 35
The Preacher's Son 38
Bombon dulce despedazar Candy Tears................................... 43
Angie's Magical Lamp... 44
Shattering Historical Moments (A Chronology)....................... 48

ACT II 79

- Mothers – Side B 80
- Fortification of my Inner Conscience 85
- My Most, Best Three 99
- War Interrupted What Could Have Been 101
- Some College Days 104
- The Road Ahead – Quiet Influences 109
- "Rex and the Surprise" 111
- A Retelling with Fictitious Names, except Rex 12-11-2012 .. 111
- Rolling Good Times 114
- Modeling with Warren 118
- Senegalese Sun 122
- Code Name: Tony King 129
- Humming Birds Do Fly 135
- Acting (Alone) 139
- Glad I Asked 150
- Black Henry 155
- Moments in Time The Best Days 156
- *History (Firsts) 162
- A Continuation of Moments in Time 162
- Careers 171
- Sangria Sound Bites 185

ACT III ... 207

- Violins ... 208
- Thaw ... 209
- Dialogue with Myself Some Inner Workings ... 209
- Smiles ... 212
- Voices ... 215
- Inside my Heart ... 219
- Diagnosis FMD ... 230
- A Thank-You Blanket ... 259
- Lee Malik (Mine King) ... 263
- The Transition that got Away ... 267
- Thirteen Days ... 270
- ~Shahada of Adrea Adams~ ... 281
- Coming Out of the Dark ... 285
- For My Mother A Song Unsung ... 287
- Reclaiming my Identity ... 290
- In Memoriam ... 299
- I Fill Better ... 323
- About the Author ... 325

Prelude:

The Why of (My) Life's Opera

The recently strained dynamics of my individualism broadcast the emergence of the need to quench my hunger towards self-actualization, the pyramidal height of chronic need of human fulfillment. This work represents a pinnacle acquired because I have purposely strengthened the foundations upon which my autobiography, (My) *Life's Opera* presents itself. My strengthening and rejuvenation process is ongoing, but I gave myself, associated environments, persons, and unfolding events, proper pause and observatory analysis before the undertaking of this most engagingly cathartic and cleansing process.

I believed I had a book in me worthy of distinctive attention and I trust you will believe the same. (My) *Life's Opera* holds back a lot; it is not a tell-all; far from it. Rather it is representative of a spliced blend of defining instances. I must trust that my revelations, experiences, and shared responses can and do, in some small way, lend help to others similarly affected. In whole truth, I wrote my memoir for lasting dimensions of enhanced health.

ACT I

Dedication to My Father

West Virginia born and bred, a handsome, sprig curly haired, blue-eyed man,

My father

Could do the hambone and sing a country tune

A hardworking, tractor-driving dad

A family man, a joke-telling man

An own your own home kind of man

A Sunday "pancake breakfast" dad

A walk to the bus for church with a daughter in each hand dad

My Father

Swivel stool drugstore ice cream treats for <u>his girls</u>

A dime saving father

He'd play ad infinitum Solitaire

Sober and somber

My father

I loved him,

"Your old man" is how he referred to himself on my *Phonemate*

Only saw him cry once, at his mother's funeral as I sat to his left

I miss him

My Father

Homestead Days

The curvaceous, lush slopes of Philippi and Buckhannon, West Virginia in all their idiosyncratic glory are staples of my mind. Inherent in the ridges are a deep history of once self-segregated peoples; because of their mixed racial ethnicities (former and not so slaves, black and red, and free whites). My father's origins were of this Appalachian group, some atop Chestnut Ridge. My father was a farm boy on a sprawling stretch of land to which I was introduced as a toddler, after escort and delivery by my father via Greyhound through outskirts of Ohio's corn fields, beef, and dairy farms. I loved summers spent with my beautifully sweet fraternal aunts, Rose and Kathleen and their respective offspring, my cousins.

Aunt Rose lived in the house my father was born in. In the 60s, the floors were still stripped boards, no indoor plumbing; we used a large tomato can to urinate in, in the dark of night; rather than to traipse up the back yard to the solitary gray planked 'outhouse'. Interior design included a wood-burning stove, a monstrous thing, on which Aunt Rose cooked fresh snapped neck, drained, and plucked home fed (from just outside the kitchen door) chickens (some messy things). Another of my favorite things prepared by Aunt Rose was oatmeal flavored with sweetened dollops of thick homemade preserves and whips of real 'everybody take turns' churned butter. We 'city kids', my siblings and I, did not drink the warm straight from the cow milk (strained three times through cheese cloth to catch wee pebbles or grass bits), but Brenda and Tommy did. Baths were taken in the kitchen in a large tin tub filled with stove heated water.

Cousins Brenda and Tommy were Aunt Rose's grandchildren; their father, Rose's son, Quentin. We had a pure D ball, romping in the haystacks in the barn, running wild, pumping well water for fresh drinks. Playing with giant frogs, my favorite, putting chicken feed in a found brown medicine bottle with water and then force feeding it to Mickey. I loved cows, still my favorite farm animal. We'd hitch rides "to town" on the bed of anyone's pickup. Once, Quentin showed us how to make beer. I don't remember all the steps, but was enraptured to see foam when salt was sprinkled in the brew; my first non-classroom science lesson, of sorts.

Aunt Kathleen and Uncle Dick, both quiet and reserved, were also very special, but lived in Buckhannon on a huge spread, where I learned to ride horses and what an electrically charged fence was, churned a lot of butter, and made homemade ice cream. Their teen daughter Elaine was one of the prettiest and refined young ladies I'd ever seen. Elaine wore lovely clothes bought in the city; just gorgeous ensembles. I remember one time admiring her as she hummed along to the hit 'Soldier Boy' and I vowed to dress like her when I grew up. I did too; neat skirts at the knee and matching sweaters and bobby socks. I last dressed like this in my office in 1995. I wore a gray A-line skirt, stiffly starched white shirt with gold cuff links, black loafers with white, rolled to the ankle socks. I thought of Elaine all day that day.

I last visited "The Homestead", now an estimated 300 acres with tree lakes, in the early 2000s. I took pictures of the preserved 'outhouse', my father's 'retired' red tractor, all my aunts, uncles, and cousins, and I slumbered in the down of a 'country' so calm, embracing Aunt Kathleen's home, longing to hear my father's voice calling the cows in from the fields.

For Olin (My Stepfather) MY HERO MY JAZZ MAN

Did you know, you're one of my heroes
One of my warriors
My jazz man, my beloved dad
My hero
My jazz man
So much you've taught me
The Count (Basie), Davis (Miles)
Nina (Simone)
So much more, you taught me
To eat right, to exercise,
To think right,
To do the right things
To love,
To be strong
To never give up the fight
My hero
My jazz man
My dad
My personal philosopher
My hero
My warrior
I love you
Your daughter,

Adrea
4-20-2008

Mothers – Side A

Mothers, in most cultures with which I am familiar are, by and large, the first persons to introduce to a child the human relationships of dependency and that of leader and follower. A child's development and progression is reliant upon the organization, directing and controlling of plans laid by the managing mother.

I do not hold the belief that there is one clear definitive description of the word mother, madre, mere, maman, umm, for the descriptive is related to the culture from which dictates are prescribed, anticipated or expected.

We all lay claim to a unique mother, biological or not. I'll share with the readers a bit of the unique attributes of my mother.

Situational, our mother presented to her four children a devotion and strength unparalleled by many. Our mother contracted a dreadful disease, at three years in 1936, spinal meningitis, possibly due to being allowed to play outside before she was totally recovered from either measles or chicken pox. Symptoms of meningitis appeared one day while my mother was eating lunch or dinner; she began to uncontrollably slide down in her chair and to lean her head to one side. Her mother thought she was playing and didn't think too much of it. But when the "playing" did not subside, her mother drew concern. It is unknown how much time elapsed before her mother realized something was seriously not right. My mother was ultimately taken to a doctor, but it was too late. Mother was blind and irreversibly so, as confirmed by several specialists over the years of her childhood, early adult life, and beyond. A tragic loss for all parties of concern. A precious gift ripped away. I suppose we all lose something along the path of life, just not so early in our travels.

Lee was a 5'1" beauty. Petite in build, fiery in spirit, intelligent, a snazzy dresser, a pretty good dancer, she could shake and groove with the best, could throw down in a bid whist card game. The cards were brailled in the upper corners causing some participants to jokingly remark that she and her blind partners were cheating, especially when they were winning.

I'd venture to wage a bet that most children think their mothers to be the best of mothers. Most mothers are in all probability, the best they know how to be, a woman first, bringing all the positive and yes, negative traits that the innate personality and society /culture/ familial status permits. As my stepfather, Olin, often quips "Women catch hell around the world."

Hell might be too polite an adjective to describe what my mother caught over the span of her 54 years. Mother divorced our father when we four kids were all below the age of 12. Mother never talked a lot about what led to the divorce. I'd say it was most likely due to the fact that my mother and father were, in a sense, mismatched. Mother was more citified, finger popping. Whereas father was a really laid back, quiet-type man, a non-drinking, non-partying, raised on a West Virginia farm homestead man, generally soft spoken, often tired from laborious working kind of man. They had two things in common; they were both strikingly handsome and had met at school in Institute, West Virginia. The school was designed for educating the hearing and sight impaired, of which my father was both. Both parents were fluent in American Sign Language and Braille, the former of which our mother taught to me.

After the divorce was decreed, our father left the house and moved next door and shared a tiny box of a house with our neighbor John, a very portly approaching middle age white man whose body and home had the odor of cats and an odd putrid sweet smell. If you have ever smelled it, you know what I'm talking about. I still have a picture of the four of us kids, taken in John's kitchen. John's kitchen table had a red and white-checkered cloth on it. Ah, the things you remember. That one photo evokes the smell I mention.

Mother is now free to do and be what she wants. It seems that there is always somebody over. Usually, mama's then best friend, Hattie Mae and her then three but soon to be four children. Mother and Hattie had also met at school.

On weekends, especially, it seemed that the music never stopped. All kinds of folks, good and bad came. Every kind, from family members to a few homosexuals and lesbians. Now, my mother was not a swinger of the same persuasion by no stretch of the imagination. I guess these odd sorts, called sissies and bull daggers back then simply found a safe haven to hang out in. Most of these kinds of people remained in the closet with clothes on, zippered and buttoned, but still you knew. Perhaps, my mother because of her blindness and knowing, knew what it felt like to be outcast, ostracized, took some sort of pity on these deemed undesirables and opened her home to them. I also think that these folks and even some of the family members were studying us, my mother and Hattie Mae in particular. Most of them could not believe they could not see at all, nothing, nada and behave as they did. By the latter, I mean keep a clean home, cook, and care for their children, all the things done successfully by sighted mothers.

Fortunately, or not, my mother didn't work outside of the home during our early developmental and formative years.

Mother was really big on education. I could read and write at the age of three. We all had chores and knew how to prepare at least two kinds of meals at ages well before nine or 10. Mother said she wanted us to be able to take care of ourselves, "Just in case you ever have to go to an orphanage. They'll be kinder to you if you can do things for yourself." Those kinds of comments used to scare the beJesus out of me.

We persevered, I marvel at how. Many, too many lean days. We struggled like the dickens. My father had been ordered to remit child support for four kids in the measly sum of $40.00 per month. One good thing, we didn't own a car to maintain. But we suffered because of that. Everything was done on foot or bus. We kids all hated that, but especially my sister and oldest brother, and as we aged resentment associated with childhood lacking welled up. My baby brother and I seemed to have taken most things in stride.

My mother had this thing for moving a lot, which I detest to this day. There didn't seem to be any consideration towards the impact of constant moving on the children, but what could we do but follow our leader? Well in 1979 I was my own leader, I led myself, by myself, to California's Bay Area on March 2nd and gladly and happily remained there until forced to return to Ohio in 2006.

In the by and by, mother expanded her horizons and when I was in 5th grade, my oldest brother being in 8th grade. It was decided that we should attend Catholic school. The three oldest of us four were enrolled in St. Agnes on 79th and Euclid in Cleveland. This was the same school that famed actress Vanessa

Bell Calloway attended. We were actually in the same class. Our teacher was a black woman named Miss Tolbert, a good and pleasant non-nun or Habit wearing teacher. The baby boy attended Bolton Elementary. Mother began taking Medical Terminology classes in the evenings at John Hay High School in partnership or association with the Cleveland Society for the Blind.

Mother successfully completed the course along with her mobility training with the red tipped white cane. Because of pride and safety issues mother rarely walked alone with that cane. She felt the cane just drew attention to her. My sister and I devised a code when walking with our mother in public. Rather than speaking, "step up" or "step down" at curbsides, we'd squeeze mother's hand. Mother could tell by our gait that it was an up or down step at a curb. Yeah, we had our own way of adapting. On buses, if we wanted to describe someone or thing, we'd simply speak to mother in her hand with the use of sign language, so as not to embarrass or be embarrassed, 'cause you know how kids can sometimes speak loudly when they think they're speaking low. Anyway, it wasn't polite to whisper. So, we had all bases covered by speaking silently into mother's lap-held hands, eyes forward, giggling if we wanted and no one was the wiser in having a hint that they were the subjects of off commentary.

When my sister was in 9th or 10th grade, I recall her remarking, "Mama you need to get a job. We need things." More specifically, my sister had joined the Hi-Liters at Shaw High School and needed color-coordinated outfits, so she needed things that cost well beyond my father's still $40.00 per month child support. At any rate, soon after this observatory comment, mother began training in a state sponsored food service program. Mother succeeded in this endeavor and was eventually awarded her very own snack bar in the Ohio College of Podiatric Medicine on Carnegie and E.107th. Prior to the award, mother trained at other state sponsored snack bars, one of which was located in the original Cleveland Clinic, a solitary, smooth, white cement, 2 or 3 story building located at E. 93rd and Euclid. It breaks my heart today to drive in this area; gone is the coziness and comfort of that corner. Everyone knew the other. Now Cleveland Clinic Foundation (CCF) owns the area for miles and miles around, makes me sick. CCF has even branched into suburbia. Something had to have been lost. A lot was lost. I don't give a rats 'you know what' that CCF is ranked one of the top 10 hospitals in America. It stole something from the community. Yep, it's all about the dollar. After the CCF training stint, mother trained at the Federal Building in downtown Cleveland, where a federal court deputy was immediately smitten upon spying this petite blind woman taking care of her business.

The deputy, so taken with my mother, made his love move. They began dating, fell in each other's amour, and married within a year and a half in the early fall of 1973. Olin bought us a lovely house in University Heights. So, we owned 2 houses, the one we moved from, and rented out for the $83.06 note and the new one on Raymont. I was a freshman in college by then, my sister was a junior in high school. My oldest brother had left home at 16 for sweeter dreams with my maternal grandparents, his doing, not my mother's. She would have **never voluntarily given one of her 4 gift children to another.** My baby brother was in a private school. So, we were successfully and proudly raised by then. Nothing left for my mother to do but love and care for this man and his absolutely adorable seven-year-old son, Al Kwame. We were true Middle Class, no doubt about it. We all were happy. My sister was given decorator's rights in the new house, so she had a ball in red, black and white, of which black and red ironically were the primaries at Shaw High School, the home of the Cardinals.

The struggle was long, hard, and arduous for this blind woman and Korean War Vet, but they did it. I applaud them both with a resounding standing ovation.

My mother passed away on July 10, 1988 due to complications from breast cancer. I visited Olin today, April 23rd, 2008, his 79th birthday. He remains a major ingredient in my life for I know what he fulfilled and filled in my mother who'd sacrificed so much in the name of her four gift children. My mother loved him too. I know this because his last name is on her grave's headstone. May they both be revealed in the highest honor of our Lord God. Olin still speaks of my mother with the greatest admiration and memory devotion. "Thank you" seems not enough to say. Your ever-loving daughter, Adrea.

Gifts

Four precious bundles delivered for crowning as hers to the world.

Opaque in sight to the mother her four babies, her gifts were spun into 1950's <u>Negro</u> America.

The first-born, KDA, a beautiful, strong, honey colored dip of masculinity. He grew in stature and promise, enduring most of the manly duties when the parents irreconcilably differed during that infamous 7-year itch. As a lad, he was required to seek employment as a paperboy, which he disliked very much. KDA had a strong attraction for dogs, not his own. The first puppy he introduced to the family was a black silky shorthaired male, promptly named Randy. We all loved that dog up until the day of his at-home yard burial. KDA matured to a strikingly handsome young man coupled with street smarts and well above average intellect, leading his 9th grade homeroom teacher to remark that his PLR, pupil learning ratio, was the highest he'd ever seen. KDA seemed to have, always, from early puberty, the innate ability to draw the opposite sex to him. It began in 6th grade, when he began coming home with quarters and Almond Joy candy bars, banded by phone calls from an older sounding girl. (All that aside). He maintained his studies and excelled in the top percentile of his class. Mama was not going to and did not settle for less. He became the protectorate of his mother and siblings but was seemingly a bit harsh with his sisters in play. One memory stands fresh. KDA was able to twist and hold his tongue under and with a grimace would twirl a bath towel into a hard rope and snap it against his siblings. Wow, did that sting. We would all laugh and hop around, glad to be shown big brother attention. We all looked up to him, I know, I did. I revered him and I still do. Time, observations (some unmentionable), and experiences resulted in KDA finding and I believe to a minor extent, salvaging himself. At an early age, 15, KDA aided/assisted his maternal grandmother and step grandfather in realizing his decided upon identity as KDG. It broke his mother's heart and it never mended and ripped a bit more each time he would refer to her by her first name. KDG became a success in the business world. Mama asked me once, "How does a son, my child, become my step brother?" We both knew how it all began on a Sunday afternoon on Ashbury.

The second gift was the first daughter, AAA. Entering, she sported a spiked hairdo and slanted eyes just like KDA, with a slightly darker hue than his. Like the first, she was strong in spirit and conviction and became mama's little at-home helper, seeing all that had continued from and during KDA's early years. Strong willed, yet bashful. She was drawn to the printed word at three years, gobbling all her eyes could fill and putting down, wherever, all she could, even the walls of her bedroom. She would follow and assist her mother all day. She, too, observed and experienced much that a child not ought to. She ultimately took refuge in her own body, mind, and spirit. Becoming competitive in running track and excelling in scholastics, she patterned herself in female fashion in a semi-mold of KDG, and never failing to seek the instruction of her God she continues to thrive.

Daughter TDA enters as gift number three, a fair-skinned golden haired girl child. It must have been somewhat hard for her with so much already established in and around her new world. It is said, "The third time is a charm." I imagine she did just that, charmed her way into the hearts and psyches of many. She too, was strong willed and determined, joining AAA as in-home helper. I suppose the daughters vied for the favor of their parents. When AAA began school, first grade at age five, TDA became the sole day helper, with AAA hurrying home each day to share what she had learned because she wanted her sister to be equal and not miss the experience of the classroom. TDA would later exhibit mathematical skills like daddy and an ability to understand intricacies, like matching colored phone wiring for a quick repair job in the wall jack. Not a lazy student and certainly not lacking in intelligence TDA, simply liked her rest time, thus getting up for school, sometimes was a slight chore, but I'm certain she now has no major problem in that area as I understand she is near to completing a second degree as AAA is.

MSA, Jr. was the fourth gift, a hickory-hued muscular lad. Suffering from chronic bronchitis as a toddler, he required intermittent placement in an oxygen tent for a few days in the hospital. He was the baby of the family and indeed, we babied him, coddled, and fussed over him. He was/is the spitting physical image of mama's brothers in which he takes great pride. He was full of rambunctious, inquisitive energy and excelled in sports.

One memory sets apart for me and involves my sixth sense. While I was walking from school a squealing fire truck sped past me a few blocks from home and I took off running because I just knew the engine was going to our home. I arrived a few moments behind the engine to witness two of the biggest and strongest men I had ever seen tugging with the split trunk of our tree. MSA had climbed the tree; apparently slipped, and became trapped between the split trunk. Mama was frantic but calmed when her baby was lifted safely out of the bark.

MSA's mischievous ways caused him to have to, years later, enter a private residential school. By this time, it was just the two girl gifts. I looked forward to our Sunday dinner and visits.

We would always have what MSA wanted; round steak, Rice -A-Roni and a vegetable. Most visits included a yellow-boxed Duncan Hines cake with chocolate icing and then it was time for the walk back to the 123rd street Rapid from where we three ladies had picked him up. MSA and AAA probably had the closest relationship of the siblings. MSA possesses a great deal of wisdom, an abiding love of animals, and an unmatched puzzle solving ability. He has one of the cleanest spirits I know.

****

Four Gifts, all loved equally by our parents. I believe we are all successes and possess our own satisfying degrees of happiness in our respective arenas, our breath choices. We all love, have our strengths and weaknesses like all mortals. We are not to be faulted for we do our best. There is no right, wrong, correct or not so. Only our best effort to reach the canopied ceiling of life. We do not embrace <u>all</u> of the other, but that is no reflection on our composers and producers. It simply is, that is all.

Bobby and Felicia on the Knoll

Imaginatively, based on a photograph of my mother and her brother, Robert (Uncle Bobby), circa 1936

Bobby stretched his long sinewy legs one last time, yawned. Next, he slowly pulled the covers down past his nose then his chin, drew a small right fist to his eyes to wipe last night's sleep from his glistening jet black eyes. "Could it be the odor of fried apples and cinnamon coming from the kitchen?" The day was starting off just fine and dandy and Bobby knew just what he and his little sister Felicia would do for some fun. He couldn't wait to share his plan.

Bobby was always coming up with a plan for his sister, whom he'd given the nickname Felicia, later shortening the nickname to Lee. Today, he'd decided that he was going to share with her a special kind of game of Hide and Seek that his blind sister could join in. But before they could get going more important things had to be taken care of like those fried apples, crispy thick fried bacon with the rind still on it, piping hot biscuits with home churned butter and Mama's homemade blackberry preserves. "Yep, Bobby licked his lips."

Bobby bounded from his bed, ran to the bathroom, splashed some water on his face, and hurriedly brushed his teeth. Performed a quick body wash-up and leapt into his T-shirt and dungarees. The kind with built in shoulder straps and all kinds of pockets, that adventurous boys like Bobby just loved because you could fill the pockets with all sorts of things, all kinds of do-dads, and no one would be the wiser, especially Mama. Mamas were girls, too, after all.

Mama hurriedly set the table for the four of them. Daddy was in the parlor reading the paper. Felicia was sitting with her father who read the "funny pages" to her. This was their morning ritual while Mama prepared breakfast.

Mama placed 4 plates before calling Felicia to help her finish setting the table. It was Felicia's job to put glasses and silverware beside the plates and she did an excellent job.

First, the knives were placed to the right of each plate with the sharp edge facing the plate, and then the spoons were placed to the right of each knife. Next came the forks, which were set at the left of each plate. Felicia was very careful when feeling for the tips of the knives, because at the head of the tip was where she had to place each glass. Felicia completed the placement of the glasses.

Mama didn't have to say much, Bobby knew it was his turn to help bring the food to the table and he could hardly wait because the sooner the food got to the table and was eaten the sooner he and Felicia could leave for the knoll. They had to hurry. It was going to be a busy traffic day today and that suited his plan just swell.

With each platter of food that was brought to the table Bobby's heart began to thump with anticipation until Daddy asked, "What's the matter son, got ants in your pants this morning?" "Oh nothing, daddy, I'm just hungry for some of Mama's good cooking."

Mama turned from the counter and caught Bobby winking at her.

Finally, the last dish was set on the table. Daddy blessed the food and breakfast was eaten.

After Bobby had swallowed his last bites of bacon and apples he scooted his chair back, glanced towards his father, "May I be excused?" "Yes, you may, your plate." O.K. daddy," Bobby said as he took his things to the counter. "Mama may we play on the hill today?" "Yes, for a little while. But behave yourselves." Lee excused herself, placed her dishes on the counter, returned to the table and gave her father a hug, "Don't work too hard today daddy, love you. Love you too mama."

"Come on Lee, you ready?" Bobby said, returning from his room. Bobby grabbed Lee's hand and out the door they skipped into the morning sunshine.

Mama returned to the table where she and daddy sat sipping the last of their coffee and juice. Their conversation was peppered with talk about the big changes going on in the surrounding towns. A lot of folks were moving in and out. A lot of growth and expansion and the need for new and different industry in the area were a major issue. This concerned daddy a lot. How was he going to provide for his family? The primary employer in town was the Jackson Quarry, which hired laborers to jack hammer rock out of the mountainside. But once the mountain had been opened wide enough, where was daddy to work? Growth and expansion was not a good thing for everyone. Daddy was one of the fortunate ones. He had been chosen to work an extra shift on this Saturday so he would get paid his regular pay plus one half of the regular hourly rate.

Bobby and Lee finished their trek to the knoll, which wasn't too far from their home, less than one-fourth of a mile.

While lying on their backs just beneath the crest of the knoll Lee and Bobby were each consumed with their private thoughts. Lee mostly thought about what dress she was going to wear to church tomorrow, the number of ribbons she'd have and the corresponding number of plaits, and whether or not mama would let her wear bangs. Although Lee was blind she knew she was surely the other apple of daddy's eye and especially on Sundays when she was all dressed for church and walking hand in hand with daddy, Lee on the left and mama on the right, Bobby in front.

Bobby's thoughts drifted to that phrase he'd heard or read so often lately, "growth and expansion" and it worried and frightened him. To Bobby's young mind it meant that his family might have to leave this town, their home, their friends, everything they'd come to know and love. All he knew was the road with those whizzing cars below them were possibly carrying his family's future and he wanted to do something about it, because he was mad he didn't know to whom to tell about this dilemma.

Bobby and Lee decided to take turns rolling down the hill for a little while. At the end of Bobby's rolls, he'd gather small pebbles, enough until he had two pockets full in his dungarees. Bobby described cars and pickup trucks to Lee for a bit and the occupants, too. Some of the pick-ups had kids or dogs in the back or were piled high with bags or boxes of dry goods or feed for farm animals. Other truck beds contained small furniture items. They supposed some families were already moving to Richmond, the next town over.

Anyway, Bobby had to get his game underway, so he explained it to Lee. They were hiding just beneath the knoll's crest and could not be seen by drivers or occupants of oncoming autos. As the autos would round the bend either he or Lee would toss a pebble down towards the road. Lee was hesitant to join in this game, but Bobby explained what he'd been worrying about. Somehow, they convinced their young and unthinking minds that throwing rocks at these passing autos might cause the people to stay in their town. And so, with

Bobby serving as "lookout man," he could see cars approaching the bend from the left. The pelting began. Bobby said, "Let's see how long we can hide before they seek us out." This game, if you can call it that, lasted for about 15 minutes. Ping! Pop! Crack! Screech! Crack, Zap! Plop! Ping! Kerplunk! Zing! Haha Heehaha Yow Yee!

Bobby turned his head to check on their ammo status and missed seeing the sheriff's patrol car approach at the precise instant that Lee lobbed her last pebble that bounced off the hood of the sheriff's car.

The sheriff brought his car to a screeching halt, exited his patrol car and with the entire swagger that a bored, small and sleepy southern town sheriff could muster, he approached the knoll from Bobby's side. "Uh oh, Lee, we're in big trouble. Here comes Sheriff Tolbert. We got his patrol car." With revolver dangling on his right hip and a wad of tobacco in his cheek the portly sheriff walked up the knoll, "Hey there you two youngins' what are you doing there?" Bobby's mouth hung open with fright as he scrambled up on spindly legs, while helping Lee to her trembling ones and knocking knees. The sheriff bellowed, "Ain't ya'll Ray and Ina's kids. You could have hurt somebody! Come on I'll take you home."

The ride home in the back of the patrol car was the longest of their short lives. Bobby and Lee tried to explain what happened and why but the sheriff simply smiled to himself and said, "I think ya'll better leave all of your explaining for your mama and daddy. Don't you know if you ever have a problem or if something is worrying you, always talk it over with your parents first? Your parents love you and will always give you the best advice."

I am a Negro
Soy Angelito Negro

I am a Negro; at least that is what my birth certificate states in the *Race* section. But what is a Negro? I know from which language the English word is derived. Negro in Spanish simply means black as in the color black.

During my time and place of birth, 1956, right on the cusp of the dawning or the simultaneous birth of the modern Civil Rights Era in the United States of America. I was an infant Negro at perhaps one of the best or worst times. Our society was at a major crossroads. We'd been graced with innumerable leaders, including those who'd helped to bring us up through and out of the boughs of slave ships and plantations.

We were thereafter *reconstructed,* in part, with the aid of the Congress backed Freedmen's Bureau. This period of Reconstruction purportedly lasted from 1865-1877, with freed Negroes having lost many of the rights they'd gained.

Jim Crow Laws were in full denigrating placard and poster view from the late 1800's through the 1950's with unabashed shamefulness. Racial segregation was in every venue of society. This included <u>all</u> public accommodations. The 1896 legal case of *Plessy v. Ferguson* had insured segregation in education. And here I come amidst all this mess. I would come to gain as my benefactors some of the best Black Voices of the 1920's Harlem Renaissance Period.

I was born to a very fair skinned, blue eyed Negro father and what I'll deem as a three-level melanin Negro mother in mid-Ohio, ironically one of the states where slaves would run away to or through, as it was part of the route of the Underground Railroad.

Ohio was also one of the states beckoning Negroes during the Great "Black" Migration.

As a child, I was confronted with many negative images of what it meant to be a Negro. Images and voices, everywhere, told me, one of the darker hued of us 4 siblings, that I was less than. The images and voices were in society. Some of the voices were in my family. My sister, in skin color, was closest to my father's. She has sort of hazel- green eyes, and brown hair which was straight, curly-wavy when we were young.

The image I had of myself as a child was mainly imposed upon me by society and a few family members. Some family members favored my darker skin over my sister's more fair skin, or conversely. Some people would ooh and aah over her hair, saying that familiar line still used in Negro circles. He/she has "good" hair, which would further instill in me a sense of being less than. My hair texture was more tightly curled than my sister's or nappy, requiring, (my mother thought,) Dixie Peach, Royal Crown, and a hot comb.

Our mother often dressed us alike which I think she believed would make us look more alike in physicality. Of course, the same outfits remedied nothing.

I remember at the age of about 10, a pastor's wife Mrs. Carter, made a remark to me about the "good" versus "bad" hair. She said, "All hair is good, the bad hair is what falls out." I'd never heard that before and I've never forgotten it. When I was an educator I would tell this to students who were squabbling over the hair thing. I'm now well past that. Once during my teen years, I was walking with my sister along

Terrace Road, and passed one of her friends' homes. Her friend was in her driveway. My sister introduced us and the friend let out, Ooh, T, she's prettier than you." This immediately removed the sting of Mr. Brown on 88th Street grabbing each of one of our arms, extending them alongside the other and remarking, "Look, one black one and one white one. Mr. Brown meant it as an insult.

I have no idea how it was decided that Negroes or Native to America blacks should be referred to as African Americans. We certainly didn't vote on it. Perhaps one of the leading blacks or black leaders used it in a public forum and it stuck. Once during a local Oakland, CA talk show, "SoulBeat" airing, I made a live on-air inquiry about the origin of African American, as a label for former Coloreds, Negroes, Afro-Americans, Blacks, but the host, obviously embarrassed, was unable to provide an answer to his audience.

Intellectually, I know that the word African can identify an ancestor's country of origin and American is to presumably signify the place of citizenship. Well, I am unable to directly trace my roots to Africa, albeit I'm not denying them. I am satisfied with my American Negro self. Esteemed writer and philosopher Alain Locke edited the acclaimed work *The New Negro* in 1925. I wonder what he'd think of us today in the 21st century. We have come a long way. By the way, my sister remarked to me a few years ago, "You have that good stuff (hair), like Uncle Harry and Little Harry." I had it all the time, what I lacked if anything was a length gene. Too many 'relaxers' ruined the texture of her hair and it is now kinkier or nappier than mine ever dared. But it's all good. We are both Negroes of different hues and what a difference a few decades made.

Earliest Recollections

My youngest memories are some of my fondest. I have no recall of the span from birth through my first year, but I have to believe that most of that time was a celebratory phase. I have held on to a 3" x 5" black and white photo of me taken in Mount Carmel Hospital (East) at about three days old. I was daddy's first girl and I can only suppose I was catered to by him. Mama said I walked at nine months and I can only conjecture that because I could then share floor space with my elder four-year-old brother that minor territorial spats evolved. My speaking voice arrived on schedule. I remember everyone remarking, "She sounds just like you." (Meaning my mother). We both shared deep, yet feminine voices. I enjoyed the comparison until my late teens, but keep reading and you'll see why my mindset changed. As I matured, I'd hear, "You look just like Carletha." Again, in my youth, that comparison was accepted by me, but my acknowledgement was no longer heartfelt as I aged. I was my own person. And the older I got, I justifiably feared that males of my mother's generation saw me as a replication of her in ways that I detested - keep reading. My mother was without exception a pretty woman; no one disputed the exterior.

My initial speech was normal, like everyone else's, but I developed a stutter and I'll share the most probable causative factors of why - keep reading.

I do not recall the additions of my sister or baby brother, probably because I was one and two, respectively. But then there was a family of six with my father working two laborious jobs, one fulltime day job requiring a GI-Joe green uniform with cap and a seemingly part-time night job for which my mother starched and ironed white long-sleeve shirts.

The Columbus Society for the Blind provided our family with *Talking Books* which were actual 78 1/3 RPM vinyl albums played on a heavy gray shellacked folding boxed player that housed a turntable and electrical cord. My mother and father could both read braille and use sign language, but most children's books were in print. Thankfully and gratefully we received via mail a supply of books to quench our thirst for being read to. It was a real treat for us kids to open the folders to see what was inside. I suppose there was an insert of sorts in braille detailing what the books were about and mama would let us know before Keith, (usually) put needle stylus to record, before the readings began. It seemed as if there were only two people who performed these recordings, one man and one woman. These recordings forced a child or anyone to engage their imaginations on a higher plain. I think we all enjoyed those books. I know I did. (My mother used those machines and records all our lives). My favorite talking book story was *The Man who didn't Wash his Dishes*. I remember the surprising way in which he finally did wash them, but will not reveal it here. However, the story written in 1950, is considered a classic. I also enjoyed the nursery rhyme series and *Little Black Sambo* by which time, I had a book to follow along with.

During the time of talking book stories, at about age four, I began experiencing very vivid dreams in color. The dreams were not scary –only vivid colors of images that I could see on the dark walls of my bedroom when I over- anxiously awoke in the middle of the night, sometimes crying out for my mother. These episodes became disruptive to my sleep and I was taken to our pediatrician, Dr. Gerard, a friendly, probably late 40s white man. After describing my dreams, he prescribed for me to do the following when I awakened from one of them, "Go in the bathroom, look in the toilet bowl water, put the image there, and flush it away." I did as suggested and soon the excitingly vivid dreams lessened, ultimately disappearing. However, I always dream in color, never black and white as I've read that most people do.

Spankings by my mother began at around one or two; just the kind with a hair brush on the behind, or, after the small rubber balls broke off, two glued together Biff Bat paddles were employed as I lay across her bent knees, my head resting on the top of her left leg, while her lower right leg stilled both my legs to expose my buttocks to her fiery hand. Beatings began at about age late three, just when my speech was accommodating fuller and more fluid sentences and this too is when I began to stutter. In much later years, I asked my mother when I first stuttered and she said, "When you first started talking." I let it go as I did so many things.

And then the 'party' began, even with Reverend Towns' teenaged sons Riley and Benny joining in at our home while my father was working. This was 1962.

Some Childhood Memories

I just couldn't get to sleep because it was Christmas Eve in the Almstead Apartment complex. Our family lived in a townhouse of sorts. Santa Clause still existed for me. Mama and Daddy were still awake, having coffee over small talk at the kitchen table situated in the northwest corner of "downstairs." I must have walked to the top of the stairs and said something, to which, I heard mama murmur something to daddy and before I knew it I was being lifted into wonderland by daddy. I was summarily taken over to the brimming tree and told that Santa had come and brought me some presents. My dad presented me with the most elegant and dainty, "real" porcelain tea set for serving my dolls. I was allowed to open the present. In my giddy excitement and while walking to my mother to show it to her, I dropped a cup and it shattered on the linoleum over cement kitchen floor. I felt so bad, I cried and apologized as daddy swept up the tiny broken porcelain pieces. Bet that set would be worth an awful lot today.

Another memorable incident occurring at Almstead took place on a seemingly late spring midafternoon day. Mama was cleaning the bathroom, which was at the top of the stairs, as I sat on the top step. It seems I was always near and observing my mother as a small child. The banister was situated to my left. I chatted with my mother while occupied with completing the loosening of a screw in the banister. After I'd successfully pried the screw from its anchor, I began rolling it between my fingers. I don't know where the idea came from, but Pop! It was there. I had thrust the screw in my right nostril. My 3-year-old fingers pushed it too far and try as I might I could not retrieve it. The screw seemed to sprout tiny feet. I couldn't grasp it. My chatter with my mother began to die down as alarms went off in my head. Albeit my mother was blind, she sensed something wrong and made inquiry. I hurriedly told her of my dilemma. Mama left her knees and rushed to my side. Mama tried to get the screw out but her much older-sized fingers could not get the screw. Mama was seeking retrieval with two fingers, but the more she tried, the further up it went, until the screw could not be felt.

Time now for the ride of my young life. The snow white with sirens blaring ambulance arrived within minutes. In came two young white men dressed in all Clorox white uniforms. My nose had begun to trickle red by this time. I wonder if I gave the paramedics a start with the thought of my red on their white. I remember them as kind and in a hurry. I was lifted in the ambulance, placed in the front seat between these 2 clean smelling men where I sort of scooted down as the white tornado spun me to the hospital. My mother stayed home. Perhaps she had to wait for my brother to come home from school. We arrived at the hospital's emergency entrance with personnel on full standby. Nurses were dressed all in crisp white, even their hats were white, just like the nurse wore in the hospital scene of the film *The Godfather (1972)*. I was placed on a gurney and rushed to an ER room, where an examination under bright lights was made. Within a few minutes, the doctor had extracted the screw, remarking that had it moved an inch further it would have gone to my brain. I was awful lucky that mama stopped her efforts when she did. In short order, I was approved for release to my father whom mama must have called at work. Daddy was there and took me to H.L. Green's drugstore and bought me a Valentine's sized box of chocolates. Daddy took me to mama's friend, Hattie Mae, before taking me back home. I'll always remember that day, scary yet exciting. I never put anything in my nose again until 3rd grade in Ms. Hammock's class, but this time, I was big enough to think of a way to get that eraser tip out by myself. I got permission to use the restroom where I blew the eraser into some tissue.

Another Christmas, my 6th one, I'd begged for and received an *Easybake Oven*. A true prize of a gift. I'd pre-planned that I was going to use my oven in the seclusion of my room and save that gift as the last I'd play with, much later in the day, when all guests had left. I'd decided to visit a classmate and then return to enjoy my prize gift. Big mistake. By the time I returned home, some of the visiting kids had baked and eaten every single cake. My heart was broken and until this day I have vowed that I will get an *Easybake Oven* of my very own and bake and eat every cake by myself. This I fully intend to do. I know it's a simple thing. I'm not and never have been selfish, but I like to use/wear my things first before they are shared. I refused to play with my 6th year *Easybake Oven*. Somehow it just seemed tainted with someone else's, at the time, unwelcome spirit.

My first real girl crush was on our paperboy, Zimmia Spears, when I was about 11 years old. Zimmia was a teenager in 9th grade. He had jet-black hair atop an olive- toned angular face. I couldn't wait for him to come for his weekly bill payment. He knew I liked him, but I was not in his league. I was a kid to him, just in 7th grade, but that didn't stop me from almost breaking my neck to answer his collection knocks on Friday evenings. I liked him so much; the whole neighborhood knew it. I even scrawled his name in my high school yearbook, even though; he'd long since moved and graduated from a different high school. He was the absolute finest young man I'd ever seen with my 11-year-old eyes. Once, when I'd returned to the old neighborhood some 25 years later, I was informed that my beloved crush had died in a car accident. I was devastated, but glad my neighbor had remembered that this news would be of some importance to me. I still have my yearbook, the one with Zimmia Spears' name in it. I hope he knows I still think of him.

Bitten

Bitten is the past tense of the word bite, to seize, pierce or cut with the teeth or with parts like jaws; to cut into, to hurt in a sharp stinging way.

It was a school morning in mid-winter, early 1962. The days of *Captain Kangaroo,* his sidekicks *Mr. Green Jeans*, and the *Dancing Bear.* Angie had rushed through her Cream of Wheat and toast breakfast, hugged her parent's goodbye, ran to the kitchen to get her lunch box before joining her older impatiently waiting brother at the front door.

Angie put her coat on and pangs of fear shot up her spine as she thrust her right hand in the right pocket of her coat. Her mittens were not there. Although it was a cold morning, she dared not tell her mother she'd lost her gloves a second time. Angie detested being chastised and yelled at, so she simply straightened her back and braced herself for the several miles' hike to Milo Elementary on 3rd Avenue. Boy, oh boy was it cold. On occasion the wind would whip around the hem of Angie's coat, piercing her leotard legs, but Angie trudged on, increasingly lagging behind her brother and his scowling backward glances. Angie hung tight to her lunch box, which was in her right hand; her book was tucked under the wing of her left arm. She had to get to school, but more specifically, to Miss Carter's second grade classroom.

When Angie and her brother were at the midway point. Angie could stand the cold no longer. As her hands began to ache, Angie realized that she had to turn back towards home. So, she ran to her brother to explain. Not much sympathy, just another familiar scowl. Angie didn't have time for this and turned on her heels to home.

By the time Angie reached her front porch her right hand had become one with her metal lunch box. Angie let her book slip to the cement of the front porch as she banged on the door. "Who is it", she heard her mother yell. "It's me, mama. Open the door." Tears were now streaming down Angie's face as she hurriedly explained the dilemma. The living room wall vent was blowing hot air and Mama promptly led Angie to it with instructions to stand there while rubbing her hands in order to get circulation of blood established. Mama only asked once, "What happened to your gloves?" There was no chastisement, no real yelling only an apparent acceptance and understanding by mama.

Mama went to make a phone call to the school to explain why Angie would be absent that day.

As Angie stood before the vent with its warmth, she rubbed her hands and interlocked her fingers to create more warmth but nothing seemed to help. Angie's hands were burning and stinging something fierce. Angie's feet also began to ache.

By the time mama returned from her phone call Angie's hands had glued themselves to each other in an interlocked state. Angie's eyes had closed shut. With this news mama carried Angie to bed, where she covered Angie with blankets.

Angie's condition did not greatly improve in an appropriate time frame, so the family physician, Doctor Girard was contacted. Good News. Angie was taken to the doctor. After being examined, mama was instructed in Angie's recovery care which to Angie's disappointment included staying home from school for two weeks, applying compresses to Angie's eyes, a salve to her hands and feet.

Gradually, after a few days Angie's hands divorced, her feet softened. Her eyes blinked independently and her smile returned.

One day Angie was told that it was time to go shopping. A very special outing, especially since it was not a holiday time. It was time to return to school. So, in accordance with Dr. Gerard's instruction, Angie was going to get some more gloves coupled with a stern mama warning… "And you better not lose them or I'm gonna bite you." The doctor had also prescribed that Angie wear pants to school for the remainder of the winter season. This was a big deal since girls were not generally allowed to wear pants to school.

Eyes of curiosity and envy were all upon Angie when in a cute pant outfit, she entered Ms. Carter's classroom after a two-week hiatus. The students had been informed of the reason behind Angie's lengthy absence and this prompted all kinds of questions at recess. Inquiring minds wanted to know how it felt to be frostbitten. Had frost really bitten me? Frost certainly has no literal teeth. But the agonizing pain definitely leaves an unforgivable and indelible imprint, sharp and most definitely stinging. Angie did her best to explain the seemingly oxymoron of having been frostbitten.

HATTIE and the Puppy

Once upon a time long, long ago in a semi-wooded area along the pathway of Gray Street in Columbus, Ohio there visited a maiden named Hattie. Hattie came to visit her good friend Lee most every day. Hattie and Lee were best friends, having met while students in grade school.

Now, Hattie and Lee were grown up women with families of their own. Lee had four small children and Hattie had three children. Lee and Hattie were housewives while their husbands went to work during the day.

One day Hattie came to visit Lee on Gray Street. Lee's oldest son, Keith, was at school. Hattie brought her 3 children, Deborah, Denise, and Gary to play with Lee's children, Mickey, Dianne, and Adrea.

During a game of tag in the big front yard on Gray Street, the children ran, laughed and played with Lee's brown and white dog Chrissie. All of a sudden and out of the clear blue yonder in meanders the prettiest, most beautiful dog any of the children had ever seen. This dog was knock-down gorgeous amber, gold, and red- orange. The kids were awestruck and called to one another, and then in a group ran to the newfound animal friend, encircling it cautiously. Gary and Mickey, being the only boys stepped in a little closer to get a fuller inspection while Denise stood at the perimeter, hands on hips, "Ya'll better be careful." Dianne ran towards the house, shouting, "I'm going to tell mama and Hattie Mae." While Deborah and Adrea thought just about the same thing, "Oh, she's always telling something. We just want to play."

The little animal wasn't making any noise, really. It was behaving rather nicely. After a minute or so Dianne returned with Hattie Mae who was led straight to our new friend. Hattie knelt down and embraced the little fellow right away. For all the panic that Dianne tried to stir you surely couldn't tell by Hattie's calm response.

Each of the children took turns describing the dog to Hattie Mae while she pet and rubbed the animal maintaining calm in the early afternoon sun. The dog made soft yelping noises. Arched its back and fluffy tail, while spinning its golden amber fur in the sun.

Somehow Hattie Mae was cajoled into taking the dog inside to meet Lee. A short time later it was decided that, like the dog Chrissie, the new one could stay, but how was Lee going to explain an additional mouth to feed to her husband, Melvin?

Lee and Hattie had to think quickly! It was decided that the new puppy would stay hidden in the basement. Hattie assured Lee that she would come visit each day to help care for the dog and to clean up after it. The puppy was so quiet, it hadn't barked once, so hiding it from Lee's husband would probably be a cinch.

The puppy was placed in the basement in a tin washtub. It was hidden for several days until Hattie and Lee's hearts were softened. They both got to thinking that perhaps the puppy to which they and the kids were growing so attached belonged to someone else. Lee and Hattie also began to wonder that perhaps something was wrong with the puppy; maybe it was sick because it wasn't barking at all. So, they contacted the Animal Protective League, which sent an agent out.

The puppy with its entire golden splendor was produced for the Animal Protective League agent, Bob Lowe. The agent's eyes lit up and his face broke into a half-startled smile. He addressed both Lee and Hattie, "I see you have small children in the home, has the animal bitten any of them?" "No," they answer in unison. The agent gingerly explained to Lee and Hattie that the <u>puppy</u> was actually a wild baby fox, that it could be infected with rabies, which if the fox had bitten anyone could have resulted in a very serious health matter requiring a possible hospitalization and a series of painful inoculations for the rabid infected person.

Fortunately, this would not be the case. Lee and Hattie and Bob all got a big laugh. You see, Lee and Hattie were blind; the children were too small and did not know that the puppy was in fact a fox. Lee's husband never saw the puppy in the basement.

The storyteller believes that it was Hattie's demeanor in relating to the fox that caused the fox to behave in such a tame manner. God bless Hattie Mae. There are several morals to this short story. I'll let the reader come up with his or her own.

Written
11-8-2007
For Hattie Mae Parrish
with fond memories

The Preacher's Son

I can't recall the play from which the acting class scene was chosen, but it may come to mind as the story unfolds. What the writer does remember is that the setting was during the Depression Era of 1930's America and took place between a husband and wife who were having a discussion about household expenses. The real-life actors were being trained in Stanislavski's Method Acting by renowned acting teacher and Coach Jean Shelton of San Francisco.

Method Acting requires or demands that the actor "be" in the moment of the dialogue, setting, every nuance of the scene, but to get and stay there the actor often relives a real-life event in order to act the emotion or play an action, like anger, joy or pain.

During an at-home rehearsal, the female began to "prepare," to get into character when from some long past time, a time ago so removed had it been from her mind and essence, that she was startled at the recollection which caused her to break into tears and flee her acting partner.

When the female returned to the room, her acting partner consoled her as she chokingly relived that long ago suffocated moment in time.

Benny Towns and his few years' younger teen brother, Riley, often visited the home of the female's parents when the female was a girl of six years. The young men were actually more friends of the girl's mother. The men were always around and even napped at the home. They were friendly and played with the little girl and her siblings, sometimes they were even allowed romping and cupped body napping with the kids on the bed located in a room off the living room. I can only presume this was so because the mother's attention could be placed elsewhere as needed during the course of her daily duties as a homemaker, or most likely because the mother was busy entertaining guests in another part of the home. Anyway, Benny and Riley were over at the house a lot. Odd, it seems now. They did not appear to have been enrolled in school on any level.

One summer midday, Riley was visiting alone. There was a knock on the door. The mother answered it. It was the telephone man. Apparently, the mother had requested the phone company's representative, as she wanted an additional phone line installed in the home. The mother spoke briefly with the telephone man who indicated that the wiring would have to be placed outside along the walls of the cement slab porch. The girl watched from the living room sofa as her mother crouched just outside the closed screen door, while the serviceman explained the outlay of the wiring installation.

Riley approached the crossed-ankle girl as she sat watching her mother, extending his left hand, he said, "Will you show me the basement?" They both shot simultaneous glances towards the closed door, which led from the living room down. Riley took her petite brown right hand and led her across the floor as the girl thought to herself, "You know where the basement is, because you've been down there before." But the child had a kind heart and didn't think to speak her thought as she crossed the room. Riley opened the white painted wood paneled door with his right hand without making a sound and down into the cool darkness they went. When at the bottom, Riley motioned the girl child towards the old furnace, a big bulky metal contraption erected near to the left of the stairs. He nudged the girl against the furnace; speaking in a low tone, "Pull your pants down. It's going to be ok. I'm not gonna hurt you." as the girl's mind began to swirl with what's and why's. Riley pulled the girl's pants and panties down to her thin trembling ankles as she tried to speak but the words were frozen somewhere in her brain. So, paralyzed with fear was she that she could not even scream. Riley pressed and spread her tender body against the furnace while fumbling with the front of his own trousers and suddenly yanked out a piece of brown flesh, the likes of which the girl had never seen. He suddenly and without warning thrust that foreign piece of flesh into the center of the girl's legs, into her "*tea pot*" The thrust was so forceful that it caused the furnace's metal to whine and creak. The girl was glad for the sound. Maybe mama had heard the noise and would come to rescue her daughter. But the girl had misjudged. The furnace was not beneath the front porch, so mama could not hear the furnace's cries. Riley finished his jabbing thrusts, said, "Now, don't tell anybody. If you do, I'll kill you and your mother."

They ascended those dreadful stairs, the girl glad to escape the dankness. Mama was still busy with the telephone man and did not immediately come inside from the porch.

The girl did as she had been told under the worst possible threat for a child. She held it all in for as long as possible, but she could not hold the blood in, although she tried by attempting to suck it back in by deep breaths. It didn't work. There was always a red or brown stain in her panties for many days afterwards, so she finally told her mother about her hurting *teapot* and the presence of the persistent blood. Because of the hovering threat of death, she dared not tell of how her *teapot* came to be spilling blood. Nonetheless the girl's mother took her to the family pediatrician, a male doctor for an examination, another awful experience. "Did you put your fingers in there? Did you put some bobby pins there?" An emphatic "No!" to both questions. "Did somebody put something in you?" The doctor knew what had happened. The mental response and, I'm sure the girl's facial reaction mimicked "Yes." But the girl child could not speak of the violation of her innocence fore it could mean death to her and her mother.

A few days after the doctor visit, the girl child was in her 2nd grade class and must have been caught acting up which got the ire of her teacher, Miss Carter. The girl was "summoned into the hall for a "place both hands on the wall and pull your dress up" paddling on the rear. The girl obliged the teacher. After pulling the bottom of her powder blue jumper up around her waist, she prayed that Miss Carter would see the red stains and ask about them but apparently, the teacher was engrossed in her paddling business and did not see the evidence of the leakage, so the girl had to tell her mother what had happened. Miss Carter, to the child's way of thinking, would have been most desirous to share this event with. After all Miss Carter wasn't under the threat of death.

That evening, the girl child told her mother what happened in the basement and for nearly 30 years the incident was <u>never</u> mentioned again. Benny and Riley stopped coming to the house. There were no police, no nothing, nothing ever until that fateful day of rehearsal, while employing Constantin Stanislavski's Method Acting.

Ten more years passed and the girl child turned woman had to confront the event, but this time, she decided to confront the demon to his face. After many long-distance phone calls, she succeeded in locating Riley's brother, Benny, to whom she told what had happened. Benny denied any knowledge of it, (a lie) but did let the woman know that Riley was no longer among the living. The woman later confirmed with the brothers' hometown police department that in fact Riley, the demon seed, preacher's son, had on November 15, 1969 assaulted another woman and while in the act was shot and killed by a police officer. Good riddance to bad rubbish. The Lord is indeed a Shepard.

Author's note: *The girl-child was me, Nicie, not the teen or adult Adrea I became. So, when I relive that incident, I psychologically remove my physical being from it, have to, and that is why I subconsciously wrote about it in the third person.*

Bombon dulce despedazar
Candy Tears

At conception she was sinned against
Born of a sinful act
No one cries for la nina, the little girl
No sweet treats
Except those she buys for herself
Sometimes
To savor for a while
To finger the wrappings
She cries
Sometimes
Candy tears
To cleanse and replenish
Her espiritu
Only sometimes does she let drop
Bombon dulce despedazar

Angie's Magical Lamp

The magic began when Angie was an eleven-year-old 7th grader, in junior high school growing her way to lady-hood. Angie was an intellectually bright girl, excelling in English, and the school orchestra wherein she played the violin. Although shy, because of a stutter she'd had since first speaking, she had fast running legs. She could outdistance any of the neighborhood kids including boys, (except one named Mann), from light pole to light pole on E.123rd. Angie also studied French, which she'd begun in A. J. Rickoff Elementary School 4th grade.

In the days of Angie's 7th grade, a student could, at lunchtime, opt to view a movie in the auditorium for a quarter. One week the feature was "Aladdin's Lamp." or some such similar title. Anyway, the film depicted Arabians, some of the males wearing delicately sewn slippers bejeweled with stones representing all colors in the arc of a fresh shower rainbow. Angie was so taken with the culture as depicted in the film that she confided to her mother one evening that she was going to marry an Arabian when she grew up.

Over the course of 7th grade, Angie had the good fortune to be taken under the guidance of two very impressionable academicians, one of which was her homeroom and art teacher, Mr. Young, the other being her speech therapist, a very caring and nice lady whose true name escapes but for purposes of continuity is referred to as Ms. Wenger.

Angie didn't know then what lasting affects the input of these conscientious individuals would have on her life travels. You see, Mr. Young chose Angie as his classroom helper, which aided Angie with her shyness malady. Ms. Wenger chose Angie as her guest to attend a local high school's (Glenville High School, comedian Steve Harvey's alma mater) production of Westside Story. Being Mr. Young's helper and Ms. Wenger's guest had the greatest import on Angie's ultimate carpet ride through early adulthood and beyond.

It was a warm spring evening when Ms. Wenger arrived at Angie's home to pick Angie up for the ride to the high school. Angie was dressed for the evening. While holding her mother's hand and with combed brown paper bag pressed bang curls greeted Ms. Wenger at the front door. Angie felt special, indeed, as her mother's silent pride beamed, "I love her too, take care of my child, she's my angel on the fringe of the carpet ride of life. Thank you for letting her feel the wind on her face." And with that the two departed for Angie's first live theatre experience. Needless to say, Angie was thrilled, had never seen anything like the *Sharks and Jets, Tony and Maria* speaking, singing and dancing so. Just fantastic! Now, Angie's curiosity was being piqued on a totally different level. This colorful and in your face venue could not be compared to the television's black and white performances popping forth from Sunday's *Ed Sullivan Show*. That theatre night introduced Angie to another of the world's cultures. Good thing to have one's mind and prospects advanced beyond themselves and their immediacy. Especially so if you're a shy, inwardly insecure stutterer whose two true refuges were reading or running.

Spring advanced into summer. Angie had devised a way to present her own backyard theatrical production of *Hansel and Gretel*. Alas, it rained on the performance date, and Angie had to return all the admittance dimes she'd collected in advance from the neighborhood attendees. But all was not lost; Angie began to give 25-cent front porch violin lessons. Angie was and still is the kind of person who likes to give and share her knowledge.

Years passed, Angie graduated high school and four years later attained her undergraduate degree. Over these years, Angie's shyness folded and from there pollinated a much more confident and outwardly secure young woman. A year after graduating college Angie traveled alone to New York, the setting for *West Side Story*. That same year Angie's employment training required that she travel to San Francisco, California. Angie was eager to go to the west coast. While there for her three-week training period, once again, Angie was introduced to a myriad of cultures and life themes, the likes of which were a rarity in her Ohio hometown. Angie was totally smitten and knew she'd found her home, her peace. So, upon her return to Ohio, Angie immediately set in motion, plans to permanently relocate to the west coast.

Angie moved to Oakland, CA on March 2nd 1979. She met, fell in love with and married a charming young man, named Rahim, about whom her mother remarked or rather reminded her, "You told me, when you were a little girl that you were going to marry a real Arabian. He's not Arabian, but you came close." You see Rahim is Iranian, a Middle Easterner, nonetheless.

Angie's magic lamp produced tree loving and influential people in her budding years, Mr. Young, Ms. Wenger and Angie's mother. The energies spewed by these individuals helped to give Angie great insight, strong will and determination to go forth in life, and do well.

The best of life's adventures and learning is wished for all the readers who are fortunate enough to have a magic lamp to help guide them in their carpet ride journey through earth's life. Peace, and wish you all will be positively blessed with colors of a fresh shower rainbow.

Author's Note: I saw myself as an Angie (easier for me to say than my given name during most of my pre-pubescent years). I never used the name Angie socially. I graduated to my given first name during the pursuit of my first undergraduate degree.

Shattering Historical Moments
(A Chronology)

The impetus of this piece is only to share a few disparate occurrences experienced as a child from elementary through current adult phase, with mandatory acknowledgement of two precursor moments of vicarious integration. The first happened in 1954 as a result of Supreme Court case, *Brown v. Board of Education* acknowledged as one of the greatest Supreme Court decisions of the 20th century, which unanimously held that the racial segregation of children in public schools violated the Equal Protection Clause of the Fourteenth Amendment. This ruling predated my birth by two years and garnered a more synonymous environ for my impending primary education. Getting to school was an inextricably linked necessity if my family was to integrate for an equally balanced educational opportunity. Assurance of arrival at the institution of learning was, in part, spearheaded by Rosa Parks' brave act of refusing to move to the rear section of a city bus resulting in the successful organization and yearlong Montgomery Bus Boycott. The boycott culminated in the Supreme Court deciding, in the 12 month of my life (12/20/56) that segregation on public buses or other modes of transportation was unconstitutional. Thus, the stage was set for me to seek out and receive an education on a non-segregated basis with equal protection accommodations.

Of vital import in our democracy is having a (constitutional) right to vote. Medgar Evers was a leader, among others, instrumental in educating blacks **about** and how to **register** to vote. He was assassinated in the driveway of his home on June 13, 1963. The Reverend Dr. Martin Luther King Jr., marched on Washington on August 28, 1963, with more than

100,000 fellow citizens of all tinges, and backgrounds, demanding recognition in civil rights' application to all persons regardless of race, creed, color, or socioeconomic standing.

1963 racially integrated third grade brought the wonders of a conscientiously inquisitive and studious seven-year-old. A petite, braided hair, awkward "BlackJap" little girl who was not, by choice, too proud to wear *Charity Newsie* dresses passed out from backs of organization- sponsored trucks in destitute neighborhoods in Columbus, Ohio. I was not ashamed to wear the dresses but my sister was; it was an indicator that we were poor. Hell, we were poor as was most of the neighborhood. What else could explain the reason for half of the kids in school appearing within days of the other wearing the exact dresses/pants and shirts, although different colors with same patterns? I still have my third-grade photo wearing a *Charity Newsie* outfit. While writing this piece, I used the Internet to research that organization's beginnings and was ecstatically impressed to learn that it still exists, after being established in 1907, with the Mission of Charity Newsies being "that no child shall be kept out of school for lack of adequate clothing". I relished in my role as Miss Hammock's pet, my second time in such designation. I was smart, would breeze with ease through assignments, especially the 'Scholastic' reading exercises. Now, when occasionally during doctor appointments, I see one of those books in the children's section of a waiting room, I rush to pick it up and thumb through for comparison sake. I remember one question from my time: When someone says, "just a minute", how much time are they really speaking of? And then there were four choices. I am sure I selected the right one.

The right one…? And then came the Friday before Thanksgiving, November 22. Around 1:30, someone came to our classroom door to summon our teacher. Miss Hammock left and returned about 10 minutes later. Immediately upon her return, her jovial demeanor had changed to a teary-eyed semi-dazed piece of porcelain. Miss Hammock informed us that the principal was to make an announcement over the Public-Address System... and then the trembling yet steady voice of our principal told his student body that our beloved president, John F. Kennedy had been killed... further that because of this tragedy school was being dismissed. We were instructed to return home immediately. Disbelief was not a word readily available. Still 50 years later, the adjective phrase still fitting best for me is shocked sadness. John F. Kennedy had been our right one, or so most families we knew believed. No other president or public figure had graced our walls before him. We didn't have a 'Jesus' only him. Stilled in the glorious prime of his being, he was a fallen hero, for all of us. The First Lady, Jacqueline Bouvier Kennedy summoned all courage, dignity, and unparalleled grace in providing the country's men, women, and children a masterful display of the grandest celebration of our president's life, including John-John's poignant salute of his father's casket as it passed. In our mangled hearts, we, too, saluted as one nation that mournful Monday.

- People! Remember that the Voting Rights Act of 1965, ushered in by President Lyndon Johnson, is just that, an act, <u>not an Amendment</u> to the U. S. Constitution. Wake up, do not snooze and let certain (current) powers chisel away at one of our most basic of freedoms; lest you yawn and find a return to proof of literacy and a poll tax. That is what it looks like to me and I'm not paranoid. Just an observatory thought. On June 25, 2013, The Supreme Court effectively struck down the heart of the Voting Rights Act of 1965 by a 5-to-4 vote, freeing nine states, mostly in the South, to change their election laws without advance federal approval. **Also, never forget** the murders of James Chaney, Andrew Goodman, and Michael Schwerner, three civil rights workers who unselfishly sacrificed the ultimate gift for freedom in a Ku Klux Klan infested county in 1964 Mississippi sweltering summer. The names of these three men are indelibly imprinted in the forefront of my mind. -

Continuing the exacerbation of the demand for sameness in opportunity and furtherance of a self-serving agenda was Malcom X who succumbed to assassins' bullets on February 21, 1965. Alex Haley penned the autobiography of his life and by the time of my ninth grade the work was required reading.

In November 1967, I was in seventh grade, and received an English homework assignment instructing the class to watch the mayoral election returns, and present a minimum two-page report on the results. My mother sat and watched the television accounts with me. I wish I had that 'A' paper now but I do remember my closing sentence, "The returns were in, the news was out" ... Cleveland, Ohio had elected its first Black mayor, Carl B. Stokes, the first Black to preside over any major city in the United States. And we celebrated!

Martin Luther King, Jr. continued the non-violent struggle for equity in civil rights, but once again, another champion was failed by an assassin's article of exploding steel on April 4, 1968. And we wept once more!

The nation was nearing total exhaustion, but we trudged on with Robert F. Kennedy, John's brother, carrying the ignited torch for democracy. And while in the midst of applauding him, he too, was murdered by that coward, Sirhan, Sirhan in June, 1968; this before we had finished dabbing our watershed of two months prior. Have Mercy, did we have the stamina or enough tissues for dispensary?

And... then the rains of bullets came literally in my yard in the Glenville area of Cleveland, Ohio; dubbed *The Glenville Riots* of July 23-28, 1968.

My mother, sister, oldest brother and I lived on Ashbury and 123rd Street, from where we had moved (just around the corner when I was in the 7th grade). Our backyard faced Lakeview Avenue which apexes Ashbury. My sister and I were visiting what I will describe as an influential, respected, and dignified couple of the neighborhood, Troy and Blanche Wallace, near Ashbury and 105th. I do not recall how my mother knew them, but I was glad she did. Troy, Blanche, and their late- teens daughter offered me respite from the doldrums of our home. I was educated on a higher social level when in their company. I felt expansive and worldlier. I could sense their deep admiration of my mother. But, more importantly for me, being around the couple, especially Blanche, I received an appreciation of my spirited child self who in another life might have claimed the likeness of the Wallaces as my parents. Both were soft-spoken and spiked with grace. I adored them. Plus, they offered me my first pomegranate and taught me how to partake of it properly.

It had to be that first day of the riots, that Tuesday, the 23rd, that my sister and I had gone to the Wallace home. It was a typical blazing hot Cleveland summer day, when the phone rang in the late afternoon. Blanche answered it. She never said who it was, but she called our mother and told her that some sort of trouble was about to start which prompted my mother to tell us to come home RIGHT NOW! As we hurried out the door, not knowing what lay ahead of about a 10-block walk, we ran with Blanche's stern, "Now go straight home, your mother's there alone," at our backs. We arrived home to a frantic mother nearly in tears who we calmed. Brother Keith was not there yet, but arrived within minutes. We waited, semi-huddled in our living room until the sun set... and we waited, until all hell broke out on Lakeview.

Darkness descended and the music began with the lead crescendo of rat-a-tat-tat, repeated in choral unisons of pop-pop-pop, boom, boom, and boom! Wailing sirens, screeching tires, and helicopters' impaling search lights were unrelenting, vying for attention. This orchestrated melody of artillery and first responders was accompanied by loud running and shouting voices all around our house, particularly in the back. Everybody was scared, even I was, but in the midst, I decided I wanted to see what was happening, so I bolted to the front door to look out to a chime of "No, Nicie get down, stay down!, but I looked out anyway, and saw a trail of dark figures running, east on Ashbury, then north on Lakeview, and the music and foot activity kept up for a good while until the overpowering sound of the loudest vehicle engines I had ever heard rumbled down Lakeview accompanied by bullhorns instructing us to stay in our homes. No one budged; just kept still with local television news crews giving updates from just beyond our back yard. At one point our front window received a ding, not a direct shot, but we remained collected for the most part, unaware that Black Nationalists (BN) were occupying a home on Lakeview and had had a shootout with police who were surveilling one of the BN members. Three white police officers were killed as were three Black Nationalists and one Black male civilian who had transported a white officer into the killing zone.

Extensive burning and looting of businesses on Superior took place over the next few nights. My mother didn't want him to, but one night my brother Keith and his best friend Anthony went up on Superior and brought back a smoky Halloween orange with black stripes sofa bed. We welcomed that sofa into our empty side room; cleaning it later. Keith and Anthony did not riot or loot. The sofa had been left on the curb of Superior. During the musk of one of the riot days, I ventured up to Kresge's Drug store and gingerly walked through the aftermath of fire, smoke, and water and selected for myself a few packages of panties and socks. The Fresh Meat Market where we bought our Sunday round steak was gone; that saddened me, yet I was happy to have much needed undies and socks, in this 12th year of my teetering life.

My big brother, Keith, left us soon afterwards to a much safer town of Williamson, West Virginia, and the guardianship of my maternal grandmother, Mama Ada, and arms of Daddy Gregory. We remaining three meandered for a while in the lull after the summer storm. I gave violin lessons to neighborhood kids on our front porch, pantomimed Peaches and Herb duets with my sister, received my first love-crush letter from neighbor Flowers' vacationing teen son, ran relays from light pole to light pole on 123rd, and waited for 8th grade at Harry E. Davis which I began with much excitement, but then we moved after about two months into the school year. OK, mama. The schools were supposedly better in East Cleveland, but I was one of the best students where I was. I was traumatized to the point of being sent home for three days in order to adjust. I did adjust, but not before going back to my old school and teacher, Mr. Eugene Young, who assured me through my profuse tears that I would be alright.

...and the Vietnam War raged on. Keith joined the marines and Cousin Daniel (Skipper) the navy...both returned home, but more than 50,000 did not...and we still mourn them, the average age of whom was 19, (the infantrymen).

As a young child, these series of events could not but insist urgency in my psyche, a sense of having to do something...something, but what...and who was to lead us? We dug deep, scratching, clawing, with indefatigable tenacity, tossing aside quiescence and arrived at a destination of Si se puede, yes we can, and elected President Barack Obama, the first African American to win two consecutive terms, 2008 and 2012. Although physically handicapped, I rigorously and with vigor campaigned for him in Ohio in '08 and California in '12 as a volunteer and am a continuing financial contributor to Organizing for America (OFA).

I never forgot Mr. Young or Troy and Blanche Wallace. I always sought them when I visited Cleveland. Blanche died a few years after my mother. I visited Troy and Blanche's last home together on Herrick Rd. in 2003 to see Troy, but as I turned to leave the porch their daughter drove up, remembered me in her greeting, as she said Troy had recently passed away; that she was just checking the mail- oh, the floodgates opened, I was left to yearn the smile and hug of one I so long ago had adored, but never forgot. Whenever I see or eat pomegranates I remember the Wallace family. Mr. Young and I are friends. He suffered a severely debilitating stroke several years ago. I remain in contact with him by letters and last visited him in July, 2013. I also drove through the *Glenville Riots* area as I always did during my returns since I left Ohio. A vacant overgrown grassy lot now occupies the space of our former home on Ashbury and the building where the shootout took place has been replaced with new homes.

Author, Thomas Wolfe, penned *You Can't Go Home Again.* I know and understand, but vestigial remnants of home remain for me, with my reliance on the good of all the bad and ugly.

**Harry Thomas Cox, ca 1930- Carletha's father
- Ada Gregory collection-;**
(An ancestry.com April 1, 1940 Census shows his birth as "about 1901, Virginia")

Ada Mae Rumley Cox-Gregory, ca 1995, Carletha's mother

**Harry Cox, Jr. (Uncle Harry) and Carletha Cox, ca. 1940-
Ada's private collection**

Carletha and Robert Cox (Uncle Bobby) with unidentified woman, ca. 1940;
Ada Gregory Private collection;
Adrea imagined Bobby and *Felicia* on the *Knoll* from this photo

Aunt Ruth Singleton-Maroudas, ca. 1973- Harry Cox, II Collection

Aunt Gertrude Thomas - Campbell, ca. 1985, Harry Cox II Collection

Carletha and Melvin, Institute, W. VA, ca. 1950, Graduation day from high school; Ada Gregory Collection

**Carletha and Melvin Adams, Columbus, Ohio, ca.1962
Elaine Wright Collection**

Carletha and her four gifts, Front row, TDA,
Middle row, MSA, Jr., AAA, and KDA.
(Hattie Mae's daughter, Deborah at right) ca. 1962 –
Elaine Wright Collection

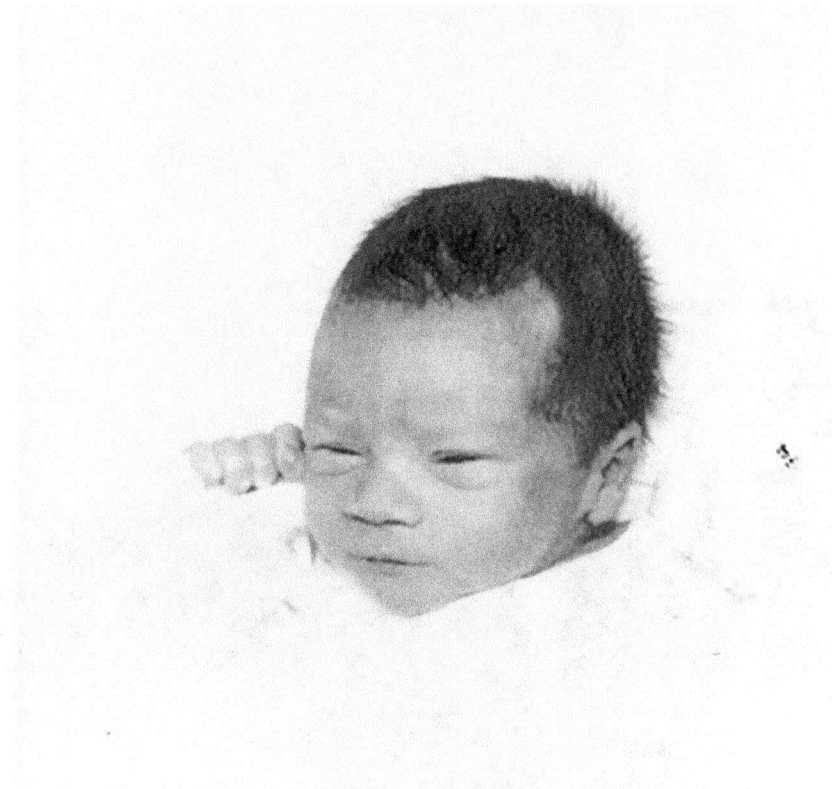

Adrea Anise Adams, approximately two days old, January 21, 1956

Below is Adrea's first piece of jewelery, her Hospital ID bracelet

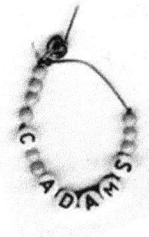

Back Row: L-R Dwaun, Keith (Buzz), Ronnie, Daniel (Skipper), Darrell (Butch),

Front Row: L-R Gina, Little Harry, Tona, Mickey, Nicie, Terry, Cathy, ca. 1961 (Cousins)
Sadie Cox Collection

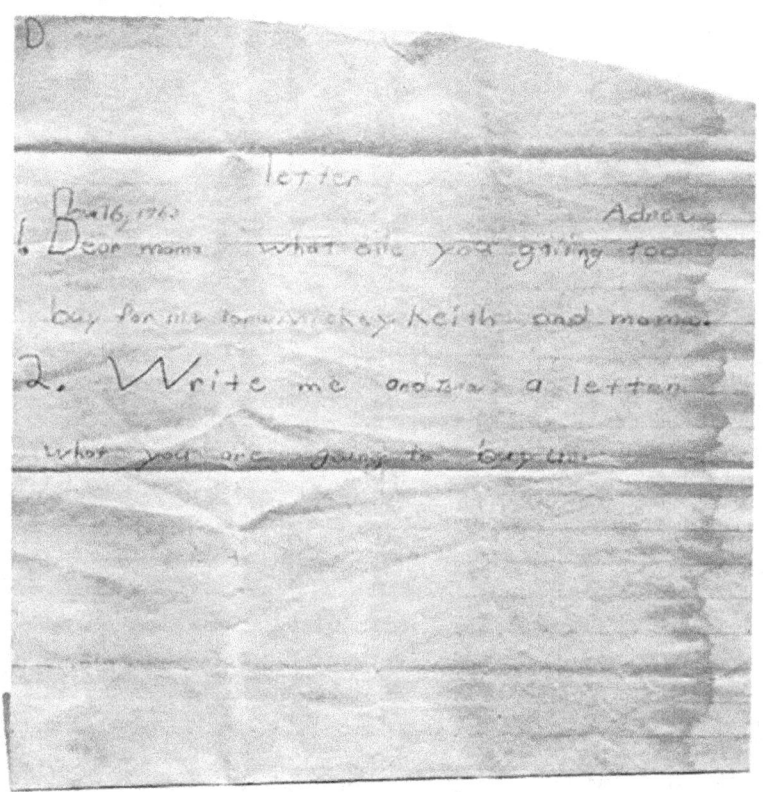

Adrea's Letter Dec 16, 1962 to Mama Ada

> letter
> Nov 2, 1979.   "Mama Ada"
> 1. Dear Adrea what are you going to
>   buy me and Daddy & Keith?
> 2. Write me and Daddy a letter what you
>   are going to buy us.
>
> Dear Nieme,
> This is a letter you wrote me years
> ago. You can see I don't throw away
> much. I do love you so much and
> hope the best of everything in your
> adventure in the big city of San Fran-
> cisco, Calif. Do take good care of your
> self but if you find things are not
> what you want or expected don't be too
> proud to come home. You know you
> will always have your family behind
> you. I know I didn't write in para-
> graphs the way I should but that
> is just me. I know better but
> this is the way I am.
>   Much luck and happiness always.
>   Love, Your Grandmother
>   Mama Ada.
> Please send the letter back to me.

Mama Ada's Response Nov 2, 1979
(I'm sure Mama Ada sent something for Christmas)

Adrea (Nicie) and cousin Dwaun, Third Grade 1963

Adrea (Nicie) and cousin Dwaun, March 29, 1978

Adrea top left to right fifth and sixth; bottom left to right eighth, and ninth grade class pictures.

Adrea Adams

Adrea's Ribbon and number for 200-yard relay race in 1969, Junior Olympics.

Cleveland Public Schools
Elementary Division

AWARD

For Honor Citizen

Presented to Adrea Adams
NAME OF PUPIL

SCHOOL — PRINCIPAL

June 16, 1967
DATE — TEACHER

Recognition For Perfect Attendance

This card certifies that

attended HARRY E. DAVIS JUNIOR HIGH SCHOOL each DAY OF THE ____ SEMESTER 19__ 19__

HOME ROOM TEACHER

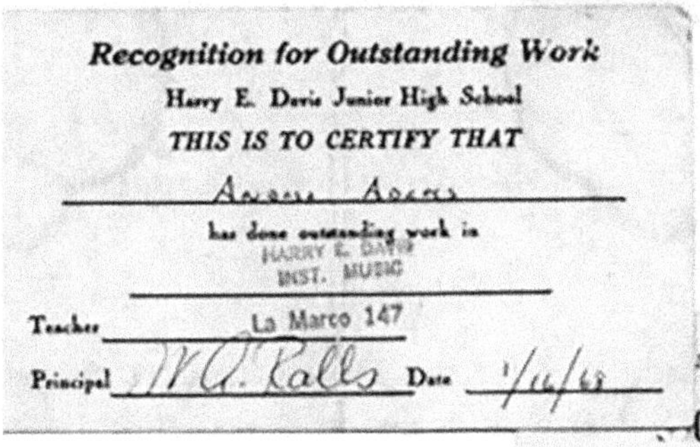

Recognition for Outstanding Work

Harry E. Davis Junior High School

THIS IS TO CERTIFY THAT

has done outstanding work in

HARRY E. DAVIS
INST. MUSIC

Teacher La Marco 147

Principal W. A. Ralls Date 1/16/68

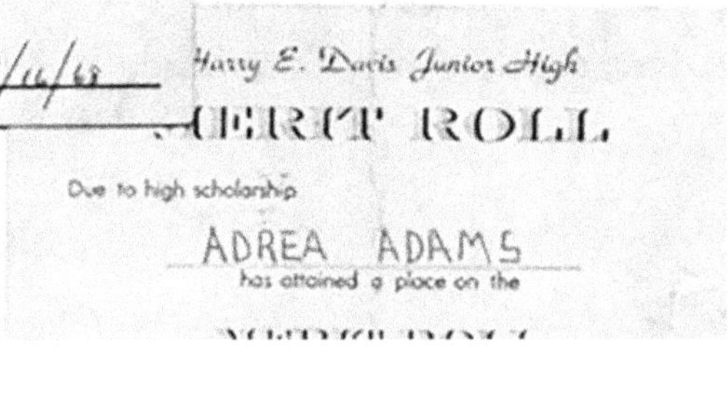

Harry E. Davis Junior High

MERIT ROLL

Due to high scholarship

ADREA ADAMS

has attained a place on the

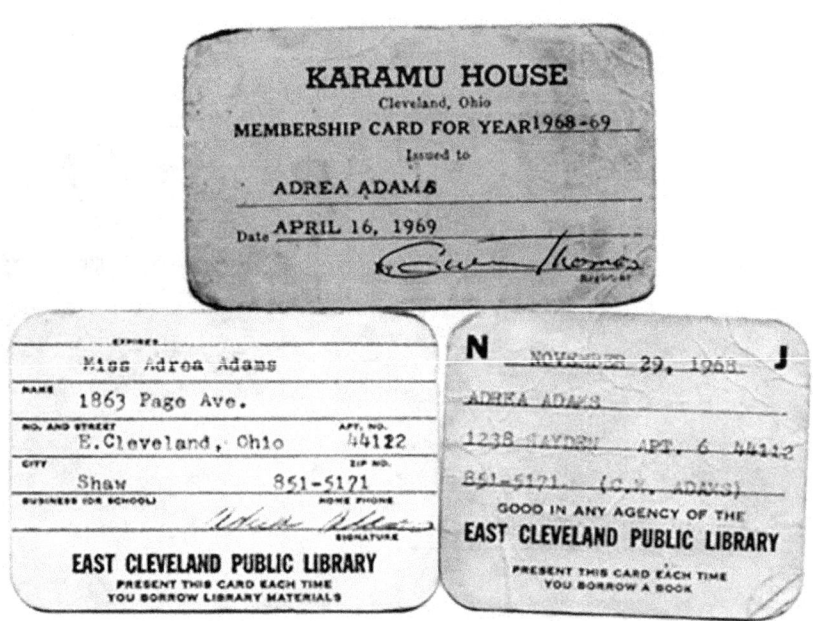

Adrea studied modern dance at Karamu House in Cleveland, OH

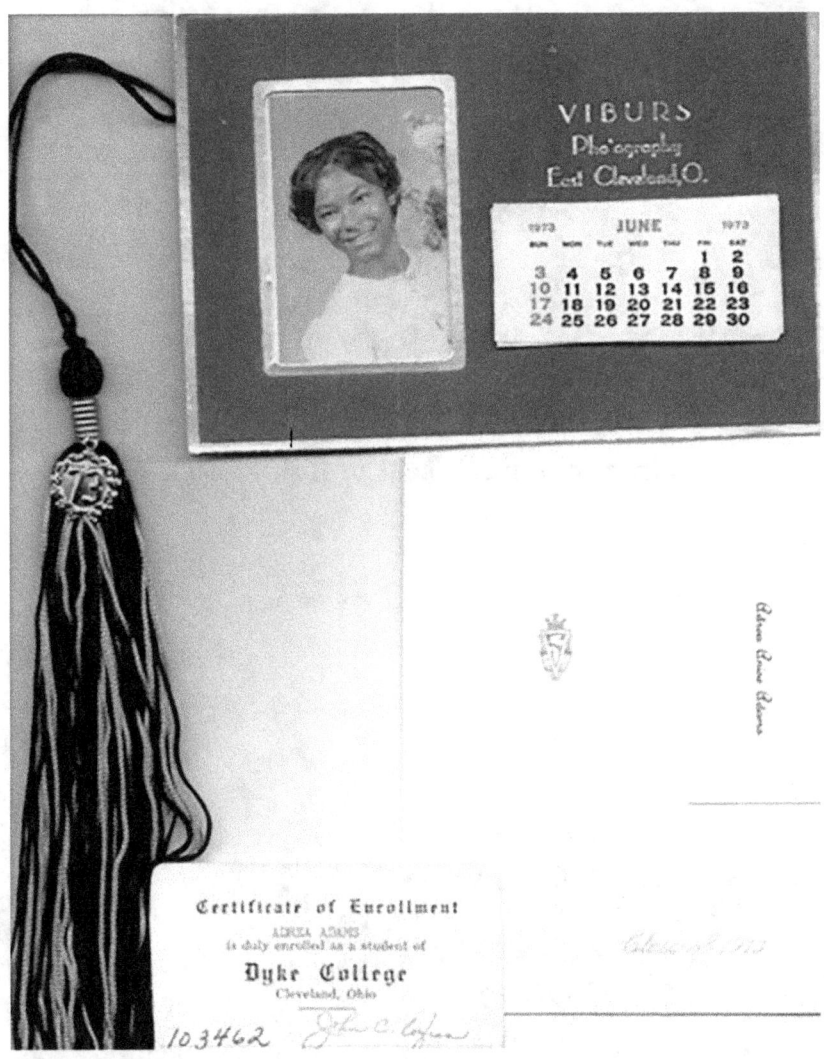

Adrea in driver's seat of Homer's TR-6

Four Gifts, L-R: KDG, TDA, AAA, and MSA Jr., ca.1996

Carletha and Olin on their wedding day September 1973 (Ann Adams (Whimpy) hosted their reception).

ACT II

Mothers – Side B

My mother divorced Olin after about three years of marriage. I never fully understood the reasons why; albeit a lot of friction was introduced into the household by my female sibling. I will not go into all of what occurred, but will lend that arguments abounded concerning my sibling's youthful dating and subsequent disrespect of household rules. My mother's health was grievously affected because of untoward behavior by my sibling who would phone my mother on her job and spew venom. A bevy of these outbursts within the home helped to widen any chasm existing in Olin and my mother's marriage. Ultimately my mother decided to divorce Olin when I was a junior in college. I personally think my mother wanted to simply not be a wife anymore and (get back out there to unregimented activities and behavior) without regard for the effect on me or anyone else for that matter. The night of the final blowout occurred during my and my mother's move from the home. Olin was very hurt and I was extremely disappointed and distraught to the point of being locked in their bedroom with forgotten loaded guns. By the time this was realized, I was adequately calm. I was not a violent individual; thus, my thought processes had never considered the use of possible deadly force to quell a situation. It tickled me to see the three of them, Olin, my mother, and sister standing in the hall after the skeleton key had been turned to release me from my temporary cell and to hear them remark almost in chorus, "We forgot there were guns in here when we locked you in, so come on out."

During my lockup time, consensus was reached that mama and I could remove the twin beds Olin had bought for me and my sister when we moved into the house on Raymont. The beds we had used on Page had been left there for my Cousin Skipper's convenience. Skipper had moved into our vacated home on which my mother paid the $83.06 monthly mortgage. After several months, Skipper moved out and my boyfriend Homer took over. My mother still paid the mortgage because Olin was absorbing the note on Raymont.

We, my mother and I, moved to a two-bedroom apartment on Euclid Heights Blvd. in Cleveland Heights. We struggled financially since my mother had to assume responsibility of all household expenses. In less than one year, my mother was not working and began receiving her Social Security (SS). She quickly saw how much fun it was not; being without someone around to care for and about her (a husband). Some of her male students at the college had convinced her that I should be the one to step in, fill in the gap. I had no intention of pulling the majority of her weight. I focused on my studies and steadfastly refused to fry burgers. When she asked me if I thought I was too good to do so, I told her, "Yes, I am." And that shut her mouth. She stayed drunk. Oh, well. I was finishing my degree, unencumbered by her bullshit. At one point, she broached me in a roundabout way of performing sexual favors with men for money. I never did. She must have been out of her fucking mind. She knew Homer and I were a couple, but even if we had not been, I would not prostitute for money. If I refused to fry burgers, I damn sure was not selling my body.

Anyway, things got so bad, that my mother told me to go apply for welfare. I did and began receiving a General Assistance (GA) check and medical benefits, but no food stamps because of the total household income which included my mother's SS check. To insure we had food, I implored a friend of mine who unloaded trucks at a super market to give me boxed dinners and canned goods, for as long as possible. I contributed my entire GA to our finances. Because Homer still paid the mortgage (by cash directly to us) on Page; that along with my GA brought in more than one-half of our current apartment rent.

One afternoon after my classes, I came home as usual, walked into the apartment, glanced to my left through the kitchen and into the dining area and was temporarily shocked at my mother sitting in inebriated gay conversation with a man I had not seen since I was six years old; this dog of a specimen and my mother's half-assed attempt to have me join them by saying, "Guess who this is, this is Benny (Towns)." I immediately recognized him as the older brother of Riley, The Preacher's Son who had raped "the little girl." I rolled my eyes at him, mumbled a barely audible "Hi" to them both and kept walking to my room where I remained until that dog had left. What the hell? What kind of mother or person period would thrust and twist a jagged, double edged sword into their child's theretofore stilled nightmare? My mother, that's who!

At some point my mother decided to stop remitting the note for the Page house and she began spending it. Rather than return to Page, economically affordable but, (a step down to East Cleveland, from my mother's perspective), she opted to have us remain where we were with rent almost exceeding $300.00 plus utilities. Granted, in winter, heating costs on Page would have been higher, so we stayed on Euclid Hts. Blvd. until my mother decided to move way out on Lakeshore Blvd., (cheaper rent, I think, but a greater distance from everything and everyone). One day, Homer received the formal Notice to Foreclose and I had to tell him what my mother had been doing or more to the point what she had not been doing, as evidenced by the Notice. Homer was forced to move. My mother didn't care. She'd temporarily ingratiated herself once more. The house fell into disrepair and with no heat in winter, the pipes burst, heavily damaging the lower level hardwood floors my sister and I had kept polished on our hands and knees for many years.

In early 1977, my stressed out senior year in college, I took a part-time job as a cashier at Open Pantry on Coventry and Cleveland Hts. Blvd. I was able to place my books under the counter and read and do some assignments between customers during my 3-11 shifts. I graduated August 14, 1977, and at my urging, Olin escorted my mother to the Bond Court festivities. They both beamed pride and I was happy to present a feigned semblance of a supportive family unit to my professors and friends. I was 21, degree in hand; very soon, had a "good job", and was on my way to my life with my integrity and reputation unsullied.

Before we moved I had taken another cashier job and shortly thereafter was hired by Fireman's Fund Insurance, and I knew this move would be my last with my mother. I was totally exhausted from her selfish disregard. We stayed on Lakeshore for about a year, perhaps not that long and then my mother decided to move again. I let her know, I was not moving with her, but on my own. I rented my first apartment in Indian Hills (195th St. and Euclid Ave.) and exhaled. My mother found her way to 250th and Euclid and I continued to assist her as needed or as I was financially or physically able. She wanted to "be out there" and so she was and remained by herself until her death 10 years later. I never abandoned my mother from my life, just tired of her manipulative non-altruistic mannerisms.

After I had moved to California I visited her at that apartment three times; in 1980, bringing my fiancé, Rahim, for her to meet before we married; the second time, I surprised her for Mother's Day, in cahoots with my sister who kept her on the phone during my drive from the airport. I knocked on her door and still talking with my sister she said, "Who is it?" I said, "It's me, Mama." I heard the phone drop, and the door flew open and she fainted. I stepped in folding her in my arms as she fell to her knees. We had a good visit. We talked a lot, while I brightened by hand with bleach water, years of thick layers of the nicotine stained walls of her kitchen; evidence of alone hours filled by excessive smoking. Recognizing the beginning of her descent, I truly felt sorry for her, in her aggregate woundedness. The last time I visited that apartment was 1983, during the time of my 10-year high school reunion. I knew she had to get out of there, and we discussed her exit. Before she moved for the final time of her life, I had her flown to California and during that visit, she attempted to have me agree to move her to San Jose, but I refused. It was later decided, without input from me that she move to Columbus, which she did. Over the course of the next five years my mother underwent extensive intervening treatment for contracted breast cancer. I would fly to Ohio for procedures on a moment's notice and surprised her once when she awoke in ICU after her mastectomy.

Adrea Adams

Fortification of my Inner Conscience

Preamble to Genesis

Everyone has a beginning, segue to a divide or not. My mother's birth occurred in 1933, a circa and focus of depressed national social economics. Mama's parents Harry Thomas and Ada Mae Cox resided in Lynchburg, Virginia. Preceding my mother, Carletha, were sisters Ruth and Gertrude. After my mother came Harry Jr., and finally the fifth child, the baby boy, Robert (Uncle Bobby). At the time of this expository, all are deceased excepting Uncle Harry. It has always struck me as odd that my grandmother's marital beginnings as they were, began with Harry Cox, and yet many of my current family members have no knowledge of him. For instance, my second cousin, the grandson of Ada's first son, Harry, had no knowledge that his true (blood) great grandfather was Harry T. Cox. This was until he visited me in 2010 and saw a photograph of his blood great grandfather hanging on my wall. Amazing that his own grandfather, my Uncle Harry, had not been instrumental in identifying his own father to his first-born grandson; or so the implication. Also, further confounding me is that many of my family members have relished in pride at the exponentially negation of their biological lineage to ascending generations. It is an abomination on high, in my opinion. I'll leave it up to them to reveal the truth to those shielded from the knowledge as documented in verifiable genealogy records.

My father, was born in 1932 in Philippe, West Virginia on a farm. I descend from him in the 8th generation of <u>his</u> father, Everlyn Elza Adams (b. 19, Oct., 1882- d. 21, Sept., 1961), and mother Loreda "Lori" Newman (b. 23, Nov., 1890 – d. 13, July, 1966). My father was the youngest of 10: Burchell (10 May,

1910- January, 30, 1983), J. Wilbur "Jay" Adams 5 Apr 1912. He died on 23 Oct 1972, Rosalee Margaret born on 3 May 1914 in Berryburg, Barbour County, West Virginia. She died on 27 Feb 1999. Dorsey Elisha, Mary Kathleen, born on November 7, 1918 and died in Buchannon, W. Virginia, 2005; Lenora May, born January 31, 1921, married Doctor Alfred L. COLES M. D. (son of FNUK Coles and Margaret L. Pettyjohn) was born on 25 Dec 1910 in Morgantown, Monongahalia County, West Virginia. He was educated. Dr. A. L. Coles came to Zanesville, Ohio area from Indianapolis where he had practiced since 1956 following his discharge from the Army Medical Corps. A native of Morgantown, West Virginia, Dr. Coles attended West Virginia State College. He obtained his science degree at the University of Pittsburgh and his medical degree at Meharry College in Nashville, Tenn. He served his internship at Lincoln Hospital in Hamilton, Ohio. While in the Military service he was stationed in Denver, Colorado and at Fort Riley, Kansas. During the late 1950s, Dr. Coles opened an office at 126 Pierce Street in Zanesville, Ohio.

Everlyn Elza, Jr., was born on 28 Apr 1922 in West Virginia. He was a School teacher and High School Principal in Barbour County, West Virginia. He was also a farmer for many years. He died 21, Sept., 1961. He was married to Lillian Dalton (daughter of Leroy Dalton and Maggie Trimble) about 1946. Lillian Dalton was born on 9 Feb 1919 in Barbour County, West Virginia. She died on 20 Apr 1976 in Barbour County, West Virginia. She was buried in Chestnut Ridge, Barbour County, West Virginia in the Welch Cemetery. Henry Gordan, was born on 11 Jul 1925. He died on 3 Nov 1948. He was married to Georgia Ellen "Duty" WELLS (daughter of Brisko WELLS and Bertie MAYLE). Georgia Ellen "Duty" Wells was born on 7 Apr 1927 in Philippi, Barbour County, West Virginia. She died on 9 Jul 1965 in Mercy Hospital, Canton, Stark County, Ohio. She was buried on 23 Jul 1965 in

Chestnut Ridge, Barbour County, West Virginia in the Welch Cemetery. Lillian, was born on 17 Aug 1929, and Melvin Slydell (my father), born 29, Sept., 1932 and died October 30, 1990, Columbus, Ohio.

I actually traced my father's genealogy back to first generation of entry into the United States to Ann "Dorton" Dalton, sentenced in Devon County England to be transported and arriving in 1750 in Prince Georges County Maryland resulting from the charge of having a bastard child, Henry. (http://familytreemaker.genealogy.com/users/b/a/r/Glenn-W-Barnett/FAMO2-0001/index.htm)

Maternally, I traced my grandmother, Ada Mae Rumley Cox Gregory to times of slavery. Arthur Jerry Eldridge b. 1853 – d. 1918, was my grandmother's grandfather, and one of 21 slaves owned by Daniel B. Eldridge (1860 Forsyth County, N. C.). My maternal grandmother, Ada Mae Rumley (b. 10/27/1911- d. 2/12/2006), born in Rural Hall, North Carolina, descended from parents Lindsey Rumley, b. 1873 and Maggie Rumley, b. 1874. Ada's siblings were twins, Paul and Silas, b. 1877, Cleo, b.1895-d.1980, Eva, b. 1897, McKenley, b. 1899, Annie, b. 1907 – d. 1978, Laddie, b. 1901, Edna, b. 1904 and Arthur, b. 1909. None of my grandmother's siblings remain. My grandmother was an enterprising individual, succeeding during a time of great tensions and turmoil. Ada, attended and graduated Porto Beauty School, Lynchburg, Virginia and Barber College at West Virginia State College. Ada married Garrett R. Gregory, a mortician. Their respective skills and talents meshed to form Gregory Funeral Home in Williamson, West Virginia; concurrently Ada continued to operate and manage her own barber shop, built as an annex to their family home. The funeral home was situated on the other side of the home on Harvey Street. (My maternal grandmother's family origins were

Fortification of my Inner Conscience

My 58th birthday was yesterday. No cause for celebration. I do not celebrate my birth. When it was important to me, my 16th. I had waited as many years for *16 Candles*. I was a 'Sweet 16'. (had barely been kissed, was definitely a virgin, had bolted from the first teen boy, Jon Sylvester, who received an erection during a slow dance at a party in neighbor, Wanda Ingram's basement; awoke that morning, dressed for my 11th grade classes, walked to Shaw High school, barely got through the day from hoped for surprises of acknowledgement when I arrived home that afternoon.

I returned home from school walking west on Terrace Rd., then north on Page Ave., my street. I skipped down the half block and ran up our walk way. I loved that house, mostly because we had lived there for the longest period of time in our still short lives. The three story with beige trim wood framed house had been built in 1920. The front porch, bordered by 5' hedges was gray painted wood planks. The front door was of heavy carved mahogany wood with a 2" thick beveled oval glass pane. Even the door knob was ornately carved. The door opened into a vestibule of marble floor and to the immediate right was another door with heavy floor to ceiling beveled glass which opened onto the slickest wood floors highly shined with Johnson and Johnson liquid wax. Those floors were our pride. The living room stretched about 20' and in its front center were three double paneled windows set in glistening mahogany wood frames. At the far end of the living room was a fireplace with built-in book cases on either side. And for good reading measure there were two built in benches that had raised seat/lids. On both sides of the fireplace was a window and one window was also placed above the front bench. These three windows contained exquisite inlays of lead décor.

When I walked in I half-heartedly expected a few balloons to be in the living room with my mother sitting and smiling on the sectional with a burst of "Happy Birthday, my sweet sixteen", but nothing was floating in the air and there was no gift-wrapped package, so I simply mumbled a dejected "Hi, mama", which brought the inquiry, "What's the matter?" I let her know. That was one of the too few times, I let my mother know how I felt. I deeply regret not speaking my mind and thoughts to her about so many, many things. I got over that birthday and threw my own wonderful 16th party when I was about 28, but you can never recapture lost moments in time even if they are only slivers. However... late(r) you can expel feelings and thoughts, but you can never expunge the slate for what has in fact occurred. One of my favorite songs for choice of lyric is *The Living Years* by Mike and the Mechanics and when I initially memorized the words, I thought they were indicative of what my brother Keith might have harbored about our father, Melvin, but the lyrics turn to me in regurgitation for my memoir.

Necessarily, I preface the following, because some family members, close 'friends', or associates may be learning this for the first time. My intent is not to lend negativity or to alter an established opinion, but to share my truth. If you disagree, that is your truth. I will contend that some readers had knowledge but steadfastly refused to accept the reality.

To a fault, I honored my mother in her living years. I do not regret any kindness, generosity, or love bestowed her. She was my mother, the only one I knew, and I refused my grandmother's offer to leave her at age 11 because I felt sorry for my mother and in all sincerity, knew my sister could not handle the household had I accepted the proffering of Mama Ada and so I stayed with physical abuse continuing against my sister and me. The beatings were not daily, but when they occurred, they were almost savage in nature. The first time I remember being bloodied by mama was when I was about five, perhaps four. We lived on Gray Street in Columbus. I have no recollection of what I could possibly have done to deserve being picked up and with great force flung across the room, where I landed on the floor and slid left face/eye flush into a steel bed frame corner. My eye gushed a stream of non-stop blood for many minutes. Finally, Keith looked at me and expressed concern and mama shouted "Too bad, well, she's going to have to walk to the store by herself for Band-Aids." I should have had emergency room stitches, as evidenced by the gash still remaining in the corner of my left eye today.

Another kind of abuse against me was my mother's forcing me to take her to a bar just before closing, in the dead of night. I was about 5 or 6. Daddy was working his second job. Mama would get me up or not let me go to bed and then I'd lead her to the bar where she would buy a 6-pack of Blatz or Pabst Blue Ribbon beer. I guess when she had extra change, she'd buy me an ice-cream or Heath candy bar. I detested the sexual leering of the male patrons. My mother couldn't see them, but I sure as hell could. My mother didn't care, apparently, about the perceivable danger we were in. A blind woman with a small child in the sapphire blue ink of night. We'd return home, go into the kitchen where she'd talk until the 6-pack was gone or my head hit the table from sleep deprivation. She'd talk to me as if I were an adult, drinking, smoking cigarettes, non-stop.

Sometimes she'd wake us up in our beds and beat us from our sleep. Imagine being pummeled through a blanket in a dark room with a stupid remark like, "Who left the so and so, thus?" These sleep beatings happened primarily in Sullivant Garden Apartments in Columbus when I was in second but primarily third grade. Third grade also saw the beginning of mama going out and partying more on school nights. One of the persons mama night-clubbed with was named Caleb. This was the time of "Evening in Paris" perfume, Betty Brooks and her kids, "I got a whole house Betty", -son Tyrone memorably said one day at about age three or four- and daughter, Joanne. I loved Betty and her kids, but they or especially Betty coming over sometimes meant late, late nights out for mama. One time mama got in so late that she overslept and did not wake to comb our hair as usual. I combed my hair for the first time and (I guess) I was so good at it that my days as family hairdresser began. From then on, I was combing, Lilt and Care Free Curl perming, French rolling, chignoning, my little hands off. I was really good at styling hair; could look at a magazine photo and style hair (any style) before I was nine years old and in hind sight, this talent may have been one reason my grandmother wanted me, since she was a barber by trade.

We moved so much, could never really establish ourselves. Mama would hear a damn song and decide to move. I vividly remember this on 88th St. in Cleveland. She called Uncle Harry on a summer Friday night and he agreed to come get us the next day. So, early the next day, we got up, went in search of boxes, and packed. Keith had a job at the stadium for baseball games (bless his heart). He was growing up and really needed things, like more than two pair of pants to wear to a Catholic school (for which mama could not really afford tuition, but we finished one hellish year). Anyway, Uncle Harry arrives and loads the truck. Mama is in such a rush to go that she leaves

Keith a message and Greyhound bus fare with Mr. Jones, the apartment building manager. Damn! We load all furnishings, Nanette, our German Shepard, and us two girls in the back of the truck. Uncle Harry had brought his son Dwaun, so we four kids (Dwaun, my younger sister, brother and I) got in back, and threw macaroni out an air slit over the 132-mile drive. I hated that move; didn't make any sense, especially since we had no new home to move right in to. In 16 years of education, including four each of high school and four in college, I attended 13 schools. (In fourth grade I attended four schools; two in Columbus and two in Cleveland). I never got put back a grade. We had no choice but to adjust; but I never had friends. Fortunately, and thankfully, I was book smart, so I could escape.

Mama's beer drinking and intake of other substances began to spiral when we returned to Cleveland for the last time, and to my second 6th grade school, Mary McLeod Bethune, off of 123rd. I began to blossom a bit. I was nominated class President and I joined Mr. DeFranco's orchestra, playing flute, but settling on violin. I suppose I was saving my lung power for running. I did, too. This was when I discovered my talent for running competitively. I ran like the wind. One boy, Reuben, even complimented me on my 'big, pretty' legs. I was perplexed because I was skinny in my body, my teeth not having caught up with my head so, I was teasingly called 'skelly' by some of the girls. It was cool. I was a boys' girl, playing their sports, yet I was feminine. This is when jealousy and bullying by girls began to escalate. I ignored the girls and kept on running and playing my violin, excelling in French and English Literature, and writing. I was a good Second Violinist and asked daddy to buy me my own instrument so I could practice any time. Daddy personally delivered my violin to me. I'll never forget that day. My own violin with extra strings, rosin, and a case. I was ecstatic going to school the next day toting that shiny case, almost as long as I was tall. It was a grand moment of special bond between father and daughter.

We lived on 123 Street for about one year, then moved around the corner to Ashbury. Helen Jefferson, her husband (we called him Jeff or Old Man Jeff because he was senior to Helen by about 20 years), and their seven daughters: Sheryl, Regina, Antoinette, Sonia, Daphne, Deidre, and Tarae, moved into our former house. Immediately upon their arrival, my sister and I introduced ourselves. Mama and Helen became fast friends; they had drinking in common and similar personalities and we nine girls became close. Helen and mama went out sometimes. The Jeffersons had no car, just like us.

My sister was a year younger than I was but always two grades behind me because I began first grade early at age five. Anyway, at this time, winter 1967, I was in seventh grade and she was in fifth, attending separate schools. My junior high, Harry E. Davis was a longer distance from home. One snowing afternoon, my sister arrived home to find mama out. By the time I arrived, she was frantic. We waited and waited but no mama. As dusk began, we really got worried and went to ask neighbors had they seen mama who we were told was with Helen. We looked and searched until darkness fell and then we (along with some of the Jefferson girls found them not far from home (about a block and a half); passed out cold in a deep snow drift. I don't know how we did it, but we got them home. I guess Helen caught flak from Jeff, but my sister and I spent several hours trying to get mama to wake up. She kept blacking out and finally told what she had taken in addition to alcohol and it wasn't marijuana. We kept watch over her; my sister freaking out, crying for what to do. Somehow, I knew we had to warm and monitor her simultaneously. I think we did a damn good job; saved her from possibly freezing to death or overdosing on illegal substances. The drug she'd mixed with alcohol could very well have brought an end to her life. My point to sharing this is my mother's disregard for the emotional affectation that her behavior impinged upon us; just totally selfish disregard in the name of a good time. We kids never told, of course not... but neighbors knew. Someone always knows. To say the least, we girls were traumatized. But the partying days did not end by a long shot. I continued to escape into my books, school, play-acting in the mirror, and violin playing. My sister, well, she hung in there, but began rebelling outwardly. Jeff and Helen transitioned many years ago. However, I remain friends with the Jefferson girls to this day.

Fast forward to Page Ave. and 10th grade. I could read music, even had a sheet music stand for practicing at home. I'd played the Pomp and Circumstance in my 8th grade graduation from Kirk Junior High. Mama didn't attend as she had a job by then, so Aunt Hannah came for me.

One day when I was in high school, mama called from her job to tell me to meet her at the store when she got off the bus from work; to bring my violin as she had sold it to a lady for the lady's daughter. I began to protest, but mama insisted she needed the agreed upon 'bargain' price of $12.00. I did as I was told and delivered my prized property to Wolf's Liquors on Euclid and Page and witnessed my mother give my violin away for beer and cigarette money! That woman knew she had made a killing and my mother never saw her again. My mother was always thinking someone was her friend when they were only using her. I didn't speak up and I should have, but it's too late, now. I sulked for a long time, and hurled myself into my studies and Hippie Dom.

Physical beatings continued and especially verbal confrontations between my mother and sister. My sister rebelled. I was never rebellious; did as told, (except once *I broke curfew) out of respect and a slight fear of being beat in my sleep if I did rebel. I rebelled by wearing mama's good clothes when she got drunk. My sister and I would wait until she passed out, then wake her just enough to get a groggy "Yeah, girl", when we asked if we could wear an outfit.

The last time I saw mama damn near kill my sister was when she was about 15. Just a rage. My sister told my mother she hated her and wished she was dead and mama flew at her, grabbed her and picked her up and threw her in an iron cast tub and beat her bad. I kept yelling and grabbing at her for her to stop, but she kept at it. See- we never ran from mama even though she was blind because we had to go to sleep. People asked us all the time, "Why don't y'all just run, she can't see you to come after you?" and that's what we told neighbors, "We have to go to bed," especially when we were younger.

*The first and only time I broke our 11:00 curfew as a teenager, I had gone to the family home of the Evans' boys. The Evans lived about a 15-minute walk from our home. I had visited there a few times with my friend and neighbor Wanda Ingram who was dating the eldest son, Dwight. The other two sons were Alvie and Dwayne who was in my class at Shaw High. I liked visiting them because theirs was a true family unit, a mother and father, children, warm and inviting with good food aplenty or so it seemed. On this evening, we teens seemed to become famished as the evening wore on. I delayed my departure hoping to be fed, share in a meal before walking home. At about 10:00, a spaghetti meal was finally begun and I was impressed at how it was fixed without any tomato sauce (I think the delay in meal prep was probably because of my extra stomach, them hoping I'd leave), but I was hungry and not much awaited me at home. So, I stayed, scared to call mama. Around 11:45, Alvie walked me home with their family protector Shepard in tow. As we began to walk up the hill to my house, my heart pounded until at the crest, I saw the yellow headlights of a car parked in the street at the top of the hill. My instincts told me it was the police because cars were not allowed to park on the streets. I was right. As I crossed over to my side, I thanked my escort and said goodnight. The car cruised slowly toward me as my heart thumped. The officer stopped in front of my house, rolled the passenger window down, leaned over and said, "Are you Adrea? Your mother is worried about you, you better go on in." I slowly walked up the walkway and five steps, turned the key in the main door. I stepped into the vestibule, turned slightly to reach for the other door, but before I could place my hand on the knob, it flung open into the pitch-black living room and out came the fierce hammer of my mother's bludgeoning fist on top of my head. She knocked me out. When I came to, in utter bewilderment, I forced myself up on wobbly legs and felt wetness dripping down my legs. I thought the blow had caused urine to leak. I pushed past this creature, ran upstairs to discover that she had shocked my menstrual blood to flow. My head throbbed, my tears streamed, as I cursed her under my breath, cleaned myself, and went to bed with a violent headache, with her bitching in the background. Why had that officer left? Again, no one to rescue me. My mother had set the scene with her conniving ways; get the police on her side as a (concerned?) parent, then lay in wait to mete out another round of her fucked up abuse. If she was so concerned, why were all the lights off in the house... all of the lights? She did that shit on purpose, she knew the officer could have probably seen her strike me. Mama was blind in her eyes, but not her brain, I guess. Maybe she was a little off balance.

Anyway, that was the final time she caused blood to spring from my body.

    Mama jerked her head into a tense, "Come here." I walked toward her in the same hall from which she'd thrown my sister into the tub. I walked with a plan to end this crap. I looked at her, sized her up, and simultaneously as if commandeered by Allah, I recognized that I was looking down on her head and outstretched balled up fists which I, to her great shock, grabbed at the wrists, jerked them down so she'd know I wasn't afraid anymore. I forcibly squeezed her wrists and almost wrung them as I yanked them down and held them firm. A slight smile broke on her face. She knew I had control over her but what sealed it was me gradually, with firm meaning releasing her wrists but instead of letting them fall, she calmly reached out to me, felt up to my shoulders and neck and said, "Well, I'll be damned, you're taller than me" and I meant it when I said without hesitation, "Yes, I am and I'm not letting you hit me again, I can beat you up, now." We both chuckled lightly, but she knew I was dead serious about it. She never hit me again and to my knowledge the bath tub beating was my sister's last. I was the big sister and I was not having any more of this shit, for myself or my sister.

    I shared here some episodes of abuse by my mother, albeit there had been lots more, categorically. It's not about forgiving, but I didn't hold on, have never venomously held on to others' hurting of me. I reiterate, I honored my mother in her alive years, and now she's forever asleep. I trust she is resting well. I cared for her when no one else did and I am the better for having done so. A lot of it I choose to believe she could not help. It is easier to believe her abuse and excessive drinking stemmed from frustration at vicarious loneliness affixed by her blindness at age three. Otherwise, she was, at times amazing and if the mood strikes me, I'll share some of the marvelousness in another title of memory.

In plausible concrete psychoanalytical probe, I deduce that my mother's abuse was likely a twisted manifestation directed toward her eyes: my sister and me, who served as her lost sight.

Seven Laws

Aside from the five pillars of Islam, I have judiciously tried to adhere to the recognition and integration of seven life principles by engaging in activities of alignment for their respective furtherance. The laws are: the **law of difference** which has decided my rewards in this life by fueling my passion for distinction, **law of mind**, essentially (anyone's) true thoughts predicate reality, **law of recognition**, meaning I am aware every minute of my multitude of blessings, **law of two**, or simple multiplication; the difference between my life seasons is the one who sees me; the difference between my poverty or prosperity is one person, **law of place,** I go where I am celebrated, not tolerated, **law of honor,** who I honor/respect can be a determinant of my future, and **law of seed,** planting a long-term imperative for my future.

My Most, Best Three

~I heard it said, was in fact told by a de facto non-congealed mother-in-law in waiting, that men get three "good" women during their lives..."and you're the third and last for my son." This observation revealed itself in 2001. I believe the mother desired for her son to recognize what he had in me and that his life's term was 'perhaps' nearing. As it turns out, the son did succumb nine years later. ~

My first love remains Homer, an essence never to be undone or replicated. It was an instantaneous attraction in 1973, from his first step into my family's living room at 1863 Page Avenue in East Cleveland, Ohio. Everybody knew and still knows, 40 years later. Pure and unadulterated was our best love. Secrets whispered; still protected. Justifiably at 20, I refused his proposal of marriage. We remain the best of friends, loving, sharing, and caring from afar, forgiving all, which dictated such.

My second most best is Mirrahim (Rahim), my former spouse. He loved me and I loved him right back. Oh yes, I did. I will forever love him. We married in our mid-twenties, probably too young for this economically-driven Persian man and budding young African American woman executive. However, the ideas and ideals were good, honest, and passionate. There was a ripened variety of passion. (Multi-layered passion, particularly ideology). We unintentionally hurt each other. Neither of us right nor wrong, simply unyielding, imploring to be noticed. I chose to stop hurting and I wept divorcing him. I think he believed I was going to marry someone else, but he was most wrong. He was my best husband and I doubt I will join thus again. I am not excluding myself from the tepid notion of becoming another man's "Darling Sunshine."

My third and most best is Henry. He is the most forthcoming, steadfast, and unyielding in the intricacies of support. The one who knows me most and the best for all spans is Henry. Ours has endured despite its ornery self. Our love has no beginning or end in 'your' time. I have memorialized him poetically, so I beckon you to delve more to see what I have experienced most best.

War Interrupted What Could Have Been

Don't know how or when precisely the awareness took hold that I've never been much afraid of anything or anyone. Certainly I possess the innate and protective fear factor, for it governs survival tactics. An absolute must to save life or prolong death. To my way of deductive reasoning, there is no such thing as saving life, for we know that a debt of death is owed by us all.

I've had many encounters with near "too soon, too young to die" circumstances involving scenarios which in the macabre director's climatic scene would have surely ended in the worst.

Some life scenarios outdistance others. Inquisitiveness led me towards many streams from which I drank or in which I toe-dipped. One of the keys for healthy survival is identifying putrid materials in your journey through the valley of the shadow of death or in one gentler word, **life,** which is simply to what this passage in the biblical Psalm 23 refers.

My high school days in the early 1970's brought engagement and curiosity in and of many realms ranging from the *hippie* movement to the Foreign Exchange students at my high school or those attending Case Western Reserve University, where I would commune on occasion for intake of nourishment. I wore jeans with patches sewn on them in some unmentionable places, hitchhiked Euclid Avenue, sometimes hailing taxicabs. My hitchhiking days ended when I graduated college in 1977, a year before Lawrence Singleton picked up hitchhiker, Mary Vincent, in Berkeley, CA, raped her and cut off her forearms. (My mother expressed concern that something like this would happen to me, but unknown to her, those days had ceased for me).

As far as I knew I was the first Black female in my high school to go braless, after the disbanding of mandatory uniforms; middy blouses with "dickies" and skirts at the knee. My tastes in music ran the gamut from Classic to Reggae and of course Mick Jagger, my heartthrob, to die for crush, and the Rolling Stones, and Jimi Hendrix.

****

Those were some fun, educational and gratifying days for me. I even attended some *Black Panther* meetings at the church on my street. Of course, I did not join this group, but I wanted to. My mother would not have stood for it. I did not find them radical or anti-government. What I was drawn to though was the fact that the members espoused education, fighting poverty, and providing food for needy Day Care children. Those were the messages I received, to which I was drawn, and remember most.

Always, I loved my books, reading and writing. My worse poem ever was one I wrote to music in 10th grade for Mrs. Linson's Black Literature class. Classmate Jackie Banks gave the best presentation; her poem being set to Marvin Gaye's *What's going on?* I don't remember what the poem was about but the tune was a pop hit all by itself.

I didn't go to many neighborhood parties. The few relatives I hung and partied with as a teen did so with close male friends of the family. At one of those black light with faux velvet Astrological sign wall hangings, with ceiling nets, and smoky room sessions, the lyrics "When I heard my mother say, Hey, what she say, what she say? She said, you been slipping into darkness. Pretty soon you're gonna pay," prophetically imploded out of the treble and bass of the speakers.

Those lyrics had a most profound and defining impact on the direction I chose to take in my life. I looked around that room and at the faces staring, a few nodding in the haze, and I knew how it could continue or turn out. I'm so glad I had the ability to foresee the tragedy which befell one of those partygoers. I said, "Not me, no way in hell. I'm going to not be that way." That one partygoer is still partying nearly 40 years later. What a waste! Those lyrics by the band, *War*, interrupted what could have been but for the grace and favor of my God, and my own desire to do and be good. I wouldn't let my family, my nucleus down. I did not slip into darkness, but many I knew did and will never return to the light because they are no longer alive.

Some College Days

How I Got There

Carolyn Smith (Ms. Smith), was my high school counselor. She once remarked fondly, "You're everybody else's Adrea, but you'll always be my A<u>n</u>drea". That was cool because I liked her. I suppose it began in the early part of my senior year that intense counseling sessions began, albeit, tracking began years earlier.

I wanted to go to college to become a teacher (I'd wanted to be a teacher since about age five when I taught my stuffed animals, dolls, and younger siblings as they sat on my red toy box) and I shared this with Ms. Smith. She reflected on my transcripts from eighth grade onward and explained why she felt I should major in business and that she had a Huntington Scholarship for me if I chose to attend Dyke College, a private institution in downtown Cleveland. Ms. Smith was very persuasive and I acquiesced and agreed. Unbeknownst to me, my best friend since eighth grade, Linda Jackson, was extended the same offer. These acceptances set us on a course of friendship continuing for 45 years.

At the appointed day and time Linda and I took our ACT exams, qualifying us to proceed. Later in the spring of 1973 we would join again for our photo in Cleveland's downtown outdoor mall. We were both excited. I do not recall who took possession of that group photo or for that matter what organization sanctioned it; probably the Huntington folks. Anyway, we were off and running, with initial plans to attain only an Associate. The pace of time, mental and social maturity quickened. Before we could catch our breaths, we were on the cusps of becoming juniors and bam, just like that one day Linda said, "I think I want to get a Bachelors, what about you?" We mused about it for a few days, then informed Admissions, Financial Aid, etc. and we continued on while many dropped out. The program was strenuous with stiff math and accounting components, but I hung in there. Linda was good in math and I countered with my written language skills.

My math was really bad, but I did my best; finally receiving a solid C in my statistics class the summer we graduated, 1977. I took great notes in class and passed them on to Linda who had designed a plan to take certain classes after I did, so she had an advantage, a bit. Anyway, it all worked out. She supported me and vice versa.

In the meantime, we had fun, fun, fun. Linda always worked, even in high school. I had only worked summer jobs as a teen. Linda's uncle owned a dry-cleaning business and she worked there after classes. Linda also, owned a car (s). We started off in a sea foam green Rambler until it rambled no longer. Next came Linda's black Mustang, sometimes requiring a spray to the carburetor before we could go home. We ended college in Linda's Nova. Linda would pick me up every morning on time, no matter Cleveland's winter weather. In four years, we were never late, never missed a class; might have been a bit hung over, but we got the job done on time in four years- Lynn and Adrea.

Ultimately, there were four then five in our clan, Linda, Brenda Alford, Sandra Herron, Adrea, and then Lakeita. We played cards (bid whist) every day in The *Driftwood*, ate grilled cheese sandwiches prepared by Connie Rosan, generally took over with the sounds of Marvin Gaye, Barry White, The Rolling Stones, Cymande, The Independents, Elton John, Rita Coolidge,

The Steve Miller Band, The New Birth, Christopher Cross, The Doobie Brothers and so, so, many more, and grew up.

All sorts of things took place in the *Driftwood*, from discovering different nationalities, to me hanging a Playgirl centerfold of a buffed Fred (the hammer) Williamson on the mirror in the Ladies Room. At one point, I took calls on the pay phone from members of the Cleveland Cavaliers: Bingo Smith, Jim Chones, or Campy Russell, the latter of whom was trying to get me to visit their training camp. I refused, to the chagrin of Campy, because I had visited his beautiful home and seen a pretty home-baked cake on a marble counter top and instinctively knew that a woman had baked it. When asked about the cake Campy did admit that his girlfriend had made it. Good. That's all I needed to know. However, one Sunday night, I was finishing a paper just before *Kojak* aired on television and my phone rang. It was a woman identifying herself as the wife of one of the Cavaliers. I assured her that I didn't know her spouse, that one of the three named herein must have given him my number. Boy, oh boy did that call unnerve me, plus I had my very first toothache besides. I was pissed. Those men or one of them, probably Campy, had passed my number out. Oh, hell no! That did it. I was done with them. They all had met my mother the day I met them in Higbee's Department store. Bingo was intrigued with my mother's sassiness and blindness so he would call her on occasion just to say hello.

After we learned that Lakeita was transgender, she and I stayed close during my remaining time at Dyke. All we saw was a female wearing nice clothes and Flori Roberts make up, using the Ladies room, always well groomed, manicured, and a lot of fun; the girl who'd brought a shopping bag of Alex Haley's *Roots* and sold them to us at discount prices. I still have my copy. This was the lady who kept me in toiletries and once told another female student, who'd picked at me, "You got a song to sing, well sing it to me. Ain't nobody gone mess with "A". With that our friendship was sealed. She sometimes took my phone calls from the Cavaliers. She was my friend. I don't know what happened to her after the rest of us graduated, but I saw her a few times in later years. I doubt life was kind to her. In fact, I highly suspect it was very unkind to her. She was born male, had even been married. We never discussed her transformation; only that she was going to have a sex change. I supported her through that; was one of very few to visit her as she convalesced at University Hospital. I don't know how she met a once R&B chart-topping, but then struggling and waning in popularity, all male singing group, but she did. Near one Thanksgiving, she mentioned that she had to go shopping for them and take some things to their hotel. My step father had arranged for my weekend Avis rental, so I agreed to go with Lakeita as she "shopped". Lakeita could shop. I walked idly around near her as she selected products for the group. When she finished, she said, "OK, that's it, I'm done." We walked out of the store, her carry-all bag bulging. As I drove her to her destination, a dingy motel on Euclid Avenue, she spoke of her selections, something like, "I had to get my babies some goodies, Epsom salt, Preparation H, girl please, they're hurting. I was shocked at this knowledge, but more surprised to see an approximate 8 ½ month butt- naked pregnant woman having relations with one group member when the door swung open to the group's room. Damn, what was going on? Slowly other men sauntered into the room, glaring at me inquiringly as Lakeita produced her bag of goodies. Lakeita left the goodies and I hurried her out of that dank place, and sped her to her home, as my mouth gaped when she revealed the name of the group's lead singer and the balance of the male members, which I will not reveal for obvious reasons. They sure were happily relieved to see Lakeita and her bag of soothing goodies. I presumed they performed better, later that evening. Wink, wink.

Linda and I were some cuties, back then. Budding into discovery of early womanhood. We both had pretty legs and naturally long fingernails. Linda's nails grew straight with a slight bow. Mine were very hard and naturally curved. (We did our own manicures with most girls envying our nails. Acrylic nail salons did not exist). Our hair was always 'whipped, at least Linda's was. (She went to a salon). I did my own hair, primarily wore it straight back and pinned. What I lacked in the hair department, I made up for in clothes. I mean, I dressed; had what I thought to be the best over-all wardrobe among the Black girls. I wore pump heels, ensembles of every description, Homer inspired and supplied Nik Nik pure silk blouses accessorized with silver, coral, and lapis. Not every day, but watch out. Once I donned a felt hat with ostrich feathers to a basketball game, courtesy of a guy who liked me. Linda dressed more casual, probably because she had to go to work, but Linda had some very nice outfits. My favorite on her was her 'farmer' jeans or 'painter pants', just darling on her, with her voluptuous shape. I was thin, having lost my 'baby fat' over the summer.

The Road Ahead – Quiet Influences

Funny now, but then it was not: totally innocent offspring of youthful naiveté.

One of my professors, an Indian from India had a 'crush' on me, but I spurned his advances; no reporting, nothing newsworthy like in the 21st century. I accepted it as a compliment from this family man. On the other hand...

I had a crush on a teacher. He probably knew it and was used to it. (Perhaps). I never flirted with him or anything, just was intrigued by his black waxed in sideburns and admired what I deemed brilliance. He was probably no smarter than I was 15 years ago. However, I took it upon my young silly self to find out where he lived; to see his books. I don't know how I did it (most likely, just the phone book), but I found his address without the non-existent Internet or public media. I told Linda and she drove me to his house one evening. My intent was to tell him how much I admired him, try to engage conversation on an intellect beyond the classroom. The boldest Adrea traipsed up his walkway, one clear autumn evening, rang his doorbell as Linda stood off to the side. When he opened the door, the well-lit room spilled onto the walk. I glanced past his seemingly pleasantly shocked face to see a woman he was apparently entertaining. I immediately apologized and got the hell out of his zip code. I was later to discover that that most innocent of search and locate was instrumental in me recognizing a skill which I mastered into private investigations. Isn't life something else?

Another teacher took us as a class to his Baskin Robbins franchise, to understand better how to operate a business. Although my mother operated a snack bar in the Ohio College of

Podiatric Medicine, that teacher made me want to have my own business. I launched Triple A Investigations in 1994.

In the final analysis, we kids enjoyed ourselves, took care of business before anything else, and had mostly clean fun, supplying each other with supportive essentials as we could. We accomplished our goals without violence or extreme jealousy. We recognized ourselves as an entity, many of us historically striding and illuminating a guiding pathway for those traversing now. Oh, I wish they could see, know, and understand with enraptured hardiness.

"Rex and the Surprise"

A Retelling with Fictitious Names, except Rex
12-11-2012

Cleveland's (Ohio) *Collinwood Area* is dotted with neighborhood bars- a mix of corner pubs previously catering to Irish and Polish communities, but by the mid-1980s and early 1990s African Americans were gaining commercial entry on the periphery of this hard-working middle class enclave.

Enter, dapper Don Watkins, managing proprietor/operator of Don's Place. A thumping always "Happy Hour" if head bar/Cocktail Waitress, Antoinette, had anything to do or say about it. Antoinette was and still is the prettiest woman to grace her family and indeed the nightclub scene; could spin a conversation, 50-dollar bill, or Courvoisier, like nobody's business. Contrary to whispered innuendos, Don was not a "ladies man, only one lady, his Miss Lucy. "All that money... You know they're doing well. She got a *good job* too... he can get anybody he wants...I know he has to be messin' around...," had gotten back to Lucy. However, then again, things had cooled a bit in the loving department in that bungalow- or had it? Mostly though, Don worked and I mean diligently hard in Don's Place. Don was indeed enterprising, hardworking, admired and respected for his business savvy, had married ladylove Lucille or as he called her Miss Lucy, so it was with exuberance when he announced his great business deal. He had scrimped, saved, and manipulated a deal to purchase two adjoining plots of land, buildings included. On one lot rested the bar. On the other lot sat an unassuming bungalow with a finished basement.

Lucy had forged her demure way into corporate Cleveland as a receptionist for a mortuary and did not participate in nightclub festivities, savoring private toasting and intimate moments, exclusively with Don. Thus, Miss Lucy's evenings were spent sheltered in the bungalow under the protective eyes of Don's German Shepard watchdog, Rex. Lucy and Rex became constant, inseparable, dependent, evening companions. Rex had a loyal and protective kind of temperament, just as most 'good' dogs. Just like Pavlov's experimental dogs, Rex received a reward for a job well done. Rex enjoyed quite an easy, peaceful life. Rex spent his days lounging with Don who slept or tended errands Lucy could not accomplish to or from her mundane receptionist duties. No real 'life' or thrills at the mortuary, just sad mournful souls drifting in and out. That is what Lucy began to do, a hesitant journey of drifting. Lucy longed for the touch and comfort of her dapper Don as she started to embrace some of the whispers.

Unbeknownst to Lucy, how could it be known, several of the bar's employees and selected patrons decided to surprise her with a private gathering in the bungalow in the twilight hours of her birthday on Friday after the 1:30 a.m. closing time. Because neighborhood cars parked in close proximity neither Don nor Lucy would gather suspicion, so Don was chided into leaving a few minutes early with the selected patrons and staff eagerly anticipating walking next door for the celebration.

Don entered the side door, gently yelled out to Miss Lucy, and got no response. At this, Don motioned for the guests to enter quietly and they obliged him, with Don calling for Lucy- but still no response from Lucy or guard dog Rex. Odd, it was indeed. Just through the kitchen was the ajar door leading to the descending staircase of the finished and apparently soundproof basement. Don began to descend the stairs followed by giddy tiptoeing guests who were still remarkably well behaved. Two steps from the bottom, Don glanced over to the laundry area and there he spied Miss Lucy stark butt naked, straddled atop a pile of laundry, dripping in peanut butter with Rex's lungs and tongue panting in delight, just as Don and the guests simultaneously shouted. "SURPRISE!!!!"

Rolling Good Times

~ "I've had enough merde thrown on me all my life, that I've used it as fertilizer"~

Eartha Kitt, April, 2008

I heard Eartha speak these words with conviction in a taped introduction of a live recording of the song *Alone* in one of her last concerts filmed at Cheltenham (England) Jazz Festival. To my immense pleasure and delight, the video of this performance shows a former junior high and high school classmate, Tony Award winner, Daryl Waters, accompanying her on piano as musical director. I was not surprised to see the two of them perform together since I'd seen them in these conjunctive roles twice before, in Emeryville, California. Wow, two of my favorite persons of this world, this life! Daryl doesn't know it, but I made Eartha aware of it during our first meeting backstage in her dressing room at Kimball's East venue. I was simply ecstatic and quite anxious when I walked to the stage's edge and introduced myself to security while sharing that Eartha was my idol, had been since I was a child; that I had to meet her personally. I was granted the opportunity of a lifetime, led backstage and into Eartha's dressing room where I was honored with the pleasure of being introduced to Eartha and Eartha's daughter Kitt Shapiro. I hurriedly told of how I was then planning to prepare to be considered for the role of Eartha, if and when her life story was brought to film. I apparently convinced Eartha of my sincerity, to the point that Kitt wrote her (Kitt's) name and phone number down on one of the pink concert card notices. I still have that card in a Ziploc bag of memories. But most of all I own all three of Eartha's autobiographical installments personally autographed by her when we met. I remember distinctly extending to her with pride my hardbound, First Edition copy of *Thursday's Child*, copyrighted in 1956, the year of my birth. Eartha asked Kitt, "Do we have this one?" (Meaning an original) and Kitt responded "No", which brought a quizzical glance from Eartha to me, but I said, "Oh, no, Eartha, I can't part with it". Eartha understood why and obliged me by signing my copy. Ironically, I was born on a Thursday on January 19. Eartha was born on January 17, 1927, a Monday.

Standing there talking with someone I so admired was among the most fantastical moments in my life. I have met and conversed with many famous personalities, Isaac Hayes, Barry White (before he was a household name). Barry had a crush on my sister but she said he was too big, so she spurned his advances), The Dramatics and The Stylistics, Whoopi Goldberg, Curtis Mayfield, Melba Moore, Joie Lee (Spike Lee's sister), even slow danced with Clifton Davis at a Black Filmmakers function, where I also met football great Jim Brown, one fine, intelligent brown man!!!

Surprise of my Life

I had, with mastery, refused to accommodate Homer's prodding for intimacy for nearly 9-10 months. Homer was becoming agitated. We dated exclusively and as far as I was concerned, there was no problem. I'm sure the problem began with a full erection in my living room as we sat, petted and kissed, cooed, and suddenly, I spied this dark wet spot come through the top of Homer's jeans as I released my lips from his. That did it. He was not going to wait anymore, my mind said, but I did not relent; holding steadfast for a good while longer.

I had met Homer's mother a few weeks after we began dating. Homer had shared with me that he had been robbed in his car on Chester Avenue not too long before we'd met, so when after about 10 straight days of seeing each other from our first introduction I didn't see Homer for three consecutive days, I found my way back to his mother's home where Homer still resided. I had visited there in his mother's absence. His extraordinarily attractive mother answered the front door and I nervously told her of the car robbery, of which his mother had no knowledge until that moment. Millie, as I would later call her was obviously shocked with my news. In my young mind, I couldn't imagine not telling my mom about something such as this. But I soon learned that men do not always reveal such accounts to their mothers. Homer was not home, but his mother assured me she would have him contact me as soon as he returned. I am certain this was the moment that Millie realized I was in love with her son. She was pleased. Homer called me that night. He later confessed that he had been away because he had to finish breaking up with his girlfriend. What? I was naïve but in a good way. So, we became a couple for the ages, those wondrous ages.

Then one gloriously warm, sunny day, a Saturday, Homer and I had been spinning around town in his pretty red TR6 convertible when Homer suddenly yelled at me in an agitated voice, "We are going to have sex and I mean today. I'm taking you to a hotel right now and I mean now!" I tearily became frantic and vehemently protested. Homer sped the car west on I-90 and into downtown Cleveland and onto Euclid Avenue near Cleveland State University, into the parking lot of the Holiday Inn. My protests had become stronger to the point where Homer had to hold me tightly because I almost ran once my feet got on steady ground. Homer damn near yanked me into the elevator all the while assuring me it was okay, that he would not hurt me, that he loved me, "so calm down." I was trembling with fear, my head spinning with all kinds of thoughts. I was a nervous wreck, hair windblown over my head, a kind of orderly yet attractive chaos. I took gulps of air and tried to compose myself as we rode the elevator up to the penthouse where we stepped out and across a foyer to a door which opened from the inside. The all-embracing surprise of my life unfolded. There to greet us was Millie, astoundingly pretty Antoinette (Toni) Homer's sister, and then Curtis Mayfield with a grand smile entered from a sitting room.

Curtis Mayfield was appearing in concert in Cleveland on the heels of his richly successful soundtrack for the blockbuster film *Superfly*. Toni was Curtis' common law wife and they lived in Atlanta. We all laughed at ourselves, had small talk and left for our backstage and front row seats at the concert hall. I had a grand time, oh my goodness gracious. I was welcomed into the family and in a large sense, I remain. Curtis left us in 1999 and Millie transitioned in 2005. Thank you both for helping to make that day the best 'got cha'. I knew I was loved and wanted.

Modeling with Warren

Warren Browne, a childhood and close friend of Homer met me with Homer in Homer's mother's sitting room. That summer day, I was wearing a pair of shorts and some navy-blue canvas shoes with the heel out as I sat cross-ankle on the sofa. Warren was visiting, had not too long ago graduated Colorado State University with a degree in photography. Homer later revealed how proud the neighborhood was of Warren, who on this particular day was laden with an expensive leather bag boasting a high speed SLR top notch Nikon camera and loads of 35 mm film. Warren possessed an apparent innate gift of extroversion, accentuated by a handsome perfectly oval pecan colored face, tied together neatly with small bow lips. Warren was a fast talker, like he was trying to hustle you, when he really wasn't. Just his way of trying to convince his audience.

I could tell he liked me; thought Homer had made a good choice. Warren verbally admired my legs and asked if he could take some pictures of them. Homer gave permission with my approval. There was no posing, just sitting naturally as Warren shot my calves. That session marked the beginning of my days as Warren's studio model and of Warren making me aware of my body in terms of photography. Later I would spend endless hours with Warren in his studio when he opened it. Warren reminded me of Anthony Perkins' character Sean, in the film starring Diana Ross, *Mahogany*; only Warren was a Black male version absolutely not lacking in performance abilities with females. Warren was cosmopolitan all the way. Warren, the first black person we knew to do so, even bought a used pale yellow Volvo. Warren sought the limelight.

Warren never paid me, he didn't have to. It was a sort of quid quo pro. I assisted him in perfecting lighting, staging a mood for product presentation, model body positioning, (C, I, or S) hand, chin, eye, shoulder movements, etc. I learned that make up for color photography is very different than for black and white film usage. I also discovered my bad and good sides. Actually, for head shots I favored my left side. I took a decent straight on head shot. After I was placed in a modeling agency at Warren's referral, I discovered I had voice-over potential, when reading a script for a diamond commercial. I spoke the three syllables in the word diamond, whereas all the other girls only said the first and third sounds in the word. I also learned that I did not like runway modeling, although I did my share of it in later years in California. I was 118 lbs., 5' 7" tall, but not tall enough for big budget runway modeling. Ultimately, Dorian Modeling Agency represented me at a rate of $60.00 per hour, listing me for hands and legs, also.

I kicked it with Warren for years in his studio, even after he met and fell in love with Karen. Homer and I were still dating and nothing untoward ever occurred between me and Warren, albeit I knew Warren really liked my personality.

One of my favorite pictures of me by Warren, and I know one of his favorites, is a black and white, taken in my home's vestibule on Page Ave. My barefoot toes sported a dark Flori-Roberts lacquer, while I wore hip hugging jeans; a genuine rusting medium-sized ball and chain draped my manicured hands as I wistfully gazed out the screen door.

Karen was an exceedingly pretty, fair-skinned "mixed black chick" with straight raven black hair worn in a very flattering cropped pixie, kept shiny and in perfect place by a new hair care product line, *Pantene*. Karen and I both came from humble beginnings, although mine were (unknown to her) humbler. In my opinion, Karen was kind of insecure about her physical appearance. She finally got braces and perfected her smile, but I could tell she was jealous of me for some reason. I never knew what it was, but I liked her nonetheless and tried to remain friendly. On the eve of my moving to California in 1979, I phoned Karen to tell her I was glad we were friends, etc. that I'd never had a friend as pretty as her. Karen seemed materially possessed, but anyway she and Warren married and moved to Cleveland's Ohio City. In the early 80s she and Warren moved to San Francisco. I don't recall how I became aware of them being in the Bay area, but one day, I drove to my office in San Francisco and arranged to visit their apartment home on Fell Street. I wore a capped sleeve powder-blue belted linen dress by my favorite local designer *White Duck.* At Karen's prompting, we revealed our respective wedding bands; hers a heavy solid gold band with carved slits; mine a white gold band with five engraved hearts with diamonds in each one. My engagement ring consisted of a center baguette diamond surrounded by 12 more. Once more, that comparison thing crept up, her remarking that she had short fingers and therefore her hand looked better with just a band; while mine were long, therefore justifying my 2-ring set. Gee, she was 5' tall, so her fingers fit her body as did mine. That kind of silly envy or jealousy I never understood from anyone. Anyway, I got out of there within an hour. I never saw her again. Warren and Karen did not gel, business wise, in the Bay area and relocated to Chicago within about two years, where Warren opened another studio. Warren prospered financially, but he and Karen divorced. I located Karen about 15 years ago. I phoned her and learned she was well in Washington, D. C. and dating a GI man.

Warren's sister resides in Oakland and he visited her in the early 1990s. We met at his sister's and then for cocktails during his visit, at my favorite night spot on Lakeshore Ave., *The Fifth Amendment.* Before he left town, I asked Warren to take some headshots of me for my acting auditions. Warren had not changed, still eagle-eyed as to outdoors locale and quick speech in his direction and master of light. The setting was near my home by a local church in late afternoon. I wore an acid-washed, zippered front jean dress and my pixie cut that I had worn on and off since 1970s college days. Those photos are fantastic, I still have them. Warren had not lost his photographic knowledge of me and I revealed my best face side as he had taught me. We made a great professional pair and innumerable negatives from 35 mm film flashed through the lens of his favored Nikon. Warren is still living in Chicago, remarried to an attorney with their daughter, who according to Homer looks just like him. I bet she's all over the walls of Warren Browne Photography.

Senegalese Sun

I suppose I should blame it on Donna Summer's "*Last Dance*." Anyway, I wanted to dance to that song in a Disco Club. In preparation, I bought a red wrap around skirt with spaghetti tie strings made of lightweight material. And a black body suit that fit tight enough to make my 34B's believe they were C's. Having graduated college a year earlier, I was without a car, thus, I borrowed a friend's powder blue Volkswagen Beetle for my trip to the club. I perfumed and powdered my body, dressed with black pumps and drove to a near Westside spot. The air was ripe with night light pollution, cars of every make and model, and a hundred or so sparkling with anticipation, warm, damp bodies making their way towards the club's entrance. I was giddy and nervous, not frequenting clubs by myself. I hoped I'd find someone to ask me to dance.

Upon entering the club, I located a seat near the dance floor as I'd heard that guys ask girls to dance if they were seated close to the floor. In a little while I was joined by a slender, tall and very dark drink of a man dressed in a dark suit with white shirt and tie.

Over the course of our chatting I discovered that he was fluent in French. I spoke conversational French and in that we had something in common. The young man lived in New York and was employed in some sort of diplomatic position. I shared that I was planning to visit New York in a few weeks and we exchanged personal information, telephone numbers. We chatted for some time, had a slow dance and maybe one drink. Near to the end of our evening, **my** song came on and we danced. My practiced moves were not in comparison to the gyrating bodies of most of the other ladies but I did okay with my more classical line movement. It felt so good to have danced in a real Disco club to that song. I was on Cloud Nine. The soft-spoken gentleman escorted me to my borrowed wheels and off I went with thoughts of my impending visit to the Big Apple.

Over the next week or so, I talked with my newfound associate a few times and learned that because of his diplomatic status that he was going to afford me the luxury of some of his benefits. With the understanding that I was going to spend the majority of my time as I'd planned with a family friend/play cousin, Linda who was a model, I graciously accepted my new friend's offer of complimentary tickets to an upscale club, *The Wiz* (On Broadway) starring Stephanie Mills, and *Bob Marley and the Wailers* at Madison Square Garden.

I packed for my trip, dressed in a 2-piece baby-blue *Ship and Shore* ensemble, navy blue pumps and purse. My purse had red leather interior. There were 2 outside compartments and 3 inside compartments. One of the 3 was a small zippered area with a mini-sized gold trimmed oval mirror affixed above the zipper. The other small compartment was big enough for a small makeup compact. Inside the small zippered section I placed a small gift bag of Columbian Gold for my friend Linda.

Upon arrival at the airport checkpoint conveyor belt area I placed my gray Samsonite Overnight case on the belt, then my purse. The case was scanned, as was my purse. However, before I could continue on, the female scanner looked at me then at the scan image and said, "Ma'am..." That was the longest pause of my then short life. Together we glanced at the scanned image where I saw my gift squigglies as did she. At the very same instant I uttered a barely audible, "It's" But my good common sense said, "Don't tell her shit." "Let her find it." And without delay, 3 white men in black suits and white shirts seemed to ejaculate themselves from the cement wall and float to the conveyor belt. They stood opposite me with the lady scanner. One of the ghost men grabbed my purse and at the same time told me, "I have to search your purse." I shrugged agreement while doing all I could to prevent my urethra from spilling on the floor. My knees were knocking as the ghost man shoved his hands in my purse's compartments, all of them, but the zippered one. Surely the scanned image was not fibbing. I was cleared to go and go I did straight to the Ladies room where I let out water enough to fill one of those red aluminum gasoline cans. I was a nervous wreck.

My God and one of his Angels were on duty for me. The ghost could have simply unzipped the compartment, but I chose to think that he didn't want to waste his time on such a small gift. There was no doubt about the scan.

I boarded the jet and sat in a 3-seat row with a married couple. We chatted the whole time to La Guardia and I was grateful for the talk as I relaxed my nerves. We'd agreed to share a taxi's expense uptown to Manhattan. I was dropped off at my diplomat's Park Avenue apartment building where the doorman greeted me and rang up the diplomat from Senegal. My bags and I were placed in the elevator and up I went to his unit where I was warmly greeted and responded en Francais. After exchanging pleasantries, I phoned my mother and friend/cousin Linda. I reminded the diplomat that I was not staying with him for the duration of my trip as my plans had been set in motion before our meeting. He seemed to understand and in gentleman fashion did present me with the promised show tickets and a letter of introduction to the club. I spent that evening with him, nothing sexual although he wanted such an engagement.

While in New York, I went most places by myself on the subways. I had to see Harlem and the Apollo Theatre, so one day I ventured there, just to see, and smell the sites. I happened upon a young man pushing and pulling 2 purse racks on wheels. The purses were those clutch bags, so stylish in the late 1970s. The "salesman" beckoned me to browse, take my time, make a selection and when I had, he'd be back. I don't know where he ducked to, some doorway probably as he spied me fingering his wares. I selected two clutches, brown and a dark burgundy. Suddenly the salesman appeared with a paper bag, took $20.00 and bid me on my way.

Another day, I'd bought some strawberries but the grocery had no whipped cream, so while in Harlem I went in search of some. I went to three stores, but nothing. At the third store, I saw for the first time a bulletproof casing around the cashier's station. I made a remark about it, which gave hint that I wasn't a New Yorker. The clerk also told me, "Lady we don't sell whipped cream in Harlem." With that dejection I returned to Linda's.

One afternoon Linda took me to a fancy day spa. It was a hot and pretty day. When we stepped outside and began to walk away a crowd began to clamor at our rear. I heard ooh's and aah's, turned to see what was going on just as Sidney Poitier advanced towards us. I wanted to speak, but Linda yanked my arm and said not to. So, I did nothing but look as that icon of a being stepped from the curb and hailed a taxi that accommodated his apparent request to leave his onslaught of praising fans. It was not a bad thing, to perhaps want some privacy.

I believe it was during my search for my strawberries topping that I met a West Indian man who invited me out dancing. I agreed and gave him Linda's number. A night or so later West Indie came to pick me up in a Chevy sedan. I had him come inside so Linda could meet him, and see what he looked like. It was the proper thing to do according to how I was raised and conducted myself on dates for the first time with a stranger. After telling Linda where we were going, I left with Indie. On route to the club Indie informs me that he has to stop by his apartment for something, which I thought was strange. He parked outside and we walked up to his 2nd floor flat. I took a seat not far from but facing the flat's front door. Within less than two minutes there was a knock on the door. Indie hurriedly answered the door. Immediately alarm bells went ringing and flashing the brightest red my mind could recall. I went into direct survival mode. The visitor's darting eyes towards me told me more than I wanted to know. In an instant I knew I was going to at best be ganged raped or at worse raped and killed. Before Indie and visitor became chatty, I told Indie that I had to call my cousin; that she was expecting my call from the club, at which we should have been by now. Indie allowed me to use the phone and I'm sure visitor's penis died in his loins. I let Indie know there was an emergency and that he'd have to return me to Linda. He faked a disappointment at the news. Dead penis left as quickly as he'd come. Indie returned me to Linda; maybe he remembered that he'd be able to be identified physically by Linda. But another thing he did not know was that while he was making his acquaintance with Linda, I'd pre-arranged for one of her children to go outside and get his license plate number. This latter ritual was also something done at home when my sister and I dated as teens, just in case. The plate number wasn't needed because my God and Angel were still on duty.

The diplomat's upscale club was nice and essentially uneventful. Stephanie Mills performed her ruby slippers off in

The Wiz. But by far my most fun time was the evening on which I attended the concert at Madison Square Garden. I dressed in another *Ship and Shore* floral print and snake skin heels and matching bag. I rode the subway to the Garden, walked the short distance to the entrance's line. It was a clear, warm evening. My feet had begun to ache slightly as I stood in line. As I entered the Garden and looked around quizzically for my seat, I was approached by two attractive females who asked me whether or not I wanted to sit up front. I was also chided for wearing heels to a concert. We laughed as I removed my heels. We ran and leaped seats to the front. The band tapped our souls with Island rhythms and then Bob Marley and his female backup singers hit the stage. Irie!!! Bob and the Wailers hammered it out for 2 hours. To this day, that concert was the absolute best I've ever witnessed. The *Kaya* album had recently been released and it seems as if all cuts from it were performed. In addition, most songs from the Positive Vibration album were given to the audience. It was an unabashedly beautiful evening of lyrics and rhythms. Yeah, Bob. We miss you positively!! Your vibe still lives and influences.

I spent one more night with the diplomat before leaving for home. How, other than with words could I say thank you? I called my mother and she suggested I cook a dinner for him. I prepared a not so tasty chicken and vegetable dinner. Actually, the meal from my perspective was regrettable. The next day, I bid my farewell and returned to Linda's in readiness for my flight home. With the diplomat's permission, I made a few phone calls to home, my mother, even my job, I guess because I'd never been on vacation from a job before. I doubt I'd call my workplace now, while vacationing, unless it was my own business. Ah, youth!

I'd been back to work for about 2 months when I took a call at my desk. It was a phone company operator asking me to verify calls I'd placed from the diplomat's home. I verified them and was then summarily told that the diplomat was seeking monetary reimbursement. I agreed to pay the thirty odd dollars, no questions asked. A small price to pay for a piece of Senegalese Sun. I'd rather pay with my money than my body any day.

Code Name: Tony King

I remember the afternoon well. I remember the first time being home alone. It was a beautiful spring day, just warm enough to delight the birds in their songfests. The doorbell rang and broke the silence of the 2nd floor rear flat. I thought, "How odd, I'm not expecting anyone. My husband is not due for a few more hours."

I opened up, peered out of the front door, and glanced to the left across the landing, shot an inquiring look down the stairwell. A seemingly non-descript man was looking up at me. He was a white man, 40ish with a mild suntan. He was dressed in light colored clothing, khaki pants, pale shirt covering girth he was about to give birth to, and comfortable walking shoes, probably Hush Puppies.

I greeted the man's purposeful, unrelenting, but rather inviting calm demeanor, with mild suspicion and a friendly "Yes, may I help you." That was his open. The man began to ascend the steps explaining the purpose of his being there; "I'm conducting a survey about pain medications," etc. OK. He was in my living room now. I was not concerned about him, but my antennae were up. My neighbor was home with her toddler daughter, Pola, and I knew she'd hear me if something happened but whoever this man was he had been highly trained and was skilled, with a decidedly smooth monotone timbre spewing over his lips. He began his verbal questioning about pain medications, which I assured him neither my husband nor I took unless it was absolutely necessary. In fact, neither of us took medications during that time and if we did it was infrequent and our choice of pain reliever was Excedrin.

The man seemed not to accept my explanation, and inquired further about what drew me to my choice of Excedrin. I responded, "The green color of the bottle." At length, the man grew a bit exasperated. He'd been in my home about 5 minutes and the conversation really wasn't advancing, I think, as he would have liked. My impatience began to show. I wasn't nervous, but, more importantly, basically still a newlywed to a possessive husband. I was beginning to feel uneasy with this man. I'd not been alone with another man since I'd married. It was time for Mr. Pain man to leave. He got the message and produced a typed survey questionnaire for me to complete and for which he'd return another day to retrieve. I let him know that I'd oblige him. I just wanted him to leave. Mr. Pain thanked me and said, "We can't pay you, but you can keep the ink pen, he'd handed me for completing the questionnaire.

I placed the form on our table that also served as my husband's study desk, turned from the dining table, said my goodbye, and watched Mr. Pain descend the stairs; his non-descript khaki's melting into the same color carpeted steps. Mr. Pain drifted out into the sunlight. Being in the rear I was unable to see the directions from which he'd come and into which he exited.

I picked up the questionnaire, sat on our 7'x3'x3' couch and began to study it. There were a series of questions covering about 3 pages. I quickly deduced from the nature/format of the questions that this was some sort of psychological test to determine whether a person was fickle or firm in choices. At any rate, I waited until my husband's return from the university before further consideration was given Mr. Pain man's questions.

An hour or so later, my husband brought his pleasant spirit through the door. "Hi. My darling, what's going on?" I drew breath and waited for him, to put his things down and relax a bit. I served him his tea or as we called it chai. My husband placed a small cubed sugar on his tongue, let the warmth of sips of chai swallows slowly melt the cube. I mixed my loose sugar right in my cup. We chatted about nothing in particular for a short spell. I'd begun dinner a bit earlier and the rice was ready to be turned out. I'd become an expert rice maker. Today's rice was prepared in the form of a golden-brown cake laced with vegetables. The cake form is achieved by allowing most of the water to be absorbed, by placing a paper towel over the pot, securing a lid on until about the last 8-10 minutes of cooking time. Then place small pieces of butter atop the rice and along the inner circumference of the pot. As the butter melts under the right temperature, a tasty golden crust is formed encasing fluffy kernels of rice. The rice cake is then turned out on to a platter, very pretty. We ate our dinner of rice and lamb.

"Honey, we had a visitor today." I regurgitated the events of earlier. My husband didn't think too much about it. I explained my thoughts about the questionnaire, and then let it go. I'd answer the essentially generic questions in my husband's absence.

A few days later. I was relaxing when the phone rang. It was a young man seeking participation in another survey about soda pop. "Had word gotten out that I was a stay-at home wife and had time for surveys?" My antennae went way up but not in direct response to my aside question. It was because of what was being asked by the man on the phone? The call lasted no more than 2 minutes.

Next came a phone call a week or so later for a survey about restaurants. My husband worked as a waiter in a restaurant, *Charlie Brown's* on the Berkeley Marina. I did not reveal this, only that my choice of restaurant for an affordable quick meal was *Denny's* and that I felt comfortable, in part, because of the then, décor/colors, lilac and gold, of the pleather covered booths.

A few weeks afterward, my husband returns from the university, excited about a new job prospect. He showed me the application that had no company name on it. I wanted to know how he came to possess it. He said he'd gotten it from someone at the university. I didn't believe him but I kept mum. My husband was very intelligent, spoke three languages fluently, was discreet, came from a well-to-do family, and was seeking a graduate degree in International Economics, so I was not surprised that someone was interested in his talents. Eventually my husband completed the application. I let him know from where I believed the application came. He seemed surprised, caught off guard that I would think this.

A week or two later, I'm informed by my husband that we are scheduled to meet with someone, a man at *Denny's* at about 6:30. We arrived in casual but attractive and sophisticated dress and were greeted by a handsome light-brown-skinned man with Asian features. He stood about 5'6". He gave his name as Tony King. I was a bit uneasy, just a bit, we all struggled at forced small talk. My husband and I ordered coffee and a chunk of carrot cake, the new rage then. We weren't hungry, or big dessert fanciers. We were being polite. I found the icing too sweet. We chatted for about one hour, probably less. I had put it all together, in the instant and like a flash, when my husband had revealed the location of the meeting.

A bit of time passed. I went to work in September for a firm in San Francisco.

Seemingly, within a few weeks my husband received word that he'd been accepted for that job that Tony King was pushing and that he'd have to fly to Virginia for some written exams and interviews.

We were both excited and nervous. My suspicions grew almost on a daily basis. I had figured out what the deal was a long time ago and NOW I was being followed. I went to work on the bus and when my husband had no classes, he'd walk the short block to meet my bus, I looked forward to that. On days when he wasn't there, I'd see this same plain car parked on the side street leading to our street, occupied by a man at the wheel. One day, I decided to mess with him, so after I passed by the car I stopped at the rear passenger side and let him see me write down his license plate. I never saw him or the car again.

I prepared my husband and packed for the trip. For his interview, he was to wear the gray suit in which we'd been married with a white Yves Saint Laurent shirt and gentile blue cashmere pullover sweater. I cut his hair as I always had, drove him to the San Francisco airport in my white Monza, kissed, and hugged my husband goodbye, drove back home and waited for his, "I arrived safely" call. He was gone about 3-4 days. What were they doing with my beloved? I had a pretty good idea. Language tests, translations, all sorts of things, we'd discuss upon his return.

****

It was all worked out. Even what was to happen with me, where I'd be located, as well as my husband.

I do not feel at liberty to discuss the details or intricacies of the positions we were offered. All I know is they were ideal and for an excellent cause, excellent salary and terms. The ultimate decision was not mine to make. I'd given a resounding "Yes." I was the wife and demurred to my husband.

My husband decided to decline acceptance. Years later, he would confide that he believed he'd made a mistake and wished he'd taken the offer.

I maintained the phone number and Tony King information for years and one day it was gone, perhaps as the result of a move to our new home. I kept it in a brown spindle folder. It disappeared in 1983.

Sometimes as I view world events today, I can't help but wonder as I know my former husband does, what would things be like if he had said "Yes"? I believe we would still be married, probably with a grandchild or two, living peacefully, nestled in our love and allegiance.

****

Once a dossier always a dossier. I'll leave it at that. Que sera!!!

Humming Birds Do Fly

Most of the stories compiled for my autobiography have common woven thread, integrated in varying patterns of my life's opera.

After my husband and I divorced I relocated to a quaint 1940s stuccoed wall apartment with hardwood floors. I occupied a first-floor walkup unit in a building duplexed into eight units on Park Blvd and 5th Avenue. The building was in an area east of Lake Merritt and Lakeshore Blvd., but below Interstate 580; technically a "nice lake area" since it was within walking distance of the lake and exclusive shops lining upper Park, Lakeshore and Grand Blvds.

I was to learn later, that I had some quirky neighbors including one directly above me, a single white male who turned out to be a paranoid schizophrenic with an adverse response to necessitation of garbage removal or perhaps even toilet flushing. The stench (a sweetish dung odor), mixed with perspiration became so unbearable that it permeated the hallway through the pores of the occupant and with the mere opening of his unit's door for entering and exiting. This male would be seen walking up and down the street rubbing his full body on telephone poles as if hugging them. I would burn incense to help remove the odor. It got so bad that I summoned police, out of concern that a decomposing body was in the home carved up in plastic bags. Two officers responded to my report and stopped by my unit after inspecting the upper unit and when I asked what was causing the odor, one officer remarked, "You really don't want to know, but we have had similar complaints about him at his previous apartment." Soon after this complaint, the man moved during which time two pickup trucks were used for hauling the apartment's wasted contents. Because I had contacted police, the man called me a fascist. I didn't care as long as he got the heck out. A few years later I saw him exploring the railroad tracks in Emeryville. The young man was clean, well fed, and seemingly better adjusted.

First floor next door neighbors were a strikingly handsome husband and wife consisting of a beautiful fair-skinned African American wife, Tori, and a dark brown-black husband from Guyana (the locale of the Jim Jones mass suicide of November 18, 1978. Tori had borne a beautiful son. On occasion, I would visit Tori, sit in her pretty kitchen and chat over tea and English biscuits or toast. I was intrigued by Tori's shielded intelligence, and knew she was being mentally and/or physically abused, but I could not aid her. She feared her husband who ultimately alienated her from family and friends by moving her to a mobile home park in Sonoma County.

Above Tori resided the owner's daughter, Janice Kang, and her fiancé whose last name was Simon; they became Simon and Simon Property management, I'll always believe as a wedding present from owner- dad, Ed Kang, who was not going to have a non-titled man as his son-in-law. Mr. Ed Kang was a retired engineer from Bechtel in San Francisco and owned residential properties throughout Oakland. When I moved from Park Blvd., I moved into another of his buildings closer to Lakeshore, more conducive to my tastes. But before I left I had the ill pleasure of running into another distant resident in the area: David Barnard aka "Devil Man" (DM).

I didn't know his name then and had never spoken directly to DM; only saw him doing normal things like driving his two-toned emerald green and beige Volkswagen Beetle to and fro, or in a local convenience store on occasion. DM was what I describe as a reddish brown-black man about 5'8" with a semi stout build, unremarkable and expressionless facial features absorbed in faux staid folds, dull dark 2" unkempt afroish hair, the top portion haphazardly split and spiraled into two points, one on either side of his upper head, distinctly and purposely yielding the desired effect of a pictorial of a *"Red devil Hot Sauce* emblazoned emblem. To add insult to this self-inflicted injury was a body cloaked in 1970s double knit pants and matching (or not) cape, just enough to give anyone a start, chuckle silently, and ask, "You cannot be real because you are not dressed in all red, but are you human?" No, but there was something there, most definitely, and I couldn't put a fix on it. And then one afternoon, I visited Albany Bowl with friends and who do I see but DM on an apparent "family outing." I had seen his teen daughter before, but this time, I saw her alone in the restroom, so I approached her. I knew something was very, very wrong. Her eyes, aura, and even the odor of her nearly shivering fear begged me to inquire. I did ask, trying my best to cajole her frozen timidity into confidence unfamiliar to her, but the engulfing fear would not thaw even just a bit, so my eyes and truest heart told her I knew and would pray for her,. Her eyes, instantaneously reflected two rays of appreciation and thanks as we parted into the gay noise of the bowling lanes, and fresh grilled cheese sandwiches and fountain coke conversations.

A little less than two years passed by and then state and local newspaper headlines screamed, "Devil Man Molester given 342 Years." His daughter who'd been sexually molested by him, and was by then 18 remarked he "probably got less than what he deserves." She also added that she wished he could live the 300 years (in prison). Conjunctively the mother was arrested, convicted, and sentenced to a long prison sentence, for abuse and threatening the daughter harm if the daughter told of the horrors. Coincidentally, the mother Suzanna Barnard had been a local school district psychologist for 15 years. I envision this teen evolved into a young woman as a humming bird, soaring to heights of unimagined glorious destiny.

Acting (Alone)

Upon relocating to California in 1979, I had no job initially. After about two months, I began cashiering at a one block away convenience store, *Shortstop*. I liked my job, had a chance to meet and greet members of my community home. I was glad to get out of our tiny apartment. My then fiancé, Rahim, took the car during days to San Francisco to his University of San Francisco (USF) master degree classes and then to his waiter job at Charlie Brown's in Berkeley from 5:00 until midnight or so. I worked various shifts, but primarily from 3-11. I was happy, in love, and simply glowing at 23. I made new friends, mostly Persians, but really from all nations.

There was Soon Pai from South Korea, Ronald Kojima from San Francisco, but whose parents were Second Generation Japanese immigrants; a favorite couple, a husband/wife from Morocco and Iran, respectively, Nancy Osorio whose parents Aida and Pepe had migrated from El Salvador (Nancy later married Rahim's best friend, Abbas Mahallatti), my neighbors, Piran and Fourough, and beautiful daughter Pola from Iran. There was a plethora of others encased in some capacity. Soon was like a mother hen to many of us. She dated a white American and had a small terrier, Hop Lee, a female. Hop Lee had a pup, named Mickey Lee; both just adorable. When Sue, as she preferred to be called, visited Korea in the summer of 1981, I kept her dogs, to Rahim's dismay. Soon also briefed Rahim and me on marriage aspects, even purchasing a book for us. Rahim and I found the book embarrassingly graphic and just thumbed through it out of courtesy. We looked up to Sue, often played volley ball with her in Berkeley or surrounding areas or enjoyed personalities, different cuisine or music from six continents.

Rahim and I met many people from all over the globe. I know many seeing us together were intrigued. If I must say so, we made an exceedingly striking couple. We would often get stopped on the street or in a grocery store. Once at the Hyatt in downtown San Francisco, a vacationing couple from Japan engaged us for a few hours to the point of taking pictures of us. The wife asked for our address and promised to send some photos to us. Rahim was skeptical, but I believed her. A month or so later, we received the pictures with a note. I still have the envelope with the contents intact. Those photos reflect the softness of the love Rahim and I shared, the innocence of ourselves, a very special time indeed; I believe the wife of this couple saw themselves in us.

Some time passed. I had not thought of my modeling days in a long time, I was so busy doting on Rahim. One day, I shared with Rahim some of my studio shots, my friend Warren had taken. I also showed him some photos of shots taken of me for a Higbee Company advertisement. Rahim liked the pictures, but seemed reserved in the knowing that I had been photographed by another, a man. We dealt with that; nothing major.

Later, after I began working at Hanover Insurance in San Francisco, Rahim took a second job, telling me he wanted to retire by age 40. Essentially, I remained moot, but began to put a plan in motion to help alleviate my nighttime loneliness. One gay employee had nicknamed me Betty Boop. In my evenings, I began to reminisce about my high school days. While thumbing through my Shaw High senior *Memories* book, I stopped and read attentively the entire book paying particular attention to the "Plans" page near the back of the book. And to my wondering eyes, what should appear but: **SHORT RANGE…** sub caption TRAVEL California, the first among other cities

LONG RANGE... sub caption: CAREER: <u>Actress.</u>   Just like that it came to me, but how and where to start?

The next day, I made inquiry of the mail clerk, Charles Dudley, a worldly, lovable soft-spoken man who I would later learn was also gay. Didn't make me any difference. Charles gave me the name of Jean Shelton, a noted Bay Area acting teacher. Jean was holding classes in a tiny space in Berkeley with an associate, a female named Jo. I auditioned a few weeks later and was accepted. I began classes with Jo, having to earn promotion to Jean's classes. Classes were held on Tuesdays from 6:00 until 8:00. I studied with Jo for about eight months and then was accepted into Jean's classes now being held in San Francisco on Sutter Street up the cable car hill of Powell Street, intersecting famed Union Square. I promptly paid my first $200.00 in advance and nervously awaited instruction.

Retired now, Jean was, and I presume still, a great teacher, having perfected her craft under tutelage of Stella Adler and Lee Strasberg in 1940s New York. In my estimation, she is the finest of ladies, fashioned from the mold of a Bette Davis; an ever-present cigarette and arms gesturing, with a minimum of verbal instruction; but when she spoke, you listened intently. Jean studied you as an actor; were you the character, were you consistently believable in the moment, were you <u>being</u>, were your actions strong? Just a few of the components required during Method Acting. If you were not believable, she would tell you, then tell you how you could become so. Mostly the believing had to do with the actor's life experience or internalizing even the minutest of affectation. I was young, not a wealth of experience, yet. But I was working on it, while yet to recognize that I owned a wealth of untapped emotions. It took me a while, nearly one year, to fully understand what all the fuss was about. Jean knew when I had been struck by that bolt of knowledge when in our weekly 'scene' presentations, I finally was totally believable, had garnered the full attention of all class members and then at scene's end Jean remarked, "Well Adrea, you are an actress", to applause of my onlooking fellow thespians.

I continued studying with Jean, but the acting bug bit, and I began to audition in local theater on a regular basis. My first audition was for the director of the Oakland Ensemble Theatre in Oakland. I do not recall the production's title, but the audition did not go well. I was described as 'green' but I kept on. Next, I auditioned with The Lorraine Hansberry Theatre in San Francisco. I definitely had stage presence, but I had to kiss a man full on the lips during the audition process. I had never done this in acting class and it was obviously an uncomfortably painful episode. The man lay on a sofa and was ready, but I just could not do it. The director was disappointed; ultimately offering me a non-speaking role as a ghost/apparition. Given the status of that theater at that time, I probably should have accepted the role, but I had been offered a speaking role at Jean's theater in *St. Carmen of the Main*. Actors want to speak, or so I thought. But some of the best acting is done without words, with total reliance on body and ocular movement, a silent tear droplet, etc. Oh, well, another lesson.

I accepted the role in Jean's theatre, feeling comfortable, going to rehearsals after work. I would commute home by train, eat, freshen up, drive back to San Francisco, and come alive in my Chorale role of a mini-dress, blond wig wearing, heavily made up lady-of-the-evening. I was the only Black actor in the production, and I loved every minute of rehearsals. Opening Night! I asked Rahim to take off work at Charlie Browns and come support me and the play. Rahim very reluctantly rode with me in my car. We parked in the Union

Square parking garage, about 2 ½ blocks from the theater. Our opening was hugely successful. At the performance end, the cast decided to go for a celebratory drink around the corner. Rahim did not care to understand the importance of this for me and adamantly insisted that we return home. For the first time, I defied my husband and stayed. Rahim left me, taking my car; he had driven and kept the keys. I changed into my jeans, forest green velour top, and went around the corner with my cast members and had a good time while thinking about my semi-spoiled first Opening Night. I returned home by bus and train. Rahim never liked that I was taking acting lessons and further that I was on a stage with people (men) looking at me perform. There was no getting around that fact. Rahim refused to quit his second job from midnight to six in the morning. I begged and begged, but he stood firm and kept right on working until he finally took a third job; pre-lunch hour helping a friend open a restaurant in San Rafael. I never met this friend. Anyway the third job didn't last but a few months, and it certainly put a strain on our marriage. I worked full time and Rahim's waiter job brought good money, especially tips. I let him do his thing, begging for an occasional night alone, just me and him. He only gave in to my request two times during our marriage. He never went on vacations with me. In order for me to marry him, I let him know he had to meet my family. He did oblige me this and returned to Ohio for our marriage. Otherwise, "No, my darling", was his response, 99% of the time.

    I continued acting in local theater including San Francisco's Fort Mason.   Rahim did come to see me in my second play, in which I had a strong lead role of Millie in *Trouble in Mind*. Millie was a somewhat sassy bourgeois married actress, so I was stepping up character-wise. She was one of my favorites, but I had a slight problem, as far as the director Curtis Sims was concerned, in making my pelvis undulate when I was in character. I distinctly remember him, in rehearsal placing his fully opened palm on my stomach just below my navel and pressing in on me in attempt to have me know my pelvis movement and possibilities. He knew I knew what he was doing and I let him know and he never touched me again. I let him know my walk was my walk and that was it. Rahim sat in the very front center seat in the small Black Repertory Group (BRG), launched by Nora Vaughn (now deceased). Rahim received my second performance more positively, but still wanted me off the stage.

I kept on acting and Rahim kept on working. Unequivocally, I supported Rahim in all he did; even convincing him that he should open his own donut shop. I suggested how he do it and he followed my lead and finally found a suitable location in Alameda. About two years after the shop opened, we separated and later divorced.

I kept acting and discovered that most parts offered me were for portraying characters with more than tepid sexual innuendo. In essence, I was being type-cast and I abhorred it. I succeeded in landing a starring role as a mother in a dysfunctional family. I liked that part. I persevered and landed more roles in theater.

At one point, I received a call from the director from my first audition. Benny had been referred to me by his girlfriend, an actress with whom I'd performed in *Being There*. Artistic Director, Benny Sato Ambush, told me of a voice over/ radio commercial for KJAZ for the Oakland Ensemble Theater's production of Boseman and Lena. I visited the studio and was given the job on the spot. I was even allowed to select the background music, (a most high compliment). I recorded the radio spot in two takes and was out the door. Boy, was I soaring, just a bit. I was in rehearsal or actual performance when the spot first aired, where backstage in the dressing room, all cast was waiting to hear me. And then it came on. I was extremely pleased even though I could sense the envy of some people, especially the BRG staff person I was dating at the time. I'll refer to him by his last name here.

Fontaine had been acting for upwards of 20 years in the Bay Area and had not done as well as I was seemingly doing in less than three years. Before the radio spot, I had starred in a dramatic one-woman reading of *Rampart Street Liturgies* in San Francisco to which Fontaine attended. At the end of the reading I received an extended rousing applause, with director Lois coming on stage inviting the entire audience to meet me in the reception area of the theater. I was shocked; had never been so well-received. Still in costume, I took my place in the receiving area. It was as if I was bum rushed. I appreciated the acknowledgement, but was extremely uncomfortable. I did not enjoy the questions or people unexpectedly touching me. Fontaine stood off to the side watching this 'people's' reaction to me and I could see on his face a litany of emotion which translated to jealousy. On the quiet way home, he complimented me again, but no happiness was in his words. And I said to myself, "OK, I see now."

I kept on acting, even received repeated casting for radio comedy dramas via Rebels without Applause. I loved working with this group. I did several voice-overs for them, but never thought to ask the producer for a copy of the tapes.

Theater work continued, but I was tiring of it a bit; just a bit. I only tired because I was working full-time; had to memorize lines at work on my lunch hour and spent most free time memorizing lines, rehearsing, or performing.

In the spring of 1986, I received a call from a film casting agency, once again referred to me by Benny of Oakland Ensemble. I was told that director great Francis Ford Coppola was casting extras for the film *Peggy Sue Got Married* and was I interested and available to start filming in a few days. I assured her that yes, I was. My height, weight and hair length was taken by phone with instructions to wet set my shoulder length hair the night before the 12-hour day shooting call began. I was told to arrive on set at about 6:00 a.m. with my rollers in and to bring a pair of comfortable high heels.

I was working for CSE Insurance in San Francisco; never called in sick or took time off, but I was taking off the day of that shoot. I called my mother and let her know what was going on. I asked if she could call my job in that morning and tell them I was in the emergency room. My mother could hardly contain herself. I had had her flown here in 1983 and taken her to Whoopi Goldberg's production of *Moms* in San Francisco, where we met Whoopi briefly. Also, I'd given my mother a private performance of *Rampart Street Liturgies* which she with bursting pride enjoyed very much from the foot of my marital bed. So, the night before filming, I gassed my car, called supportive friends, washed and expertly rolled my hair on hard medium sized spindles, nervously awoke about 4:00 and showered, then drove to Santa Rosa, arriving on time to have my wardrobe presented (a very pretty 1950s yellow print dress accentuating my shoulders and a perfect length for my legs. I looked very nice). Next came my hair; expertly styled in a trailer by a lady who when done said, "You're my favorite of the day." The stylist had removed my rollers seemingly with the sweep of a single motion, brushed, fluffed, stiff sprayed, and glossier sprayed, until I thought my hair would never move again. Light powder was dusted over my face and then I was given a mirror. I was stunned. A line spoken by Natalie Wood at seeing herself for the first time in a full-length dress and hair done up from the film *Gypsy,* crept to my mind, "I'm pretty mama."

The work was not hard, just long, but we all knew it would be. I say we because about one-eighth of the 'working' black actors in the Bay Area were there for the Negro nightclub scene. I was partnered with a man at the bar, opposite of which were booths into which stars Nicholas Cage and Kathleen Turner entered and sat after other 'extras' had vacated a booth. My partner and I were directed to turn from the bar toward the booths, walk to them, and become seated (in preparation for the performance occurring in the other part of the split club. I add that Francis Coppola was seated the entire time directly to my left, about 6-8 feet away, and he had no idea *The Godfather* (trilogy) is my favorite film. At lunch time, the entire crew convened to the same eating area. Most people reading this have probably not experienced a movie set at lunch time. Well, let me tell you, there is absolutely nothing like it, I mean the display of fine, fine food. Any and every thing; just plenty of pretty and appealing: to any eye or taste bud palette. I don't recall the menu. All I know is I was partaking while utilizing good and properly cultured feminine manners (bringing my food to my mouth, chewing with mouth closed, dabbing my mouth's corners every so often while avoiding lipstick staining of the linen napkin, chatting and smiling with my table mates) when I glanced straight ahead at the table across from me, and to my pleasant surprise, Francis Ford Coppala was staring right at me and it wasn't one of those "just happened to be looking in same direction at the same time' looks, or was it? I simply let it happen. It felt nice; nothing flirtatious, more of a 'wonder who she is' look.

Filming ended just before dusk. I drove back to Oakland, thrilled. Not because of the film, but I was beginning to be noticed on the train and other public places like gas stations. It was kind of alarming and more so if a person got excited. I handled it with profuse thanks and a bashful yet courteous turn of my head. I received my paycheck within two weeks and still have the stub. Fontaine refused to go to the film's opening, but finally acquiesced about a month later. Again, that same paled reaction when I nearly shouted, "That's me." It was not unexpected; we parted romantic ways soon thereafter for disassociated but necessary reasons.

I continued acting in local theater and doing comedy dramas for radio, and then came the play *Freebase Ain't Free*, premiering at a nightclub in Oakland's Jack London Square. The script was written by a friend's husband. I was asked to read for the part of Portia, a rockstitute. I accepted the role, the character of which was based on an actual occurrence involving a pregnant freebase addicted woman who spontaneously aborts in her bathroom, but abandons the live infant in the toilet and goes right back to the living room to smoke drugs while the newborn succumbs. Community school children were brought in and it really shook up a lot of them; perhaps scaring them straight away from drugs. I hope so. My performance in that play was one of my best. In fact, I believe it was my best dramatic role. I received personal accolades from local news media as well as a lot of recognition by children in public places. Now, that felt good. This was in 1989.

My last voice-over was for an independent film the summer of that same year. Again, I did not ask for a copy, but it's cool. I do not recall the title but it had something to do with Mount Tamalpais.

During the span of about 1987 through 1992, I was a member of the blues band Godfather and the Family, featuring Earl Crudup, who was the godfather/lead singer. I, in the Godfather's assisting character of 'Stuff' was entertainingly described as "every rich man's fantasy and every poor man's dream." The godfather and I were guarded by Turbo and a machine-gun-in-violin- case toting Mad Dog. We four performed in local clubs, etc. particularly in the East Bay. Once, we appeared on the same awards bill as John Lee Hooker. Those guys were great and treated me well while providing some of my most fun-filled days in live theater. Our signature piece was James Brown's Sex Machine…and we tore it up while rocking the house.

In 1992, I performed as an extra in Sister Act, my final act, filmed in San Francisco, with Whoopi Goldberg.

Long before I personally explored acting, I had heard or read that several 'famous' celebrities stuttered but did not when they acted, i.e. Marilyn Monroe, James Earl Jones, and James Stewart. I suppose it's a truism because I never stammered on stage or during voice-over taping. I did not get into acting for a career or to become famous, rather to assuage loneliness, even though I was married. I stutter much less now and I'm not as introverted as I once was. The full body of my acting roles is not delved into here. Thank you, Jean Shelton. I wish you could have seen me in *Green Christmas*, working it- lead acting and singing. I succeeded in accomplishing my goal.

Glad I Asked

My most favorite job was when I worked or rather moonlighted as a cocktail waitress at *Geoffrey's*, an upscale nightclub in Oakland's Jack London Square.

I'd been in the establishment as a patron even as far back as when the same spot had been known as *Uppy's*, I'd heard that the spot was then named after or owned by an Oakland Raider, Gene Upshaw. That didn't mean anything to me, except that I figured it would be a decent and safe place to partake in a libation, meet some nice people, maybe dance a bit and go home.

I really wasn't into the club scene, but I was attracted to the movement and energy of *Geoffrey's*, and I especially liked the fact that all the waitresses and bartenders were required to wear white tuxedo shirts with black bow ties. All of the personnel seemed friendly, and professional. The female employees all seemed to hold a certain kind of physical attractiveness and to possess a certain air. It brought to my mind the memory of *Bricktop,* a famous Black Female American "Saloon Keeper Par Excellence" in 1920's and 1930's Paris. Bricktop served as hostess to all of the top entertainers, movers and shakers of the time.

Geoffrey's had been at its 2nd and Broadway location for about 2 years when I finally got up enough nerve to seek employment there. I knew and was friends with the silent female business partner of Geoffrey. However, I did not go the nepotism route. One afternoon after I'd finished my day job, I went to the club and simply introduced myself, applied for the job of cocktail waitress. Although I had no experience, I was hired on the spot, being told that a Floor Manager would train me in the proper manner to carry a tray full of drinks, and serve them without setting the tray down, count and hide my money. I was going to have a ball.

Geoffrey's catered to what one might call an upscale clientele including local businessmen and women, politicians, professional athletes from all genres, celebrities of all persuasions. Geoffrey had a quiet demeanor, never raised his voice and was quite handsome with a ready smile, always immaculate in his grooming and dress. His very special Lady friend, Delma would always greet patrons in the most sophisticated and tasteful suits and make-up you'd ever want to behold. Just good taste all around. She would later confide to me that she purchased her wardrobe in another state. I understood why.

One thing about working in *Geoffrey's* was that when your favorite song was played you could not dance. That was understood, so if I wanted to partake in the action, I'd have to leave, go home and change and come back. I usually worked until closing on the weekends, had to make those tips because I was trying to save money for my own business equipment. I made good tips most of the time. When celebrities came in, especially Oakland A's, you knew you were going to be tipped well. My highest tip from one of them was $100.00 for serving two rounds. One time a member of Wesley Snipes' entourage phoned ahead to give advance notice of his arrival. Floor Manager, Gary, asked me to prepare a table with courtesy Moet champagne which I did promptly. Wesley was a popular 'star' then. Upon his arrival, he and two other men were escorted to their table with me at the ready. Wesley refused the champagne, which was deemed an insult. Wesley ordered a Tom Collins. I served all men and I guess there was not enough "fawning female action", including by me, so within an hour they left without tipping me. Because I had no spouse or children, I often accepted solo special Sunday events for teachers, small business or political organizations etc. with a minimum tip of $100.00.

I was a straight--laced no-nonsense waitress, treating everyone the same. I didn't reveal any cleavage or flirt with the men for tips. Several waitresses attended UC Berkeley (with plans) or had graduated college already, like me. I had two nicknames, *The Terminator,* in the beginning because some of the thieving employees thought I'd been hired by the silent partner to spy on their activities. Later when they got to know me and they still had their jobs, they knew they'd misjudged me. All was cool. I witnessed a lot of stealing, I mean a lot, especially by the bartenders. Just awful. I didn't tell on them, just made sure they rang up my orders. I would watch them and not leave the waitress' station when they'd often snap, "Just leave the money, it's too busy, I'll ring it up". They'd lay the money by the register when it was real crowded, never ring it up. It would go in their champagne tip buckets. One female bartender was famous for this. One guy would sometimes ring up $00.00 and pocket most sales. I saw it, but who was I? There were floor managers and Geoffrey to watch them. I never went behind the bar in my capacity. Another thing I never ever did was drink alcohol while I worked, like some waitresses, and therefore, I kept track of my money; the tips I transferred to my bra when my cash became too much for my sales case. I also never owed the house beyond the $40.00 we started our shifts with. I was a hawk with my money, still am.

One Friday night, I was stationed in the main bar area and had to serve a table full of sparkling women who gave the impression of wanting to be approached by men (too hard). Most ordered frozen fruity drinks, like frozen daiquiris with whipped cream. I served them for about one and a half hours, (two drinks) and complained to Gary that they were not tipping, just occupying one of the best tables in order to be seen. Gary had recognized this and told me, "Watch this, I'll take care of this. They'll leave...I'm going to walk by and pass gas and the heat from the vent will rotate the odor." He did and within five minutes the ladies split. Another time, something similar happened. Again, I confided in Gary who suggested that one of those accidentally spilled drinks on the shoulder of one of those suits would do the trick; that profuse apologies and a complimentary dry cleaning would be sufficient for an exit. I loaded my tray with cocktails, walked by and oops, a drink accidentally toppled over and splashed on a female patron's shoulder. I went into overdrive apology mode with Gary rushing over to dab at the wetness and a sincere, "Don't worry, Geoffrey will pay for the cleaning bill, just bring it back, no questions asked." A $10.00 cleaning bill was better than $50.00 or more in lost sales. Just the cost of doing good business.

I was later deemed *"the mean waitress"* presumably because I didn't smile a lot. Just did my job, chatted with the personnel in the kitchen and my favorite floor managers, Gary and Kelly.

One Friday or Saturday, I didn't work. I traded that night with someone. I'd decided that I was going to enjoy the establishment. I had my pixie cut expertly coiffed, put on one of my pretty dresses, the one I'd purchased from Saks Fifth Avenue for my 20-year high school reunion. I still have the dress, a black lace, off the shoulder, with fitted bodice pretty thing of a dress. I wore lace-covered heels as well. I thought I looked nice. I felt good inside of myself as I drove my powder blue Lincoln LSC along the avenue and then when I stepped into the club.

I recognized many of the patrons, most of whom had never seen me so attired. I don't know when the gentleman first introduced himself, but we only had small chat and one non-alcoholic drink. Near to my leaving time, it was agreed that we'd go for a burger a block away.

I told him I'd drive my car there. I parked my car in front of the burger joint, we sat and chatted while listening to a song on a cassette tape, 'All I'll Ever Ask' by Freddie Jackson with Najee. The song had not too long ago been released and I'd immediately recognized it as a destined classic. I asked my car guest to dance with me. He obliged me and we danced on the sidewalk, right there in the middle of the produce warehouse section of downtown, Oakland. We danced to that song for more than an hour as the melodies spilled out of my car. I kept rewinding the tape and we'd lightly embrace and dance. We danced so long that my car's battery went dead. Fortunately, we were near the police department. The gentleman reminded me that he was a San Francisco Fire Lieutenant and that as a public safety courtesy he'd seek a jump-start from the agency, which he did promptly. An officer arrived and provided my car with cabled energy to get my engine rolling. The gentleman and I exchanged a warm thank you, hug, feather lip kiss and phone numbers. I drove him the block to his car. We saw each other for dinner a few times later. There was an attraction, an interest but no love match, but I know he'll always remember **our** dance. We both were glad I asked.

Black Henry

Steely, dark – smooth
Overflowing with passion
No one to trust it to?
You do have someone,
Wishing I could capture on canvas with oils
You, Black Henry

In Africa, beautiful ribbons of red & gold
Swirling around your blackness
A lioness there on the edge of the rushes
And you darting past
Swift and shining, barely breathing

The greens and ambers of Henry,
In the wild – sweet & pure – dashing forth
But for all his quickness, I saw the henna
On his toenails and I prayed

Moments in Time
The Best Days

The beginning of the best days really began on a warm November day during 1989 in Berkeley, California; actually, a rebirth of sorts was on the cure charts. Recent fallen teardrops over her mother's death had been pressed, dried, and placed away.

The protagonist's last stage performance had been performed earlier that year with her unknowingly last voice-over presented in June 1989 for a film. The film voice-over was recorded in a studio in San Francisco. Of late, she'd decided to prepare for the role of a lifetime, to portray her idol Eartha Kitt of whom she'd read about over the years, and had followed her career since first viewing Eartha on The Michael Douglas talk show when she, Adrea, was just entering her pubescent years. Thus, the protagonist enrolled in French classes at a local community college, albeit she had studied the language since 4th grade, through high school. But Eartha Kitt was said to speak about six languages, so she had to perfect her accent if she was to portray Eartha on film.

Berkeley, California is a rather politically progressive college town in the San Francisco Bay Area, housing the California State University, Berkeley.

In October 1989, an incident erupted in the Bears' Lair on the college's campus. Many of the student participants spilled out into the surrounding streets where a mini riot of sorts erupted. Police responded and fighting, physical and not, ensued. During this discourse, some of the involved students were arrested with complaints ensuing against some of the police officers in the days and weeks that followed. The Media got involved, as did the local NAACP. Berkeley's Police Review Commission (PRC) made demands for a full investigation. The commission was asked to hire an independent firm to conduct the investigation surrounding the complaints against the officers. The chosen firm was one located in close proximity to the Cal-Berkeley campus and at which I was one of the go-getter investigators and was, therefore, thrilled to have been one of two investigators selected to interview and procure statements from the complainants and subject officers, involved directly or in a witness capacity. A sticky and precarious situation, but right down my alley, not intimidated at all.

I was given a full briefing of the incident, provided a voluminous transcript of the Communications Center of all responding officers' radio and dispatch comments. Thereafter, I took a walk about of the Bear's Lair and surrounding streets of the UC campus. I also studied Berkeley Police General Orders, becoming adequately equipped to commence investigating. After having interviewed many officers and complainants over a two week or so period, I had become a good and unbiased judge of where the truth was spoken. Several of the officers had presented themselves with an attorney (primarily by noted police attorney, Michael Rains), which was their legal right. One unrepresented officer readily admitted that he had struck a complainant and another I interviewed, Officer Chew, drug things out during his interview, stating he had given his night stick to another officer so he could not have hit anyone. I countered this statement by asking whether he had accepted another officer's nightstick and received no reply. Allegations against Officer Chew were sustained and documented in a local paper. My name could not be mentioned, but I cut and have the clipping, as we investigators were precluded from media contact or mention.

One officer in particular presented himself for his scheduled interview, seemingly peeking into the tiny office space in which I was anticipating his arrival. My back was turned slightly towards the door when, the assistant announced the Sergeant's arrival. I turned to greet the officer walking towards him with an outstretched manicured hand.

The Sergeant's interview took place in one of the empty conference rooms down the main corridor. During the interview, the interviewee unwittingly had given rise to a new career pursuit, in just those moments of brevity. This particular officer exemplified my childhood vision of what a true police officer was and within a few months, circumstances presented themselves so that I had decided to forego my acting interests for a seemingly more stable career in law enforcement. Just like that, a pivotal moment in time.

Sergeant Paige became my mentor in the pursuit of my unfolding dream.

The preparation for the police examination phases was mentally and physically demanding, but Andi was more than up for the challenges. The Sergeant spent countless hours drilling his protégé in various police scenarios, oiling the gears for the first phase, the **written,** most agencies placed the 2nd phase under **physical agility,** with each agency differing only slightly in timed requirements for running, balance beam walking, and grip strength, dead weight dummy dragging and lifting, jumping, scaling a 6' wall or 2 walls in the running of an obstacle course. The 3rd phase of testing was usually the **oral board,** advancing beyond which part 4, an extensive **background** would be conducted. Getting past phase 3 generally meant a candidate was being considered for hire or recruitment. Part 4 generally was the **medica**l with part 5 being the **psychological exam, written and verbal.** Additionally, Sergeant Paige assisted me with physical preparatory aspects, including working out in a gym setting, running or walking a track, hand gun training. Fortunately, I had always been physically fit and athletic, so this aspect of readiness was not difficult, just tiring. I was whipped into shape and by the time of my first exam process with the city of Oakland, CA in 1991, I cleared every phase of testing with flying colors. Most females had problems with scaling the 6' wall, but not me who'd perfected my own one-handed style which some of the officers at Oakland had asked me to teach to other applicants, so visually unique was the technique: run to the wall, place your left arm atop the wall, rise up and lift the body in one sweeping motion, while pulling the right leg up, the left following, and you're over the all intimidating 6' wall. San Francisco (SF) availed several physical agility practice sessions attended by many female applicants of which I was a participant. I was nicknamed FloJo in recognition of Olympian track star Florence Griffith—Joyner, and asked to instruct the females in best running form as well as wall scaling. I happily obliged. I was not overly confident, didn't really want to cross the bay to go to work as a cop, because I was more comfortable with East Bay communities. I passed all phases of testing, but their hiring list expired.

The main obstacle surrounding the coveted position of police officer is that in and of itself. It is coveted and because of nepotism and prejudices against females or non- military persons, or it could be a Chief's preference for graduates of a particular college or university, many of the best qualified people are not selected from an established list of ranked applicants **or the time** for the established list, usually expires, thus if the applicant wants to be considered again for recruitment he or she must reapply and go through all phases again. Many people give up because of the cited impediments as the entire testing phase can take up to 4 months and must all be done while working your regular job. Very real was the obstacle of nepotism (a promise to a friend or family member) or in one personal instance, a black Chief's preference that you be a graduate of Cal-Berkeley or non-black.

While I was successful in all phases, during my first application process with Oakland, I, unfortunately was not selected for hire due to the established list's time frame element. I was heartsick, but persevered for 5 more years. Again, remember the length of the testing phases, which generally means one or maximally two testing phases in a given calendar year. But this too can be hampered, because of hiring freezes, etc.

Ultimately, and with Sergeant Paige still serving as mentor, I was chosen as the first black female police recruit by the City of Pleasanton, CA. in August 1995. It was the biggest moment of my life. I had already scored high on the Oral Board and the Written. The day of the physical agility, the applicants were allowed in a gym before the obstacle course testing began. I was inside stretching and just at the moment when I was stretching my spine, lying flat on my back with both legs extended from my waist, behind my head, when an overseeing officer walked in and observed this. This was the moment I knew that I was in high consideration, something just known. Now just go out there and kick ass on the obstacle course:

While wearing a simulated gun belt, and from a seated position of a police vehicle, open the driver's door and run to a 6' wall, scale the wall, run about ½ mile, after which perform a grip strength test by grasping two 70 pound tension-filled metal arms, pulling them until they touched, go inside the gym, and drag a 170-pound dead weight dummy about 50 feet and lift it to a table; all in a timed span of about two minutes and 30 seconds. I finished with seconds to spare and had a reasonably dry face.

It felt so good, really good, that bright August afternoon. I was glowing in my black leotards and gray drop waist short sleeve shirt, accenting my 22-inch waist, with short straight black hair, flattering eyes and cheeks. I'd aced the agility and had a fan in more than one observing officer. I just knew it in my heart and soul, but had no inkling of what lay ahead, the* _history_ I was about to make in this home base of John Madden, the former Oakland Raider head coach, current NFL sports commentator.

I'd done all of this with the mentoring and love of Sergeant Paige and while undergoing another process with the City of San Francisco; working full time, too, in Sacramento, a round trip of 160 daily miles. Oh, and did I mention that I was 39 years old but 40 when the moment of * _history_ began to unfold on a grander scale. Oh, what an opera life can be!

*History (Firsts)
A Continuation of Moments in Time

The precursor, in hindsight, presumptively began in 1977, exactly 18 years to the day of November 7, 1989, the day of my meeting with Sergeant Paige.

November 7, 1977 was the day I became the first black (nee) female hired by Fireman's Fund Insurance Company, Cleveland, Ohio, as a Claims Adjuster Trainee. I'd seen an advertisement in the Sunday Plain Dealer a few months earlier under the caption "Graduate Advisers" My mind's eye was caught and I placed a call the very next day to the Advisers' office located in Akron. This was in late summer or early fall. I'd only just become a college graduate in August 1977, but seeing as how I'd only worked as a cashier during my senior year, my mother was more persistent in her urging that I get a good job.

After making arrangements for an interview, I believe to have been on a Thursday, I set my sights on choosing my interview wardrobe. Not owning a suit, I selected a white blouse, red skirt, black heels and purse, borrowed my boyfriend's mother's car, a 1973 sage green over white Mach Mustang and drove to my interview in pouring rain. I was a nervous wreck, probably more so because of the red skirt, a wrong choice for sure, but it was all I had at the time, other than jeans and Nik Nik blouses, and partying dresses. Another reason for being nervous was the fact that the Mustang had no functioning windshield wiper on its driver's side. Somehow, I made it.

My male interviewer was cordial and pleasant enough, relaxing me in no time after my hurried rush into the building from the adjacent lot. To which when I returned I discovered that I'd left the headlights on, thus the car's battery was dead. I went back into the office to inform of my dilemma and was quickly accommodated with a tow truck driver who recharged the battery with instructions not to turn the car off until I arrived in Cleveland.

A few days later, I received a call from my graduate adviser who wanted to schedule an interview with an insurance company. I could hardly contain myself as arrangements were made.

After my second interview with Fireman's Fund, I gave my mother all the details, asking what she thought. "I think you got the job. They don't take you on a tour of the office or show you the restroom if you're not going to be working there." Oh, how green and naïve I was. She was right. A week or so later, while working my cashier job at Bilo's, I received a call from my mother stating I'd gotten the job and was to start the following Monday, November 7, 1977. Thus, it started with a gray A-line skirt, gray and white striped, stiffly starched blouse, black mohair sweater, pumps and hose. The Claims manager, Mr. Art Chloe informed me that I'd gotten the job as he'd discussed my candidacy with his family during dinner and told them that when we shook hands at the end of our walk-about interview, they were damp with perspiration and he liked that I'd concealed my nervousness. "Never let them see you sweat." Literally feeling the sweat was another matter. That old deodorant commercial owes me a whole lot of money.

Barbara, Mr. Chloe's personal secretary, informed me of my history-making executive entrance. Barbara was black, but the pressure ride was on me. I dealt with all kinds of prejudices (racial and gender based) and sexual harassment, particularly from my middle aged, girth- built white supervisor, George, who'd find a way to rub against my backside anytime he got the chance.

I worked in the insurance industry for nearly 20 years and after having found my niche, hard-core investigations. The more difficult or challenging to others in my orbit, the more drawn to it I was, producing desired results for clients solicited or referred.

Things began to change within the insurance industry; I'd seen them creeping in over the years, computers, mergers, economic slips, and pass overs for deserved promotions, and companies moving to other states. In 1993 I acted on a decision I'd reached before then, to apply and test for my own Private Investigator's license. I'd been in the insurance industry far too long to not have something of my very own come from it. Besides my then employer was about to go out of business. I needed the owner's statement of years of qualifying experience that I garnered. By one percentage point I did not pass the written examination. On route to my second written test in the state capitol, the left rear tire of my Lincoln went flat on Interstate 80. I pulled to the side of the road behind a resting trucker, called the state to advise of my misfortune. They would resend me notification of another test date. The night before my next exam, I could not sleep and actually began to hyperventilate as I rested on my living room sofa. The next morning came, I put on my best mental helmet and with my Lincoln in good shape, and I drove to Sacramento. A few weeks later I received the test results. I had detonated that one percentage point into oblivion and became one of very few black female Private Investigators in the state of California. I say one of few black females while having yet to verify the existence of others, but I suppose there were a few more before myself. This successful bid of mine was in 1994. I was happy and proud as a lark.

I said it before, but, I'm compelled to repeat it again, my grandest and most intimately rewarding moment was when I became, at the age of 40 years, the first black female to be recruited, in fact hired, by the Pleasanton, CA Police Department and placed in their academy. This moment began a few weeks after I received a call in December1995 while working in my office in Sacramento. It was wondered by the agency if I could come in that day for a drug test to which I agreed. I arranged to leave the office early; I beat the returning to the Bay Area traffic and headed to the police department where I was greeted by the person who'd conducted my background investigation, Tom Fenner. I was asked to provide a urine sample. I was told that the sample taking would be conducted in the presence of a female officer, who escorted me, per Fenner's orders, briefcase-less to a restroom and stood outside my stall while I urinated in a cup. I exited the stall, handed my untainted urine to the female officer who remarked that she'd never seen urine so clear. My urine almost had the look of tap water, it was so clear. I just smiled and remarked that it was due to the fact that I drank lots of water. I didn't use illicit drugs, so I was not concerned in the least about this 'surprise out of nowhere' request for a pee sample.

Soon after the drug test, I was scheduled for complete medical, psych and polygraph exams. I passed them all. Lastly and in January 1996 I underwent the interview with the Chief, aced it and was placed in the paid Police Academy at Evergreen in San Jose which is also where San Jose recruits are trained. San Jose recruits were in large part trained and kept apart from the other represented agency recruits. Pleasanton had three recruits, myself and a black guy, Rod Lewis, a USA ranked track person, and an early 20's all too serious/never smiling white male, a former reserve officer who suffered from a very bad case of halitosis. He and Rod would graduate the academy, Rod later being fired while still on probation for an alleged theft of a prisoner's wallet.

I was Recruit #27 of about 46. My primary training officer was T.O. Shabatura, a very nice, handsome, medium built, seemingly moderately-tanned man with thinning hair. I would later learn that he chewed tobacco. I liked him, even had a non-revealed slight crush on him. He was honest and decent. I was so proud to be there fulfilling my dream, I thought I'd burst. We underwent all kinds of training; mental and physical, weapon and weaponless, scenarios associated with penal code violations, from a basic car stop to murder. It seems as if on every other day there was a written test, amidst uniform and handgun inspections, oftentimes not with advance notice. You were required to memorize the serial number of your handgun and mace canister as you might be called upon to recite either with no notice. If you didn't respond correctly, you'd be dinged some points. Certain violations were punished by 100-1000 word memos due the next day at precisely 8:00 a.m. We all had our turn at standing guard over the locker room for which you had to arrive on site at 7:30, stand at attention like a guarding soldier until a staff member unlocked the main doors. It would be freezing. You could not show your uniform shirt during your commute time. Better not have any pennants (lint) on your uniform, spit shine those boots, name tag and watch on. Females could wear no nail polish, lipstick was ok. No one could have hair touching his or her collars. You could not enter a building wearing "cover" (your cap) or there'd be a memo if caught. I sometimes forgot to remove my cover; often enough to where I'd voiced to another recruit my concern. I never got caught by the T O's, as respects the cover issue.

- Under the stress of not do's and HIGH ANXIETY related to life dependency performance on all levels. My daily routine went something like this:

- 5:19 a.m. Alarm used for 1st time as a working adult.

- Shower and dress. White undies including undershirt; white gym socks beneath black uniform socks; black brogan boots shined and laced; uniform shirt; covering the sleeve's patches by a jacket; a 2nd or 3rd check for pennants. A quick going over with a lint brush.

- Place packed lunch in my building's borrowed 4-wheeled

shopping cart which contained my text books, gun and anything else I needed for that day at the academy; heart thumping, "can't be late."

- Between 6:15 and 6:30 a.m. out the door to the elevator at the end of the hall; hoping the rumbling cart is not disturbing my sleeping neighbors

- Unload cart into trunk of my tired and right rear side dinged, gas guzzling Lincoln

- Commence 25+ mile drive to academy

- Arrive at academy in time to unload trunk, walk to locker room and place items in locker, timed to a science after about 2 weeks

- Cup of coffee, time permitting

- Walk to classroom. I was placed on Team 2; the other half of students on team 1.

- 8:00 Team Leader announces, "TO on deck" TO'S entry into room of eager fresh-faced recruits. We all stand in anticipation of something new to learn via lecture.

- Order to take seats; any memos due are collected after which lecture begins.

- Noon, lunch. Afterwards, I rush to locker to wrap my ankles for always physical training/daily runs. I never ran without wrapping my ankles. Everything was timed. Couldn't be late to the skid, where we stretched after 2 laps in prep for 6-8-mile run.

The skid was used for warm-up exercising before runs, marching drills, car stop scenarios, and defensive driving. If you were late to it, you'd have to do 50 extra sit-ups. I was sometimes late because I wrapped my ankles every day. I didn't mind the extra sit ups; they just made my stomach muscles stronger and waist smaller.

I'm in heaven though; not the fastest jogger, but I was the top female on a sprint. I could pull out a sprint on our last stretch back to the skid like nobody's business. The TO'S never understood this when I was the slowest jogging uphill from the skid. Hey, I wasn't a jogger, but a sprinter. In the beginning, I would walk-run the hill from the skid. Once, our team leader spoke with me about it, so I mentally switched gears and the next day or so I made it up the hill without walking or slowing down. I never came in last on our return from running with my 40-year-old self among all of those 20's youngsters. There was a guy older than me, he was about 50. He did great. He'd been recruited from a local military base, Moffitt Field. We even had an English Bobby a genuine C.O.P. or Constable on Patrol.

I was having the time of my life, absolutely. However, I was far from being the best shot with the hand gun, so I had to go to range practice on my own after the daily regimen. I had to practice at an off-site range and pay for it, the range fee, and provide my own ammunition which was another expense. Pleasanton was aware of my shooting deficiency, but only availed their range to me once in five months, citing the lack of personnel to assist me. It hurts to say it, but about five weeks before graduation, I neglected to pass my last qualifying handgun test, daytime combat shooting. I'd already passed all of the others including night-time combat. Additionally, I'd passed all the shotgun qualifying shoots. I was really good with the shot gun. There was more pressure with the hand gun. Our agency's gun belts had a 2-snap gun holster which slowed your target firing time. Anyway, on the last day of qualifying in the hand gun, there were two instances of cheating by the same person. I won't say by whom. This herein unnamed recruit even left the range, just before his shoot, ran to the locker room and switched gun belts to a single snap holster. When counting up the number of holes in his target, he successfully argued with a female master that one hole represented two shots. She passed him and we all knew it was unfair. No one mentioned seeing him leave the range and obviously run quite a distance to the locker room during the qualifying shoot, return to the range while we all were taking our turns. I saw him, and I know others did too. The range master saw him return but said nothing. Oh, well. That Blue Code of silence was in full force. Fine; I'd bought into it also. And even though I had a bad day at the range and by rules had to leave the academy that very day, I never said anything about it to anyone.

My agency was contacted immediately and I was instructed to bring my equipment in that day. I was even asked to remove my department patches from the sleeves of my uniform which I never did. That was a psychological game I was not going to play.

OK, you want to play? You can have the uniform back but it will be on my terms. I returned the used (before me) 9mm Sig Sauer on my way home, no problem, the sights were probably off anyway. But by giving it back I could not have it tested and the agency knew it. I stalled in getting my size 4 uniform back to the agency, stating I wanted to clean it. I returned it with the rest of my equipment within a few days. During my exit interview, it was remarked that I was so calm. I let the observing officers know that, "Yes, I am calm, however absolutely devastated but I'd not disgraced the agency or myself; that I never lied, that no, I did not want their conciliatory job offer of non-sworn Community Service Officer. Hell no! No, I did not curse, but the three men sitting before me got the message loud and clear. I left their presence with a great big sigh of relief. I'd been used as a token. They'd done nothing really to insure my success or for that matter, their own.

I was later, a year later, told that the academy had wanted to allow me to take the qualifying range test again but that Pleasanton had refused to accept its invitation.

No one knows but me, the pressure I was under during those academy days. During it all, I was carrying the weight of an entire race of people on my back, at least in the Bay Area's police officer community. I gave it my truest best. I was not a failure, I was failed. And it truly pissed me when later that year after Thanksgiving dinner in my older brother's home, he remarked in front of guests, "You couldn't even pass a police academy." I don't know what he thought had occurred, but if he thought it was because of academics, he of course is /was wrong! Bottom line is I did it the hard way, no nepotism or grandfathering into a hire.

God Bless the family of the young woman who a few months after the academy graduation, suffered the loss of their daughter via a murder by the handgun of one of my academy team members. This particular recruit was young and had against academy rules, gotten involved with another recruit, an older female. He had a hard time dealing with that dissolution while still in the academy. The person he killed was someone else. Many of us suspected his instability while in the academy and the worldlier of us conjectured something like him stalking a female, which he'd done to this young woman before accosting her on an interstate and murdering her.

See, Pleasanton, I'm still here, didn't freak out. The academy personnel knew I was worth a second try and deep down, you knew it too. My integrity remains intact. My department issued gun belt hangs in one of my closets. My cover/cap with the Pleasanton emblem is in one of my drawers and my Private Investigator License remains in good standing in the state of California.

Careers

My first (career) as an investigator essentially began in November 1977 when I began working as a Claims Adjuster Trainee for Fireman's Fund Insurance Company of North America (FFA) in Cleveland, Ohio. I was 21 and a recent college graduate, full of energy and inquisitiveness; basically, a true fresh face in Corporate America, possessing naiveté in the highest; well at least in some respects. As I mention in Moments in Time, I was the first Black person hired in such capacity. My first day was full of wracked nerves, lots of tension, apprehension, but excitement. I was pretty cool, though. I was on Front Street, being watched by everyone (all the other young and talented trainees, supervisors (2), and manager, Mr. Chloe. I was receiving intense training, primarily consisting of reading a variety of introductory texts, including the history of insurance, investigation techniques, analyzing and interpreting insurance policy provisions or exclusions. I was being groomed for bodily injury claims, inclusive of tort law and medical terminologies product liability, etc. For the first eight weeks or so all I did was read and ask questions or take tests. Then came the day I received my very first claim; to handle from inception to conclusion. It was a very minor collision claim, but I handled it expertly and from there began to receive more complex claims involving minor bodily injuries necessitating medical payments. Then came claims involving attorney representation and evolving legal issues. After about six months, I was flown to a seminar in Indiana for a few days. That was successful and I started to feel myself expanding in my knowledge of the intricacies of corporate activities, because I had learned a few things, particularly about lunch hour.

I had never really consumed alcohol and was shocked that people did so at lunch time. (I never did while in training). The one time the company approved on-site consumption was during my first Holiday season there. At some point near Christmas/New Year's, 1977-1978, the office was officially closed for about 2 hours (12:00-2:00 (an extended lunch) during which time fine wine was served. I took a small plastic cup about ½ full into my cubicle with Hors d'oeuvre planning to sip and munch until day's end at 4:00. Around 3:00 Mr. Chloe's secretary, Barbara, came in my cubicle and saw me still sipping my wine. Barbara was surprised and let me know that I had to throw the wine out. I didn't quibble, but was told, that I should have thrown my wine out at 2:00; that we'd been open for business since then. I understood, but didn't understand how my co-workers could go out for lunch and have two or three cocktails and come back and that was accepted- but I grew to know more. I never drank at lunch at FFA; I didn't drink alcohol.

****

In July 1978 I was approaching my first year, but before I could be officially declared a Claims Adjuster, I had to undergo the last phase of training in the Home Office of FFA in San Francisco. Oh my, I'd heard so much about that place, read about it as a child, and had seen it featured in films. I along with trainees from all over the country were readied for our trip; planned with mastery detail for comfort and comport. American Express owned FFA and I was given an American Express card with a per diem expense allotment with express understanding that any excesses of any kind would be my sole responsibility. I agreed and understood. Wow! My very first charge card. (I was growing fast). Appreciated detail was given the company's selection of my roommate. I was Black, but my favorite person to take breaks and lunch with was Helen Myers, a white late 40s-early-50s woman. We had a lot in common. I always did integrate well. Anyway, my manager selected a middle-aged white woman as my roommate. (I told you, I was being watched). I don't recall her name but she was the best choice for me. She was pleasant with sprayed- to- last-three weeks frosted white hair. She had the most beautiful natural finger nails I had ever seen; she buffed them to a bright sheen each evening before putting on her hair bonnet to preserve that hair do. We enjoyed the others' company. We had been instructed on what to pack for San Francisco's cool weather and we listened. (Glad we did, too).

The throng of FFA trainees embarked on a three-week training session, in July 1978. I suffered jet lag for the first and last time ever. (My trip to Switzerland four years later didn't bother me).

Over three weeks, we read, tested, and submitted to scenarios, and had fun week nights and weekends. I believe I (explored the environs) more than most in that class. I went everywhere I could; what I thought were the hip places, like UC Berkeley campus and surrounding avenues; even Haight/Ashbury. I ventured within reasonable distance from our Van Ness Holiday Inn locale; even to the Davies Symphony Hall location where I saw Leontyne Price elegantly strolling past wearing draped mink and head wrap in drizzling July. It was sheer delight. I excused myself from the Sausalito frog races and hightailed it to Berkeley. A week or so later, I contacted former high school classmate, Demetrius Andrews who lived in the area and he and I hooked up one Friday and went clubbing. Another time, I got my hair braided with extensions and appear with them in our FFA class photo which I've held onto. By the time I returned home I had visited Rafiki at Vidal Sassoon and gotten my hair pixied out. It was an excellent cut with which I returned to Cleveland, to the surprise of my co-workers, because I'd left with near shoulder length hair.

During my three weeks in class, I discovered within myself that I had an affinity for interviewing and for property claims, (not cars), but structures, burglaries, fires, mudslides etc. I wanted to handle property not liability claims. I received all A's in my classes and was promoted to Claims Adjuster by the Home Office.

Almost immediately upon my return I requested a transfer to San Francisco which was summarily refused. One month later, I began my relocation from Cleveland plan, leaving there

March 2, 1979. Now that's a date, I celebrate every year-my liberation.

Some Memorable Claims/Investigations

I picked up my claims career at Hanover Insurance in November 1979, as a personal lines property adjuster; just what I'd wanted in Cleveland. I caught on quick and gained so much steam that eventually I was given a private room. Subsequent to that I was promoted and before I knew it, I had been placed back out on the floor to directly train and (essentially) supervise a new-hiree, Renee McDowell. In part, the idea was for Renee to observe and listen to me on the phone and during my dictation of correspondence, etc. and to be readily available for any questions she might have or to give immediate hands on instructions to her. Ultimately Renee resigned and pursued a career in Health Care from which she retired. Renee and I remained friends until her sudden death in 2010.

One day I received a vandalism claim. I contacted the insured, a sweet 40 something woman. I'll call her Betty. Betty told me that she had damages to the hems of her draperies and gouge marks in her hardwood floors, amongst other miscellaneous damages like a broken music box. Betty claimed the vandalism and malicious mischief damages (V and MM) were caused by a ghost which prompted me to draw pictures of "Casper" and write the words "boo, boo" accompanied by a smiley face in my claim file.

As I was an 'inside' adjuster, I assigned the claim to an outside, independent firm, GAB. Their field adjuster visited Betty's home, took her recorded statement and a slew of photographs, and prepared a written report of their investigative findings along with recommendations and valuations of Betty's damages. The field adjuster report informed that Betty's home had many large "attack" animals, including dogs, cats, and birds; that Betty claimed the ghost had bitten off the hems of the drapes, drug furniture across the floors, and flung the jewelry box into a wall.

Betty insisted that a ghost had maliciously vandalized her home. I found it necessary to call the field guy who told me that Betty had marred the floors with constant moving of furniture; that the drapes had been chewed off by her pets. The issue with the jewelry box was never decided. But a coverage issue was made clear. Does the policy cover vandalism damages caused by a ghost? First things first, a ghost is not a person; that takes care of that. Damage to contents or a dwelling structure caused by domestic animals is specifically excluded. I denied Betty's claim and later, by pure chance, this file was audited by my manager, Tom Jacobsen, who taught me never, ever draw a picture in a file again. We both laughed, but I understood that just like he randomly had someone pull about 20 of my cases, that an attorney could subpoena a claim file and we did not want personal commentary included.

Still at Hanover, I received an 'explosion' claim, in the bright dawn of convenient in-home use of microwave ovens. I'll call the insured Selie. I contacted Selie with the distinct thought that her new microwave oven had malfunctioned and was covered under manufacturer's warranty. Selie informed me that she had tried her oven on a few items and was interested in seeing how it could work for her dog (a small lap canine). Selie said she bathed Poochie and as she had a quick errand, she left home after Poochie was placed in the microwave oven on a time of about 20 minutes. When Selie returned, the microwave had exploded or shall I say Poochie had exploded through the door of the oven and Poochie's remains were everywhere (dog flesh, hair, innards) were all over. I denied the claim for the oven as it was not used for its intended and designed purpose. Poochie was also excluded since domestic animals are excluded under a homeowner's policy. However, I approved the clean-up of Selie's kitchen, a massive undertaking. Folks, you know the moral of this story...

Ever have debt problems and added to them is a fast-approaching Balloon mortgage payment of $30,000.00? Oh my, I feel you, sympathize and all that jazz, even though it's never happened to me. Has to be a lot of pressure. I totally understand. But do not do the following: crush to fine granules and powder about 100+ pounds of glass, remove all important documents, etc., from your house, along with yourself, drive to site of all fire hydrants within a mile radius of your ballooned mortgaged house, open the hydrants and pour the ground glass in each hydrant to prevent water pressure, set the house ablaze using an accelerant, remove yourself from the scene of the house burning to the ground because responding firefighters cannot fill their hoses to extinguish the blaze, and then file a total loss claim under your infant policy (less than one year from inception date). Total loss of a structure and its contents and you don't think Ms. Adams has a few questions. You betcha, buddy. Got to call you Buddy because you thought you had found a new friend. OK. How you like me now? You're most likely still serving your sentence for arson, insurance fraud, and a few more California Penal Code charges and convictions.

If you consume enough alcohol to register a 0.38 blood alcohol content (BAC), "we have a problem", but let's say you do anyway, please, do not drive a vehicle. A man, I'll call Rodrigo did this one evening, entered eastbound Highway 4 in Contra Costa County, California. Highway Patrol (CHP) Officer, Flash, working the graveyard shift sat atop a knoll in his cruiser spying the east and west lanes. Flash witnessed Rodrigo enter, traveling east, but in the westbound lanes. The boldly erected and well-lit with black stripes, across red lettering "DO NOT ENTER" signs were not an afterthought of Rodrigo's before Flash saw a within the posted 50 miles per hour speed limit a fully loaded big rig semi barreling down in his proper lane and collide head on with Rodrigo's car. Rodrigo died instantly in a twisted mass of steel and swirling and engulfing fumes, but he probably felt not much, courtesy of a 0.38 BAC. Rodrigo's surviving family filed a Negligent Homicide/Wrongful Death suit against the trucking company and its emotionally distraught driver. After my full independent field investigation including an interview of Flash, procurement and review of CHP report, Coroner's report, including autopsy, scene photographs, I recommended a heavily supported denial of Rodrigo's family's claims. The denial of compensatory damages was not refuted.

I investigated thousands of claims (too innumerable to affix a number) several involving transcontinental fraud (mostly involving Nigerians), deceit, and many deaths.

As a private investigator, I am not at liberty to reveal finite details of most of my cases. Most were surveillance to determine who's the other man, woman; some police brutality or improper procedure, many locates/skip-trace, assist with vehicle repossession, asset location, many process services (not my favorite, but good money; Ron Beshears, owner of ProServ is the man for this, but we shared a lot of work. If he couldn't get 'em, I did, and vice versa). I became a protégé of now retired law enforcement officer and private investigator, Donnie Nunley aka Sherlock, who trained me in aspects of Unlawful Detainer, repossessions, and lots more. Those were great times. Thanks Donnie. It was a quid quo pro-business relationship. I had fun and think of him sometimes. Oh wow, we were an excellent team.

****

One of my first cases came from Florida via my local Chamber of Commerce membership. I'll refer to the client as Lydia who was seeking to reunite with a former male lover, a graduate of an Ivy League University. I confirmed the latter and tracked him to the Bay Area where he was a very successful dentist. I spoke briefly with him only once and he lent authenticity as to why he did not desire to have any communication with Lydia, ever again. I reported back to Lydia, but was gentler with her than the doctor had been with me. Lydia almost freaked. I didn't mind. She was 3,000 miles away and based upon my knowledge of her resources, I knew she was not coming my or the doctor's way. Of course, I did not reveal the doctor's vocation or location; just that he chose to be left alone. I was paid quite handsomely for this case. Lydia was on time with her installments.

Bold maneuvering, quick decisive talk, the right outfit, brought me into the stylishly furnished apartment of a mid-20s up and coming yuppie in my neighborhood. I walked to her place, reminiscent of a New York 1940s circa Brownstone with painted flanks. I'll call her Chi-Chi. I talked my way through an opened door and a "Hi, come on in" (before my neighbors find out about me), look around. Chi- Chi had written a bad check for her hair services at the salon at which I had my services performed. In brief conversation, I visually checked for my security in her living room. No threats, so I let her have it in a nice, firm business tone. She kept denying having any cash on hand. I urged that she check her bedroom. She did, and brought me $40.00. I took it with insistent instructions to have the balance remitted to the hair dresser on or before the following Friday, otherwise I'd be back, etc. Chi-Chi kept her promise, right on time with full balance in cash, good girl. Your hair looks swell, but you have to pay, just like me, Chi-Chi.

Another time, I hooked up with Tommy Trusso, a bad mother...shut your mouth, Bounty Hunter for a ride-along, observe, assist in Berkeley. I'll call the criminal, Hyde. First, Berkeley Police Department (BPD) were notified of our intended take down and two patrol officers were positioned in their cruiser around the corner from Hyde's mother's house. Tommy had readied his arsenal of weapons, a semiautomatic handgun and a shotgun. The trunk of Tommy's vehicle was left down but unlocked, in case immediate access and retrieval were warranted. As we approached the house, I observed the surroundings which included a detached garage at the left rear of the home. Hyde's mother answered Tommy's firm knock and we entered her living room where several framed photographs of Hyde were displayed. Tommy and I glanced each other while the mother denied her son being there. Tommy and I eyed each other again. I knew Hyde was there, but we couldn't let on. So, we excused ourselves, sternly reminding her of the need to have Hyde surrender on the warrant associated with the bail he'd skipped out on (probably his mother's home had been used as collateral for bail). I could tell his mother was lying. Tommy and I left and returned to his car parked in front of the house two houses away at the right of Hyde's mother's. I picked up on Tommy's instinct to not leave, but to wait a few minutes. We couldn't keep BPD in limbo much longer. Before we knew it, within less than two minutes, Hyde burst down his mother's drive and ran towards our car. Tommy leapt from the front seat, seemed to literally reach to the trunk, grabbed the shotgun and racked it with a loud commanding "click, click" before Hyde reached the back of our car. Damn, Tommy was fast. Tommy raised his weapon at shoulder height just in Hyde's path. Hyde stopped so quick, it was like a screech from a cartoon character. I almost laughed, but I was a pro, exiting the front seat and stepping in behind Hyde's stunned self. Tommy identified himself and the warrant specifics. Hyde was pat searched, placed in handcuffs, put in the back seat. BPD was alerted of our successful fugitive retrieval and a call was placed to Sonoma County sheriffs who awaited our arrival. We drove the 20 minutes to Fairfield and without incident delivered Hyde to his fate. That was some wild exciting stuff. I loved it.

In all my years as a private investigator, I never had to expose or use the threat of a weapon. The client always received what they paid for and in some cases received what they wanted but did not pay me for. I still have a few thousand dollars outstanding in uncollected fees, but it is real cool, trust me. I've written it off as a gratuity of life. I am rewarded, now, beyond those thousands.

I opine that success in private investigations or law enforcement bears direct correlation to overt confidence in knowledge of people and a lack of visible or odorous fear, but rather innate compassion. There's very little I actually fear. Without exception, including myself definitely, all of the persons I have aligned with in this career possess four traits: intensive knowledge of human behavior, confidence in knowledge of issue at hand, importantly, command presence, and most essential, protection of identities. These traits were without doubt in peak mode for me during a commercial burglary investigation at a car stereo parts business (I'll not identify the city), Alameda County, California.

I remember the mild sunny spring day. I had made the appointment with the store manager. I wore a purple silk blouse beneath a black raw silk jacket atop a mild lightly woven black and white muted tweed skirt about two inches above the knee, black hose and 2" black suede pumps. I carried a black leather briefcase with necessities of camera, hand-held tape recorder, etc. I presented my business card to the counter sales clerk; an approximate 20-year-old fresh-faced eager to help young man with an easy, affable persona. I spoke with him for a few minutes. Before I could get to the business at hand, this young man revealed to me his second or third hand knowledge of a murder and the location of the disposed of body in another county. I couldn't believe what I was hearing. What the hell? I'm here for a burglary and this kid is telling me about a suspected murder. No, he was not kidding. He had apparently been holding onto this information and it was gnawing at him, poor baby, so he trusted me with it. I kept real calm, assured him it would be alright. I thanked him for sharing and proceeded to get on with my appointment with the manager. I concluded my investigation within about a week. I did not betray this young man's confidence... Instead, I did the best thing, which I will leave to the reader's imagination.

Teaching

Over the course of my selecting a well-preserved mélange of vestigial and unembellished memories, my career as a teacher is one of the highlights traversing still. I will forever be a teacher, amending the past, enhancing the present, and touching the future of attentive students.

High School guidance counselor Carolyn Smith had told me in 1973 there would be no demand for teachers in 1977 the year I was slated to graduate college, but as long as there is something to be amended, enhanced or touched upon, a teacher of some description or in some capacity will be needed. Forty-one years later I unequivocally find a demand for teachers. I'm not disappointed that I was directed onto another path because it led in many other positive directions and thankful discoveries.

In 2001, I was employed in the insurance industry as a Subrogation Recovery Specialist for Zurich Insurance in San Francisco. I was in my second year of a long-term assignment. The position was inside, involving tedious, repetitive computer station motions and activities. I had been experiencing debilitating pain in both hands and my arms, back, and neck for several months. My symptoms progressed to the point that I reported them to the company. I was thereafter accommodated with an ergonomically correct work station that included a wrist/hand rest for my keyboard and an Ergo chair and footstool. Additionally, a shoulder rest was installed for my phone, but my symptoms persisted, particularly shooting, burning sensations in my hands. Finally, I filed a worker's compensation claim as a few physicians had medically documented Bi-lateral Carpal Tunnel Syndrome, worse on the left as supported by a machine and needle insertions into my hands, wrists, and arms. I was taken off work, March 2, 2001 and placed under the care of specialists. Wrist braces and pain medications had not helped or resolved the diagnosis, either. Over the next six to eight months, I underwent acupuncture and biofeedback sessions, etc. However, I was rendered unfit to return to my career and thus qualified for rehabilitation. I was to receive about $14,000 in rehab funds, so my first thought was to put myself back through a police academy, but the State refused this as a viable career option. So, I decided to pursue a Master degree in teaching. I chose to attend John F. Kennedy University, one of the best for teacher credentialing in the Bay Area, but one of the more expensive in tuition. The state remitted quarterly tuition payments directly to JFK until the rehab money was gone, (in one year). I had another year to go before I could obtain my degree. I was offered the option of an Apple Loan, but I refused it. Terms of the loan required the candidate to work in an inner-city school system for five years and then the loan would be forgiven. Glad I refused that loan because as it turned out, I would not have been physically able to abide the terms.

I did not receive my permanent partial disability (PPD) settlement until early 2002, after not working for nearly a year. However, I had received monthly checks just about equaling my salary, so I wasn't hurting financially. I applied for a teaching position in Oakland Unified School District (OUSD) with glowing letters of recommendation from friends in the profession, law enforcement, and a physician friend, along with a transcript from JFK boasting a straight A including one A+ transcript. I had passed the state required California Basic Education Skills Test (CBEST), background and tuberculosis (TB) mandates and was offered a position, to my delight. I was not fully credentialed, so I had to work under "Emergency Credential" status. Utilizing this status under contract, I was afforded benefits, like healthcare and ultimately, my own classroom. I earned it too, thoroughly enjoyed my students, even the rough edges, let me tell you. I worked in this capacity for four years, until...Diagnosis FMD in 2005.

Still teaching but in a more muted capacity, I, twice a week get to experience 'light bulb' moments, student-initiated run, grab and hugs, notes/drawings, or smiling gratitude for 50 cents or a dollar rewards when I have it to give. I engaged in four-corner ball last week, with one hand. A high compliment for me occurred last week, also, when several teachers and an administrator requested my personal information for future substitution. I needed that. Moments like these, even driving in morning rush-hour traffic to be there by first bell brings a peace and normalcy to my life. For this ability, I am indebted to Lynette Calvin- Epps of OUSD.

Sangria Sound Bites

Dedicated to the Men and Women
of
The United States Armed Services
Who continue to defend, have died or been maimed
in
The Iraq and Afghanistan Wars

The sky rains blood
Sangria sound bites
I feel your warmth skip past my being
And want to melt
In the tears of the blood
The wet strikes, crashing down
Down, down
Pellets of pain on my soul pulsating
Down, down
To the earth
Sangria sound bites
The sky rains blood
Silencing the dove
What a dastardly thing to do
Catapulting your cleansing effect
How are we here in this place prescribed to
Continue on without
Our fathers, uncles, brothers, sisters, and sons.
Our heroines and heroes?
Too much, too many, too soon

Sangria sound bites
Nothing but agony and pain
My frayed spirit prays for you each night
Beloved and brave you are or were in the fight
Halt! No more!
Sangria sound bites

Adrea ADAMS $40/200
brown, brown
5'6", 7/9, 8   +

**Dorian Leigh Model Agency/ Cleveland OH
Warren Browne Photography**

Proof Sheet
Warren Browne Photography

**Adrea modeling wedding gown
designed by friend, Pamela McGhee
and male groom model.
San Francisco, CA**

My Life's Opera

Photo and Program from Adrea's first Stage Performance

**Adrea as "Mille" in Black Reparatory Group's (BRG)
Production of *Trouble in Mind*
Photo by BRG Staff, Berkeley, CA**

Adrea did the voice over commercial (KJAZZ 92.7 FM)
for the Play *Boesman and Lena*
Oakland Ensemble Theater Oakland, CA

Promotional advertisement for
"Green Christmas: The Gift of Love"
(Adrea is in the upper left corner)

San Francisco Chronicle, "Pink Section"

**Adrea as "Stuff" in Promotional photo of band
Godfather and The Family featuring Earl Crudup
Photo courtesy of Earl Crudup**

THE **Bay Area BLUES** SOCIETY

is pleased to announce

THE 1st ANNUAL
BLUES AWARDS SHOW

TONIGHT
WE HONOR
THE BLUES
TOMORROW
WE LIVE
THEM.

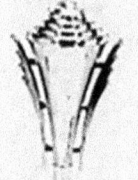

JOHN MUIR THEATER
Oakland Museum
1000 Oak Street
Oakland, CA 94612

FEBRUARY 20, 1988

BAY AREA BLUES ARTISTS OF THE YEAR

Blues Guitarist
J.J. MALONE

Blues Saxophonist
C.A. CARR

R&B Vocalist
FRANKIE ERVIN

Blues Harmonica
CHARLES MUSSELWHITE

Blues Vocalist (Male)
CURTIS LAWSON

Blues Vocalist (Female)
LADY BIANCA

Blues Keyboardist
LADY MARGARET

Blues Band of the Year
BOBBY REED & THE SIRPRIZE BAND

Blues Disc Jockey
POSTHUMOUSLY AWARDED
JOSEPH DONNELL LEWIS
KRE RADIO STATION

Blues Club Owner
PATRICK RAMANI
LARRY BLAKE'S

Blues Record Shop
JOHN GOODARD
VILLAGE MUSIC

Blues Writer
LEE HILDEBRAND
THE EXPRESS

Blues Promoter
TOM MAZZOLINI
SAN FRANCISCO BLUES FESTIVAL

Special Guests
COOL PAPA
ELLA PENNEWELL
DENNIS ROBINSON
GODFATHER & THE FAMILY
LITTLE WILLIE JOHN, JR.
TAKEZO

This picture from Fred Williamson speaks for itself; by the way his Playgirl centerfold is the one I hung on the bathroom mirror in college.

Adrea greeting NFL great, Cleveland Browns running back, Jim Brown at Black Film Makers Awards event, Oakland, CA ca.1992

Adrea with Tony DeWayne at *Geoffrey's* (my favorite work place)

My Life's Opera

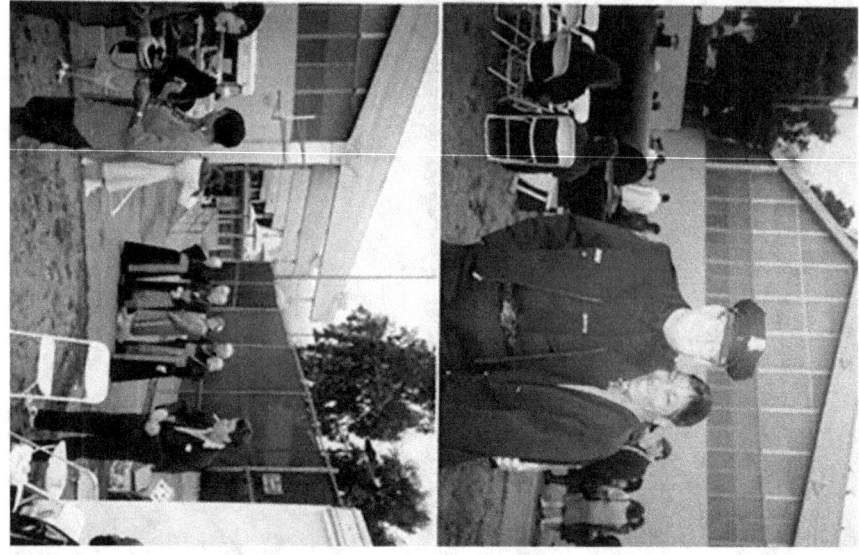

Adrea on the set of Sister Act, starring Whoopi Goldberg

Adrea as teacher and some of her Newcomer students.

My Most Best Three

Adrea with Homer, 1973

Adrea and Rahim, 7/12/80

Adrea and Henry, 1990

ACT III

Violins

Violins in sympathy
No sweeter sound
Every good boy does fine
Life's Opera should be played on violins
Grand and colorful and full of bronzes of varying hues
Electric and pale
Stirring my soul
Well-oiled is the body
~03-1990~

Thaw

Dialogue with Myself
Some Inner Workings

I suppose it depends upon many variables, like the season, the day of the week, time of day, my mood, and outward stimulus. I'm drawn to smells and colors. I deduce, then, the senses of sight and smell are my strongest and generate, by far, most of my self-reflection and the conversations I have with myself, and about myself.

No, I don't often speak aloud to myself; just enough, like you do, sometimes just to make sure the resonance or timbre is still there. Or if I stub a toe, I'll ask myself, "What's the matter are you losing your sight, girl?" Little things like that. You know what I mean. Drop something and say, "First day with your new hands?"

How do you visualize the years numerically in your mind? I mean literally. If someone were to ask you to write out the centuries from let's say 1100 until present day, with the years being given only, what would they look like on paper. I have a mental map of the years; an intricate and elaborate outlay that I've tried to explain but the party to whom I explained it could not comprehend it. I even wrote it out. It is not a simple vertical listing of the years, for some centuries, yes, I list and column but then for some reason when I get to the 1860's the listings become much more vivid and graphic. Through the 1890's the years are vertical columns but 1900 is visually horizontal with the 1 at the top. 1900 through 1919 is horizontal, then 1920 again becomes on the left, a vertical listing through 1939. Then each new decade begins a new column and continues advancing on to the right like this through 1969. 1970 becomes a horizontal plane, extending through 1999. The years 2000 through now present themselves as a horizontal plane on the right, descending. If I were more computer savvy I could probably lay it out. I'll get to that in the by and by. I hope I have enough time.

A thing that I'm good at is spelling backwards and alphabetizing words. Years ago, when Johnny Carson was still hosting The Tonight Show a guest appeared who also possessed the skill of rapidly alphabetizing words. I missed the name or technical term of this skill. I also assign numbers to letters and perform mathematical problems and solutions. I've been doing the letter and number games since I was a small child and first learned to read and dial a phone. I vividly recall associating numbers with letters when dialing those heavy black metal-based phones with the white backdrops for the black numbers way back in the late 1950's. The benefit of my self-directed mental games came in very handy on January 6, 1996, when I was undergoing a psyche exam for my police officer recruitment position. I was asked to spell a word and then to spell it backwards. To the astonishment of the doctor, there was no hesitation on my part and no mistake in either method of spelling. Thank you very much. The doctor was indeed impressed. I smiled, being similarly affected.

Often, I reflect upon the unselfish kindnesses others have given or continue to bestow upon me. The kindness of my neighbor assisting me with a brace for my hand. The continued good grace of my dearest friend, who knows who he is. He is all around, living and breathing in all I strive to do. I can never dissever my soul from his. Don't know if this is good or not. I'll continue to be his friend knowing he is mine.

On the flip side, I ponder as many others do, the heinous cruelty committed and inflicted by some against those, particularly unable to fend for themselves. I, as I'm sure you must, have lots of examples of the former and latter thought processes. All ready for a purge and thaw ceremony of their own.

I cater to an array of thoughts chronicled from first day learning through to today's news and notifications. Some thoughts are seemingly frozen, just awaiting the thaw, to be spewed forth in readiness of a percolating boil, then to be poured into a cup from which kin folk and inquisitive others desire to sip, perhaps softened by their own interpretative sprinkling of lactose.

I miss writing on my chalk or white board, my decided upon *daily aphorism*. I wonder how my former students are faring and whether or not some of the lessons I taught from textbooks and life alike have assisted in building their futures or their now daily livelihoods. I miss being one of the so-called cool teachers, one of the teachers who could talk the street lingo, flash a hip hand signal. I was caring as best as I could be, both from my gentle heart and measly paycheck. Many of my students called me "Mom." I babied and spoiled some of them a lot, maybe because I have no children of my own. I'd sometimes give them good food treats, like bananas, granola bars, crackers, milk or juice. My bottom left drawer was kept full of good stuffs, foods and films. I couldn't stand to know a child was hungry. I'll share more about my teaching experience in another expose.

Sometimes I'm perched atop a grassy knoll, flanked on all sides by angels. I'm watching, wanting to sing a song, watching, glancing, and seeing all, seeing naught. Painting myself into my next realm, a sweet calm in pale purposeful melodic spectrums. I like what I envision, and wish myself there often.

SMILES

An Observation
2-19-08

"Smile." The word in or of itself is essentially non-threatening. A lot of smiles are involuntary, automatic positive reflexive responses to direct stimuli. For example, an infant, who may or may not be cooing at you, a lover's appearance or phone call or anything a person may desire to show approval of in a non-verbal communication.

A smile represents or misrepresents us, our mood, our association or disassociation with our environment.

Certainly, our smiles are dictated by societal norms, one's position in society, even gender is a factor, and even the broadness of one's smile is predicated upon these and other elements.

Your smile is a possession as is any other part of your anatomy, to be shared or not as you deem appropriate or proper.

Some smiles are closed - mouthed revealing no teeth while other smiles reveal a range of teeth, from just a few to the completeness of uppers and lowers. The variance in a smile's range can be dependent upon one's comfort level with the overall condition or appearance of their teeth or to a perhaps lesser degree of concern, one's facial shape during smile time. I suspect these latter reasons may be why a person may cover their mouth when they smile, which often causes the receiver's curiosity to be piqued to a higher level, urging an investigation into why someone covers their mouth when he or she smiles.

History or rather historical documents offer glimpses into smiles.

On rare occasions, you will observe an elected person or head of state/government sporting a full-frontal smile in their officially commissioned photograph or painting. I suppose this is because the person wants to give the persona of seriousness and no nonsense posture.

I've often wondered why or how it is that some people smile or laugh lightly when some awfulness has befallen them, like the death of a loved one or some crime. Perhaps it's because of nerves or a smile being easier.

Certainly, some groups of people have more to smile about; are even, or, dare I say have been permitted or encouraged to smile more. Persons in traditionally subservient positions fall or have been placed in this category of permissiveness and encouragement.

Some people are just simply smilers while conversely others are not, the former probably innately as well as the latter.

Some people desire to have their morale created or enhanced by the smile of another and will go so far as to demand one or to tell you that you should smile. I find this to be in very poor taste and it doesn't matter if the tone of the seeker of a morale booster is non- harsh. Just the simple fact that someone, often a stranger, is demanding something ticks me a bit. If I want to give a smile, I will and vice versa, but don't tell me what to do. Maybe I'm having a bad day or have suffered the loss of a loved one, or maybe I have bad teeth.

True smiles are good on a physiological level, but fake smiles serve no purpose. A smile given freely, without prompt, is more beneficial than one given based on hidden agenda or motivation. A smile should be given in accordance to how one feels and not expectations.

Smiles or the acceptance of the lack thereof in our society have made sweeping changes over the past few centuries. The advances appear to be directly correlated with certain groups achieving or nearing parity with what was/is the dominant group, white males exercising their privilege.

The media now gives approval for females to be non-smilers, in all arenas including films, print and runway modeling, and the dissipating role of fulltime homemaker. Thanks, I believe to fallout from the *Feminist Movement*.

African American males are somehow seen as less threatening when they are smiling. This group went from the status of demure slave, cracking a smile, grinning to appease and entertain, tipping a hat with a smile to being partially publicly accepted without a smile in 1960's North America. This rattled more than a few folks who were threatened by this group's self-assuredness and assertiveness. But it sure made the African American woman smile a lot broader. That was a good thing. They were finally able to walk hand in hand and smile together, just because.

We were recently in the 21st century with two Democratic Party front runners, one a Caucasian woman, Hillary Clinton, the other a true by undisputed lineage African American man, Barack Obama, for whom you can bet I cast my vote with the utmost Pride and grandest Smile.

VOICES

Voices I never tired of include John F. Kennedy, Medgar Evers, Martin Luther King, Jr., Robert F. Kennedy, Walter Cronkite, Howard Cosell, Johnny Carson, my maternal grandmother, Huey Newton, my Aunt Hannah, Mirrahim - my former husband, Marvin Gaye, Olympians Tommy Smith and John Carlos, James Baldwin, and Mose Wright.

All of the above-mentioned persons positively affected me in some way. Their individual personas, messages and venues for delivery were diverse.

I was in Ms. Hammock's third grade classroom at Sullivant Elementary, Columbus, Ohio when, by the Public-Address system our principal announced the news that school was ending for the day. My visual thought pattern traded places with President Kennedy's inaugural address; his most famous, wherein he'd spoken so eloquently and with unwavering conviction about not asking what your country can do for you but rather what you can do for your country, to images of how I imagined my mother was reacting to the news at home. We students were in shock as was the entire staff. I trudged home with my bleeding heart in my throat. Mama let us in the back door. She was in near hysterics with our black and white TV blaring in the living room of our 2-story brick faced town home. The phone rang incessantly as we all grouped on the floor to watch the news unfold. It was the saddest day of my 7-year-old life.

In an odd sort of way, but maybe not, I've always connected Walter Cronkite to John Kennedy. Cronkite's reporting stays with me. His raising of his eyeglasses, dabbing at his face, the sincere empathy he exhibited, I believe, is unparalleled in television journalism. This observation in no way diminishes my respect and appreciation for other journalists or news anchors of Walter Cronkite's genre.

At the height of his civil rights and voter registration drives of the early to mid-1960s, I wish I'd known more about Medgar Evers' struggle. I was aware of his heralded efforts through media accounts and Current Event reports in school. In later years, I would come to embrace him on more than just an elementary level. He was one of my heroes.

Martin Luther King, Jr. was one of the most indisputable and galvanizing voices of the 20th century. His oratorical skills are unmatched. His message of non-violence was on par with that of Mahatma Gandhi, both of whom established and presented to global masses a higher standard of leadership via conduct, service, and unyielding belief.

I liked Howard Cosell, many didn't, but I did. I respected his intellect and ability to get to the heart and matter of the personality behind the story.

Johnny Carson exemplified true man, quick wit, and intellect on many topics, a very good dresser, and all qualities right at the top of my "man list." I rarely missed one of his shows.

My maternal grandmother had a pure soft and tender grandma voice. Even her pauses in conversation were filled with concern and love. Her "sure noughs'" were most times spoken as a query. I miss her. My "Thirteen Days" is a chronicled remembrance of our last days together.

A Black Panther was the label put upon him because of his affiliation with a group so named. Huey Newton possessed one of the most brilliant minds to which I've ever been introduced. He was extremely intelligent and essentially wanted only to do good for humankind. I admired him a lot, or shall I say I had deep admiration for his mental prowess. I met him once in Oakland, California. At that time, he was still being chauffeured by limousine. I later resided in the neighborhood in which he'd once had a penthouse. Huey's penthouse overlooked Oakland's Lake Merritt which is approximately 2.7 miles in diameter. I used to "walk/sprint the lake" for daily exercise. I'd oft times think of Huey.

Aunt Hannah's voice is soft yet lyrical, only commanding if necessary. Aunt Hannah's voice soothed my spirit for hours on end after my mother's death. I love her dearly.

Mirrahim, my former husband has or had the kindest voice, especially when he was not peeved. He greeted me as "My Darling," sometimes rolling the 'r' in darling, bringing forth my demure giggle. I knew I was adored and loved, plus he was handsome, alluring, and very smart. If ever I made a mistake in my life, divorcing him was it.

Marvin Gaye's voice through the content of interviews and song lyrics, in my opinion was a massive loss of raw talent and foresight into the pulse of the people. His musical messages expanded the globe. So very gifted he was.

Tommy Smith and John Carlos were 1968 Olympians who exemplified courage, grace, and Black pride at a time when American political and societal mandates said it was not safe to do so on a world stage. The image of two raised black gloved fists from the medal awards block-styled tiers remains unforgettably imprinted in the annals of my mind. These two men were vicariously punished for their stance, non-verbal though it was, their voices had indeed been heard, resoundingly so.

James Baldwin's keen observation of mankind, norms and not so norms fueled by his intellect and uncanny ability to reveal in written form some of the most prolific essays and exposes makes him one of the strongest voices of my life. The very first, First Edition hardbound cover book I purchased with my own earnings was Baldwin's *Just Above my Head*. I still have that book in my collection in my Baldwin section. I envied and applauded him, his writing skills and his investigative abilities. I'm left to imagine his gathering of evidence in support of his written pieces, attached the sensationalized events of society's graduation since his death.

Moses (Mose) Wright was the 64-year-old cousin Emmett Till stayed with during a few weeks of the summer of his 14th year in 1955, in Money, Mississippi. At the (trial) of the two accused, Mose Wright courageously stood and identified the accused by pointing his slender right index finger at them and said two words, seared in my brain forever, "Thar he." I was still in the womb that day, but have several times since viewed documentary film footage of these most powerful quoted words.

My composer's and producer's voices, my mother and father were the diamond and ruby from which I was hewn; rare and irreplaceable.

Inside my Heart

Dwaun T. Cox

We were as close as two kindred cousins could ever dare; we nearly shared wombs, my first, first cousin and I. He was not the first in terms of genealogy, but he was the first in so many ways. He was my first cousin, conceived a week after my own conception in March 1955. His mother, my by-marriage maternal Aunt Sadie, and my mother were seeing the same obstetrician/gynecologist (OBGYN), Dr. Cooper for prenatal care. These two petite pretty housewives. I can only imagine their excitement and mama's 5' 1" frame sporting spiked high heels. My mother had borne a son four years earlier and she wanted a girl as did my aunt for her first child. Preparations were in high gear. Aunt Sadie had bought all kinds of baby girl outfits, and I suppose my mother had done likewise, or perhaps my mother had purchased interchangeable colors like yellow, green, or blue. But anyway, excitement filled the air. Mama and daddy lived in an apartment, 'F' at 93 S. Champion; Columbus, Ohio. Aunt Sadie didn't live far away in apartment 'C'.

The OB/GYN had projected my birth for January 26 and my cousin's for January 19, 1956. Oh, the excitement swelled and as fate would have it, I was born on the date chosen for my cousin, who in fine handsome fashion arrived exactly one week later. We were destined to become so many things to the other. My cousin Dwaun Thomas Cox came to represent as a best friend, my favorite male cousin. We were as close as two cousins could be.

My memory pool is selective with this writing. Dwaun's voice has merged within my spirit so that now I am relegated to a few specifics, like his enduring ever-so-slightly crooked smile.

We also shared a permanent left eye corner scar (his, most probably because of boys' rough-housing. Factors associated with mine are recalled in 'Fortification of my Inner Conscience', chronicled within my *Life's Opera*. We were all raised to be polite and respectful to any elder with a "yes ma'am" or "no sir" and all that goes along with those words. We were obedient children, but we played hard, loved hard, protected with ferocity; all nine of us, my mother's four and Uncle Harry and Aunt Sadie's five. Aunt Ruth had two, Darrell (Butch) and Daniel (Skipper), and Aunt Gertrude (Gert) had two boys, Brent and (little) Johnny; these latter four not spending much time with us nine. Also, there was adopted cousin, Ronnie Gregory- we knew nothing about the word adopt, just that we were cousins, equal in all eyes. Then there were cousins Cathy; Linda, Robert, Carolyn, Mary, Marcella, Earline, and Anthony of Uncle Bobby and Aunt Hannah. However, these latter seven lived in West Virginia so the Columbus/Cleveland nine are the focus here.

We nine played, loved, and protected hard as young children, primarily in two places, my family's huge yard on Gray Street or at Dwaun's family home. Later as teens and young adults our meetings and times together had somewhat changed. Anyway, back to the playing. One has only to imagine nine kids ranging from age nine down to four or three years on a hot summer day; running, laughing, skinned elbows or knees, tattle-telling, cold snacks, huge meals of hot dogs with all the trimmings, "No, it's my turn to change the channel" on the boxed black and white television, the Jetsons, Highway Patrol, starring Broderick Crawford (as a child I was severely taken by his sexy voice, oh was I drawn to it. Still, for my money, he had one of the best and memorable television voices, ever). Can't forget about The Rifleman, starring handsome Chuck Connors, or Alfred Hitchcock and Ed Sullivan. ~the good 'ole days~ of real flavored and colored candies and Twinkies~

One hot summer day, eight of us (Nancy was not born yet) were enjoying ourselves, almost becoming dizzy for so much circular running around our garage/walled storage room. Dwaun ran clockwise and I countered in the opposite direction. We met at the left rear apex; paused just briefly enough to avoid running into each other, for Dwaun to kiss me on my lips, smile, and look back, as we kept running. Dwaun loved me, I knew. I've kept that day, his face, and his favorite cousin feather kiss, with me for over 50 years. Later as teens and young adults, we still kissed on the lips, in greeting. I think this was a carryover from Mama Ada, who refused to kiss you unless it was on the lips. Uncle Harry is like that, too. So, Dwaun and I carried that familial tradition forth.

As a teen, I still engaged in heavy sport with my cousins, primarily football, in neighborhood fields in Columbus. On one summer day, *August 27, 1970, we had chosen sides. I played running back, was tossed the ball and I took off, sprinting, and dodging during my run, with the ball tucked under my left arm pit. I was going to score and all of a sudden, I felt my legs lift. I was tackled, dropped the ball as I hit the ground, elbows and hands. I dropped the ball and my upper left palm area just below my baby finger came down and was sliced open by a glass shard. Stunned, I sat up to see pink meat and white tendon flowering through a faucet of red. Dwaun, took off his shirt, wrapped my hand and placed me on the back of his bike and we pumped butt back home. Aunt Sadie drove me to the emergency room of Columbus Children's Hospital where I sat for about one-half hour with my hand in an antiseptic filled bowl. A young Resident, *Dr. Brockmeyer, escorted me into a brilliant white room; spoke softly to me as he explained that I was his first stitch patient. Somehow, I felt so proud to be his first as I observed him expertly remove the flap of now dark disturbed skin, cover the area with white gauze and begin placement of eight sutures- in this late summer before I officially began my sophomore year in high school. Thanks cousin, for your shirt, what a gentleman. *I still have the dated and signed tetanus immunization card.

In our adult years, we traversed different courses, some intersecting, some not. All I will say is that during times of intersecting, we provided needed support, always love, proper amount of play, and never-ending advice for protective measures. We never betrayed the other's mutual trust, for to do so would be dishonoring. His namesake, first born son, dons a tattoo: "Death B 4 Dishonor". Because of you, my cousin, Dwaun, I knew this first. Thank you, you are a voice inside my heart, forever.

Melvin S. Adams Jr. (My brother Mickey)

You really should get to know him, love and cherish him. Him, the brother, the man, the uncle, the husband; get to know the beat of his mastered drums to which he marches. Mickey came to us all in 1958, strong-willed, and non-flaccid in his presence and demeanor. However, he presented an unexpected set of challenges my mother was not singularly equipoised to handle. I say singularly because for the majority of his young life our father was away working during the day. Keith was six, I was two and my sister was one. Mickey suffered from severe bronchitis during his first three years and frequently had to receive tented oxygen in a hospital. That aside, he was a rambunctious boy, sometimes mischievous to the point of alarm. No one apparently knew why and no prescription to thwart alarming behavior was set forth. The only thing done was strong admonishment like for the time he threw a handful of paper money into our living room standing gas burning pot-belly stove heater. All we could do was douse the flames with water and retrieve a few singed bills. Mickey was about three or four then. The next fire he was involved with resulted at his own hands, on 88th Street in Cleveland at about age six. In the middle of the night, I awoke to the odor of smoke, ran to the kitchen to see Mickey watching flames shoot up and beyond the Murphy sink by the back door. Keith was asleep in the bedroom he shared with Mickey, just off the kitchen. I rushed to get Keith out. By that time mama and my sister were up and frantic. The fire department was called but thankfully by the time they arrived Keith had extinguished the fire. And the drums continued. Mickey had a difficult time adjusting to classroom environments and did not do as well as he could have. Mama was frequently called by Bolton Elementary.

Fast forward to age nine and third grade, Mickey was expelled from Cleveland Public School(s) for throwing lit matches at a little girl. That did it. Mama (finally) made inquiries to get her child proper assistance. Mickey was placed on Cleveland's west side in Children's Aid Society where there were children similar to himself, mostly white kids awaiting foster homes. Mickey's case/social worker was Mrs. Berwald who Mickey credits with salvaging him; by instilling in him that if he continued to run away, he would never get out. Mickey did get out at age 13 when he was transferred to Star Commonwealth for Boys in Albion, Michigan. Mama never went to visit him, not once in four years citing that she had no way to get there (What about Greyhound?); therefore, his sisters never saw him either. That pained us sisters. My father and stepmother, Carol, visited him, sharing time over A& W root beer floats. At Mickey's release at 16, he went to live with daddy and Carol in Columbus. He never returned to live with mama and us girls. Mickey told me he was not mad at mama for approving his going to Michigan because that is where he learned to read and write. (I still have one of the letters he wrote in cursive from there and if the writing is not too faint, I will include a copy of it in the pages of this memoir).

Mickey has been well-adjusted the majority of his good life and this was no more evident than when he assisted me in the care of our mother in her last days. Of us four children, I believe Mickey and I endured and overcame the most, and I find it ironic that we two were our mother's primary caregivers at her end. Mickey was my mother's fourth gift of children but I doubt she fully realized it until it was demonically too late. Mickey's is unequivocally another voice inside my heart, always and forever as his "big sister."

Mary A. Cox

Seemingly incomprehensible tragedy, at some point and in some capacity, definitive or not, comes to many; it is inescapable that the deepest darkest catacombs are rustled within our psyches.

Anthony Sowell had at one time lived on my street, Page Avenue, in East Cleveland, Ohio. I remember the moment well when he approached me on the west side of our street on a summer day and loped up to me and said with a weird quirky look, "You lick your lips too much." I was slightly thrown off guard and I distinctly remember thinking, "How would you know, have you been watching me?" I quickly brushed past him and kept on up the hill, as I glanced back to make sure he was not behind me. Anthony Sowell was a weird Harold, a strange and estranged sort of person, not fitting in, in or of (our) pubescent society. I was about three years older than Anthony who resided across the street from us but closer to Terrace Road. Odd, I'm unable to recall anyone else from his family, but we all knew Anthony's presence and for the most part, we other block kids avoided him. We never went in his house like we did each other's.

By the summer of 1989, I was 33, had some street savvy, and 12 years of insurance investigation experience under my 22" belt. I was not hesitant about too many things, loved my cousins fiercely, and would fight a rock over them. And then I received the call, "Shony's missing, been missing for about a week..." I flew to Cleveland within days of that call and visited my aunt's East Cleveland home. I was informed that Shony went to the store on Memorial Day, May 29 and never came back to her two-year-old son, Eugene, or her mother, Aunt Hannah. I was told that that behavior was unusual; had never occurred, that police had been alerted. I asked appropriate questions and as I knew the layout of Euclid Avenue and all businesses (stores) along the stretch frequented by Shony, I undertook a walk and drive inquire over a span of several hours. I went in every place I conceived she would or could have gone on her way "to the store". No one in her family mentioned to me that Shony had a job at McCall's Lounge at Lee Road, which she would not have had to pass on her way "to the store".

I visited the East Cleveland Police Department and spoke with a detective who informed me that their resources were limited; that Cleveland would not assist since they were separate jurisdictions; and importantly Shony was last seen in East Cleveland so they had to work within their own department's allotted personnel. I became incensed; nearly got thrown out, before I left dejected, but imploring the detective to become more persistent in effort. I also vowed to follow up with the detective, just to keep him on track.

Upon my return to California a few weeks later, I arranged for Aunt Hannah to be interviewed for the television show America's Most Wanted. I even had a date set for the producing element to phone Aunt Hannah. For unknown and insufficiently explained reasons (to me), Aunt Hannah opted out. I didn't press anymore. However, I kept my vow and called the detective every few months.

My final call to the detective was in August, 2009, with the same lackadaisical response.

October 31, 2009, Anthony Sowell is arrested for the suspected murders of 11 women. Over the in-depth course of Cleveland police investigations combined with East Cleveland,

Sowell finally admitted (February, 2010) that he knew my cousin Mary A. Cox (Shony); that he had met her at McCall's Lounge where she had worked as a bartender. Anthony denied having anything to do with Shony's disappearance. (LIAR!)

Mary's brother, Robert, submitted his DNA for analysis testing against unidentified corpses at the peak of pre-trial discovery. Robert's DNA did not match any corpse. Mary A. Cox was the fourth of Aunt Hannah's children, the third girl. She was 28 when she went missing in her earthiness. Rest, now, sweet Shony. Your mother raised Eugene to a fine, devoted and responsible young man. Shony, we all miss you and will never dissever ourselves from you, for you are among us.

Anthony Sowell sits on Death Row at Chillicothe Correction Institution, from where he will hopefully soon be gone to an unmarked non-descript dungeon.

Patrick Thabo Chipane

Patrick was a black foreign exchange student, from Johannesburg, South Africa living with a Caucasian family in East Cleveland. Patrick attended Shaw High with me. I befriended him, even snuck him into our home after school, a few times, before my mother arrived from work. I found Patrick handsome and easy to talk with. He was very personable, soft spoken and very intelligent. He liked me and I think he thought I was attractive and smart. I believe I was one of a select few kids he trusted enough to discuss intricacies of the political atmosphere of his country. It was Patrick who told me first-hand of the atrocities of Apartheid in the early 1970s. Enlightenment about the daily life he experienced is too weak a word to describe what he and his fellow countrymen endured before and during De Klerk's Boer governing of native South African blacks. Patrick made me aware of the unconscionable repression and oppression of the majority black populous by the minority white governing body and general population. Amongst many things, I learned of the requirement to carry passes in order to move about the cities for working or any purpose and of meted punishment if the pass was not produced when requested by any white person. I learned a lot from Patrick so much so that I gave serious thought to moving to South Africa once we had graduated. I lost touch with Patrick after high school, and my efforts to locate him in past and recent years turned up nothing, essentially. There was an indication that he went on to graduate a U.S. university, and pursued the law, but I could not concretely verify this.

Patrick will forever remain a part of my spirit and I pray he is still alive, well, and that he was anyhow able to assist in fighting the good fight for his country. I think of him often and the fact that I, through Patrick Thabo Chipane, knew of the ANC and Nelson Mandela long before both were household names in the United States and long before I wrote the February 11, 1990 Cape Town release date and time of 4: 14 p.m. on a Premiere notice of the film 1987 *Mandela*. Long before anyone I knew, I knew first-hand the meaning of the exclaimed Afrikaans word Amandla! Even from across the sea, I can hear Patrick Thabo Chipane calling me.

Diagnosis FMD

July 8, 2005 was the official date upon which I was medically diagnosed with a potentially deadly and progressive genetic and extremely rare vascular disease, Fibromuscular Dysplasia (FMD). The cause of this disease is unknown and there is no known cure. The disease tends to run in families (to my knowledge, no one else in my immediate family has this disease) and females past the age of 40 are more prone to diagnosis. The disease primarily strikes the main or largest arteries of the body, by the formation of a string of bead-like material within the walls of the arteries, thereby seemingly chocking off or obstructing blood flow to main organs, like the kidneys and brain.

My symptoms of illness first presented themselves in 2004. My blood pressure could not be controlled with ever increasing doses of prescribed medication. It had gotten to the point that I was seeking a doctor's visit nearly once a week, with a plethora of complaints, from problems with weight and hair loss, low body temperature, agonizing limb pain to the point of tears. I also suffered from anxiousness and sleeplessness for which medications were given. My complaints continued for nearly a year with no relief. Finally, in late December, 2004, I was told that my right renal artery required an angioplasty procedure, this after, horrifically learning or being told by a Kaiser phone advise nurse that my records reflected renal failure, which was obviously an error in diagnosis.

I underwent a right renal angioplasty on December 22, 2004. It was a success.

Subsequent to the angioplasty I had some more blood drawn and tested. My blood pressure was under better control but other complaints persisted. In January of 2005 I was diagnosed with hyperthyroidism. This latter diagnosis was good and bad news. Good because it could be treated with medication, tapazole, which I began taking January 12, 2005. Within a few weeks, I began to feel better and my emotional state calmed a great deal. Bad news because there was no cure. Options were to have the thyroid surgically removed or drink radioactive iodine to burn the thyroid out. I opted for neither of these and continued my tapazole therapy. Very gradually things returned to a hormonal norm.

In January of 2005, I began falling in my home. Nothing major, just experiencing weakness in my left hip/leg area that began as a slight tremble. I'd sit down on the floor, pull myself across it and into my bedroom where I'd hoist myself onto my bed, remove my clothes, tuck myself in with all kinds of thoughts. I was slowly losing comfort in my ability to take for granted my walking capability. These falling/sitting down bouts began to increase in number and in public.

The first time I fell/sat in public was in a Safeway supermarket near my home. An ambulance was summoned and I was taken to Richmond, CA Kaiser. After a few hours of monitoring, blood draws, and CT scans of my brain, I was released home with no instructions but to continue with my blood pressure medication. The last time I fell publicly was in the entrance way to Pacific Gas and Electric in Berkeley, CA. After a few moments, I was able to stand after which I returned to the Goodyear lot and asked an employee with whom I was acquainted to summon an ambulance. Berkeley Fire arrived and took me to Oakland, Kaiser where I was admitted overnight for observation and MRI's.

During this hospital visit and while in the ER and waiting to be taken to my overnight room, I was able to view the hallway through which other patients were being brought for examination. On this day, I saw a fellow teacher who did not see me and about whom I'd later learn was there for heart-related problems. He was my mentor, Joseph Shields. Mr. Shields, as I addressed him, ultimately had open-heart surgery. I thereafter visited Mr. Shields as he convalesced in the hospital's care facility. My mentor, once again, asked me to start the new school year with the taking over of his class. I would have loved to take his classroom, but I wanted him in his own classroom, which would have required him recovering, so I declined the offer citing "too much stress." Mr. Shields did recover sufficiently to host friends and entertain in his newly rebuilt and remodeled home.

My fall/sitting episodes were infrequent, about 2 times per month and even began in my classroom. Somehow, I'd succeed in delaying my fall until after my students had left the room. I never let them know I was having a problem. If my legs began to tremble or weaken as I walked about my classroom, I'd place my palms on a desk or in the chalk dust tray of my board, press down, pray that I remained standing, so as not to alarm my students.

My school year began in September 2005, although I'd taught summer school to a group of Chinese American students at the Yuk Yaw School in Oakland's China Town. A wonderful and extremely gratifying experience.

The months of August and September were spent in going back and forth to my primary care physician, Laura Morgan, the last doctor I've trusted and a neurologist. After my continued complaints and half-assed diagnoses, one of which was possible multiple sclerosis; the other, possible sarcoidosis of the brain, Dr. Morgan referred me for tests/sonograms of my carotid arteries. These tests did reveal blockage in both arteries and a subsequent MRI revealed total occlusion of my right carotid artery and a diagnosis of that unknown to me or most in the medical profession, Fibromuscular Dysplasia.

Thrust into overdrive and high gear. Now what do we do? I was immediately referred to the neurology department of Kaiser, Redwood City, CA, where I underwent an exhaustive battery of tests including angiograms, brain scans of every description, including something called Spect scans. I underwent 2 Spect scans with each taking 120 views of my brain. I was told these scans were needed in order to identify the vessels to be used for a 'soon as possible' craniotomy. Actually, a brain bypass called an ECIC, (extra cranial/interracial procedure using my right temporal artery and bypassing it to a mid-cerebral artery. On or near September 9, 2005 I was informed by a neurosurgeon and an associate that I needed the ECIC as soon as possible, otherwise I could be dead within 2 months (by Christmas). You see, I was not getting any blood flow to the right hemisphere of my brain, thus the problem with the left side of my body.

I sought, through Dr. Morgan a second opinion that was to have been set up through Dr. Amgott-Kwan of Oakland neurology. I was told that my second opinion could be obtained from the University of California at San Francisco. Dr. Morgan later told me that Dr. Amgott-Kwan did not think it was practical. Practical!! I'm sure it would have been practical for him or one of his family members. Anyway, Kaiser ultimately denied my second opinion. I did not know what to do. I was alone in a major health crisis. I believed and accepted the FMD diagnosis and the impending death sentence as a real, all too real reality. I even had a friend, Karen, go with me to see the surgeon who viewed the scan results. We both felt an immediate sadness. We hugged, I cried and remarked, "I'm going to be the first to go…to die", from our small knit group of young executives who had bonded in the late 1970's to early1980's at Hanover Insurance Company, San Francisco.

I was under the gun or shall I say square in the face of the barrel of a cannon, loaded with 100 pounds of blasting powder and whose fuse was sparking. I had to do something, anything. The best thing, at the time, for myself.

The surgeon, Dr. Moyaeri and her assistant, Dr. Rao, had also told me that the surgery was needed in order to prevent a full-blown major debilitating stroke. Dr. Rao, after my inquiry even said he'd recommend the procedure for his sister, as he placed me in that associative category.

During this time, I'd recently begun to communicate with my sister by phone so she was abreast of my dilemma, albeit, she was 3,000 miles away in Ohio. I'd decided after much agonizing inner turmoil and discussion with my maternal uncle to have the surgery.

The surgery was initially scheduled for October 5, 2005 but the surgeon changed the date to October 18, 2005 and that caused my sister to have to change flight plans since she'd agreed to come with my baby brother for the surgery.

My world went into high gear as I began to plan for one of two things: 1. Return to my daily life, as it existed which included, work as a teacher, completing my Master's Degree. I had one more year to go before being fully vested in my district's retirement plan; continue rebuilding of my "on the side" Private Investigations business. I'd just renewed my

Process Service registration and bond in July with the financial aid of my friend Linda Jackson. I'd also designed and had a new brochure, business cards and color coordinated vehicle magnet done up, the latter being a gift from friend Pamela McGhee. 2. Death, of which I had and still have no fear. To me, fearing death is like fearing God, which I do not fear. It is said that fear is: false evidence appearing real. Well, God for me is true, not false. Thus, it follows that death, (we all die), is also real, not false. So, there is no fear, just reality.

If one believes in God and his works and deeds which thereby support the evidence of his existence coupled with our daily witness to and knowledge of humans dying, then why not prepare for either of my two pro- choices. Given the inherent nature of my surgical procedure I felt there was nothing else to prepare for but a best/worst case scenario.

Preparations

With the never to be replaced assistance of my dear friend, Pamela McGhee of Oakland I put every aspect of my life in order just in case I died, but, and if I lived, then I could continue in my groove. Over an approximate 2-3-week period and while working and still going to doctors' appointments, I did the following:

Died my hair red, a nice complimentary reddish brown, because I'd never been a redhead and wanted to experience the reaction to it. It was favorable. I also stopped smoking.

1. Filed for bankruptcy at the urging of my sister
2. Brought all bills current
3. Cleaned my home
4. Purchased and stored a two-month's supply of food.
5. Executed a Power of Attorney for my sister
6. Drafted letters of resignation from my job
7. Executed a Living Will and had my Last Will and Testament videotaped
8. Purchased a cell phone for my sister and brother's use while assisting me.
9. Notified a very select group of friends and family of my dilemma. None of my co-workers were informed. In fact, most of the people I knew or know were not told anything.
10. Pam transferred every single one of my phone numbers to a new book, by hand, placing a green marker dot by the names of those to be contacted in the event of my demise.

11. Purchased new sweat suits and pajamas from Target to be worn during my projected 3-5-day recovery phase.

12. Colorful signs were taped to my cupboard facings with different and varying instructions.

Instructions with city maps to the Superintendent of Schools were printed just in case I had to resign my job and retire early. I'd also completed written and legal paperwork for my self-saved pension contributions.

AND I PRAYED

Everything was prepared. It couldn't have been any better, thanks to Pam. Everything was set to go.

AND I PRAYED

Thursday, October 13th the Redwood City neurology department informed me that I had to undergo a heart stress test before surgery; otherwise the surgery could not be performed. The stress test was set for the upcoming Monday, the day before my surgery. Talk about stress, I was about to blow a gasket, in a major way.

Friday, October 14th my last day working. I'd let my supervisor know I was scheduled for surgery on the 18th.

Monday, October 17th, I underwent the heart stress test at Oakland Kaiser. I was later told by my primary care doctor that my heart stress results were those of a 16-year-old which I doubted since I'd smoked cigarettes for many, many years while still being very physically active. Anyhow I'd stopped smoking under another threat from the surgeon, that she'd not perform the surgery unless I had stopped smoking. I thereafter enlisted the aid of Kaiser's Stop Smoking Program, which by the way was excellent. I attended the program sessions on Saturdays in the midst of my preparatory stage. My sister and brother arrived at the Oakland Airport near to 10:00 p.m. I drove the 20 or so miles, picked them up, returned home and gave them a briefing on things. My coffee table was spread with folders containing instructions. I reiterated to my sister, my desire to not want to be saved or to live in a disabled manner, particularly my hands, should anything go wrong. I resided about 50 miles from the surgical center and had to be there at 6:30 a. m. the following morning. We three retired around midnight.

I can and did appreciate the anxiousness my siblings experienced.

October 18th 4:30 a.m. I leap from my bed and shower from head to toe with the prescribed pre-surgery body cleanser. I took my prescribed hypertension medication, prayed, dressed in my bath in a black with white stripes sweat suit, prayed and looked in the mirror, smiled, and performed what I hoped was not my last plie and I prayed. I'd done some flips, round-offs in the preceding week, so it was on. I did my best to energize my siblings during the pre-dawn morning and drive to the facility. My sister drove my car as nervous chatter filled the black over tan Ford Explorer Sport. It was a cool pitch morning, as the car seemed to float west on Interstate 80 and across the Oakland-San Francisco Bay Bridge, on to south 101 into Redwood City and into my destiny.

We arrived at the check in desk at precisely 6:30 a.m. I gave the male attendant my Living Will and then was instructed to go to a pre-surgery area for my prep that included vitals, brief talk with the anesthesiologist. We waited for some time. I wanted to get on with it, and in trying to help keep my siblings upbeat, I kicked into gear, "Give me my drugs." And we waited and then I heard loud voices, one of which belonged to my female Iranian surgeon. I'd forgotten her nationality at that moment. She was expressing anger about her choice of anesthesiologists not being there to assist her. Oh! My heart sank and jumped. My surgeon, of all people, was not calm. She ultimately was calmed after threatening to leave Kaiser, as her employer. I remained as outwardly calm as I could and hoped and prayed that this mortal of a woman about to drill into my life force could re-group, perform the most delicate and intimate of procedures with the steadiest of hands and get me back to my Monterey Jack cheese in my refrigerator. I wanted to flee, to return to the safety of my home, but then the ire of my sister beckoned and so I stayed moot. Damn! And Double Damn! Then it was time.

I was gurnied into the prep room, doped up, knocked out, and then, wheeled into the operating room where my red and now with black root locks were shorn.

Dogs Barking

"Are you ready? How are you feeling?" A stupid assed question. I asked the attending nurse's aide to do me a favor and write down for me my last words before my twilight began. She said she would but I doubt she did. The heavy drugs took hold within a very short time/minutes.

The expert gloved hands of the surgeon went into action, as did her mouth with instructions. First the scalpel incision into the right temporal area to locate and set my temporal artery. Next, re-clean the shorn area. The drill is placed and whirring begins as scalp is broken and blood spurts. Another hole is drilled in a vertical line just in front of my right ear and less than one half inch from my face. The scalp is pulled back to reveal skull. I'm relaxed, don't feel a thing but somehow, I knew what was going on. I was to have a direct bypass but ended up getting an indirect bypass, as the receiving artery was too small. The procedure begins, takes about 6 hours. The finishing touches are made which include a titanium screw to seal my skull. A drainage tube extending down the right side of my body. My scalp was stapled shut with about 5-6 staples. I was certainly not winning any beauty contests at that time, just a mess. I was taken to Intensive Care Recovery. I was doing good by all accounts, not much blood loss, and vitals essentially good.

A few hours later, I suddenly took a turn for the worse with my sister present in the room.

I was still drugged and unable to speak but I knew something was wrong. The monitoring equipment began to beep. My sister would later tell me that she did not notify personnel, rather left the hospital, went back to my home and went to bed because she was tired.

The next day and while comatose with a fully blown right pupil, my sister is informed that her permission is needed in order to perform a second surgery for the quelling of the bleeding in my brain. After many calls to some of my family members, it is finally decided that the second surgery can be performed. I can only imagine the amount of time it took to have my sister leave the area in which I was, take an elevator to another floor and make these series of calls, all the while that I'm hemorrhaging. My sister had been instructed to not save my life, but she had the Power of Attorney and used it to my detriment and I'll always believe it was out of jealousy and a sense of "I have the power and I'm using it as I want."

At some point I was given the blood thinner, Heparin, which has been in the news for causing death and a wealth of other health issues.

(With the grace of my God), and to my utter and unimaginable dismay I survived, to hear the words of Dr. Rao on my right side, "Can you move your legs, kick them." I kicked with a flurry aided by the thought of swimming in high school. "Name three animals" I did, "Cat, bird, dog." At the knowledge of knowing my siblings, from Ohio, (my brother being a Cleveland Browns fan (the Dog Pound) could hear me and I wanted to let them know I was back to part of my yester-self and more importantly because I wanted to bring some humor to a tense atmosphere, I began to bark like a fan in the Dog Pound. My sister later informed me that my reaction brought the response I'd wanted. My siblings laughed and my sister remarked, "She's back to her old self. In a minute, she's going to be turning flips." Dr. Rao was broken up with laughter. My first words, noted in my chart notes are, "You messed me up."

But I cried and became immediately filled with devastating and unimaginable horror when my hands were revealed to me in closed and clawed balls, unable to be opened. THE MAIN CONDITION IN WHICH MY FEMALE SIBLING KNEW I DID NOT WANT TO LIVE. At that moment, the Lord spoke to me and told me how it all came about, as far as the sibling is concerned. It was her way of getting back. And this person had the unmitigated gall to tell me I should humble myself as if she were God or God-like. I let her know that I do not humble myself to any man or woman.

I could not feed myself, even scratch an itch, nothing!!! Just lying there, with hospital breath and seething anger, hurt, embarrassment and disappointment beyond description, wanting to die absolutely. I thirsted for days and then finally ice chips. I almost died, again. A twisted face, hands and heart and a burning desire to kill that female sibling. I suppose the possibility of getting caught and going to prison prevents a lot of crimes.

Thereafter and for about a week I was in critical intensive care where I learned that the doctors were attempting to prescribe an anti- depressant, Seroquel, which when I found out, I refused it as was my right. That drug, in 2007 was later determined to cause a plethora of health problems. They tried to explain that people having strokes are depressed. Oh! Well how do you know I'm depressed, you haven't asked me? I was not depressed, but angry and extremely disappointed. Let me say here, it's not the stroke itself that may cause depression but:

Total Loss

Loss of trust in most people. I was in four different facilities over a period of two months. There were many in much worse shape than me. I remember in the Redwood City location one man, a fireman, who had a tracheotomy. He could not walk. There were many, many more. It was a dismal place, but his family was there a lot. I only recall my surgeon visiting me 2 times, never expressing any words of apology a real hard-ass with limited bedside manner.

While still in the first facility I decided to fight, to prove that although others were whispering negatives, I had to prove them wrong. I challenge anyone to undergo what I did and not come back just a bit changed. First, I demanded after about two days to have my catheter removed, as I knew that having one in for too long could lead to infection. I could urinate on my own but I refused bedpans. Hell, my legs worked, so let's try them out. So, I told the nurses, I want to walk to the toilet, shielded beneath a counter in my room. I made it on my first attempt without assistance, to the amazement of the nurses one of which kept saying I couldn't do it. Wrong. I did and kept on walking.

I arrived via ambulance at the second location about 10 days later with clawed hands, stapled head, a strong limp, and determination since I'd been made to live. First things first, call a friend for some of my favorite things. My friend Ralph Scott, bless him, brought me what I'd asked for, flowers, cheese, and strawberries, the latter two of which he hand-fed me. I'll never forget his kindness and generosity. Here is where I began to walk the halls for exercise, lurching and limping along the corridor, looking like Frankenstein's bride with staples in my head. I felt like a zombie. I was only here for a few days.

The third location is where intensive therapy began, both hands still closed. I had, over a month, about 3 different roommates, the second of which was Carol Trapp. She'd broken a hip and could not walk. She gets around now with a walker. She was very nice as was her daughter, Cathy, who brought me popcorn. My speech was not normal, most people listening to me on the phone did not know who I was. I worked hard to get my right hand back. That's the hand the therapists focused on. When I inquired about my left hand being neglected, I was told, they were focusing on my right since I was right-handed. I don't know or believe this to be the reason for such focus, but anyway within a few weeks, I was able to feed myself, open my cell phone with my mouth and dial it and wipe myself when I used the bathroom. I was assisted in the shower. While there, I had a Spanish male nurse assist me with hair removal. He'd not heard of Nair or its properties, but vowed he'd try it. I hated that place. Every 4 hours or so there was medication. You couldn't rest. The medication charts rolled the halls at night over worn and lumpy gray carpet. I nicknamed the nurses pushing them "pigeons" because that's what they sounded like.

I'd stopped smoking just before surgery and although I could have smoked in this location's courtyard, I didn't. In fact, I only went out there once for signing papers for a jury duty summons I'd received.

My best friend Pam visited often. I'd authorized her to drive my car and perform errands for me. She was great and remains one of the few people I trust. Once, I'd not had a bowel movement for a while and Pam assisted me to a bathroom a distance from my room and even went in to help me while I did my business. Now that's a loving, good friend. She's never let me down and has always been there in all times, just the best. Pam even came on 2 occasions to take me out for business and even back to Redwood City for an MRI. I even did some banking.

Not all of the nurses or rehab personnel were nice. One nurse Thelma simply did not care for me or maybe her job was wearing on her, but she brought breakfast. She'd always beat my eggs and pancakes until the heat was gone. Crappy. I stopped eating when served by her. Fortunately, I've always liked hospital food, so I didn't lose too much weight.

I prayed, began to play bingo, continued with my therapy. I exercised my legs in bed each night and I waited for my promised bed in Vallejo... and I waited. One day my primary care doctor, not the surgeon, visited me with flowers and a card. What a sweet and welcomed surprise. Dr. Laura Morgan was also truly hurt by my outcome.

While in San Leandro a good friend, Zuberi (Noonie Pete) provided me with 2 haircuts, one for myself and one for himself as a show of love and support. He delivered the barber to me. What a nice and most needed and appreciated gesture.

On the eve of the day my brother was to return to Ohio, and with permission I left the hospital to go to my home at which he was, as I'd not seen him since my sister had left many weeks earlier. He claimed he was afraid to drive my car. I went home, paid my rent. Just as I was leaving the rental office, my friend Karen was coming into the drive. I spoke with her briefly and can't recall what made me strike her in her chest. It probably was anger at having listened to her at that pre-surgery day and also to let her know I could use one hand. Anyway, I had a short visit with my brother, thanking him, expressing my regret for not being able to kick it with him as planned. We hugged; said goodbye and Pam rushed me back to San Leandro just in time to avoid being thrown out of the facility.

Hey, I got the job done, paid my rent so I'd have a place to return when discharged.

December 1, 2005. I'm transferred to Vallejo. More therapy and my re-introduction to social activities. I very much disliked being seen with my new body and still do. At one point, I had to tell the nurse to not put through calls to my room from Ohio, especially my female sibling. I was trying to get well and she was pulling me down into her evil abyss. I couldn't and can't stomach her voice. So, I purged her negative essence and got better, a lot better. My power was returning. I was handling my affairs and even assisting other patients on their way to wellness. It felt good. In this place my left hand's dead skin was removed for the first time. The staff refused to cut my toe or finger nails saying I had to pay $35.00 for that service. I summoned a friend for my finger nails. Judy lived in Vallejo and brought me the requested chicken salad prepared by her sister Tina and some tortilla chips.

The staff was wondering why I didn't have many visitors. The fact is I didn't want them; want anyone, really, to see my altered physical self. I was deeply embarrassed through no fault of my own. I know or knew many people, but only wanted to see those who I believed loved me. The truth is, most visitors only came to gawk, take a look. And assess my change- to give themselves something negative to talk about.

Home

After all the planning and preparations I'd made without a hitch, when I returned home on December 14, 2008 I discovered a *Notice of Eviction* on my front door; that before my female sibling had returned to Ohio, she'd fucked my world up. I dislike using such an expletive but it fits best.

I discovered that in requesting my teacher's pension that my sibling had asked that the check be sent to Ohio to her address as she'd lied and told state personnel I'd be residing with her. Now, how was I to pay my rent and bills? The December rent was already two weeks late as was my car note. I found out that my check had indeed been sent to Ohio so I had to retrieve it, but too late. My rental agency had already begun eviction proceedings, on December 6, 2005. I was in a real quandary.

My bankruptcy filing had been accepted with a second hearing date scheduled. I couldn't miss this one; otherwise my case would be thrown out.

I had to reapply for my Social Security Disability in California as my PA had done so in Akron, Ohio, apparently telling SSA I resided with her in Ohio, when in fact I lived in California. During my phone interview, I could sense some suspicion on the part of the interviewer who asked me whether or not my sister had life insurance on me. I don't know if she does, but it wouldn't surprise me. I know I never signed anything. As an aside, my sister knows my social security number, always has, and even ran my credit report before without my knowledge or consent.

Not having my money really impacted me. One has only to imagine. Dr. Morgan gave me $600.00. Of course, I had to call my sibling to inquire about my funds and demand their return. I was told that she and my maternal uncle had agreed that she had my money sent to Ohio, as she believed that if I needed assistance that Pam would have taken my money. Karen sanctioned this, I believe and know. Pam may not be rich or perpetrating an image, but one thing is sure, she's no thief. The thieves were in my own family. As recent as October 2007, another purported cousin, Marcella (Ludi) stole jewelry from my home in Ohio. I did report the incident to police.

The trickledown effect of limited funds was taking its toll. I was forced to make an immediate and further life altering decision. I would have to leave California and return to Ohio to continue convalescing at my uncle's home. I applied for emergency Medi-Cal benefits and was denied, seemingly because I was not literally on the street. I was given nothing by the State. By the time I received my check from my sister, I had already had a stop payment issued and received a replacement check. I purchased a Certified check for December's rent including late fees and tendered it. The check was accepted. I also tendered January's rent. Four days later, I was given both checks back and informed that the owners' attorney would not allow acceptance since eviction proceedings had commenced. Okay, cool. Now what? I was in no condition to look for a new apartment; could not drive, had no job, and no one really assisting me in any capacity. Just a bad situation.

Before my sister left, she tried to have my post office box closed. But the supervising employee happened to be Pam's sister and would not close my box based on the Power of Attorney and specifically because I had not asked her to do so. My sister, later asked me to send her my bills for her to pay for me out of the projected disability checks I was to receive, or the pension check she already had. Of course, I did not do this.

Doing so would have played into her hand of trying to have me declared incompetent, and perhaps would have given her leverage to show that she was in fact handling my financial affairs. (Yeah, right, and I was supposed to have a problem). The problem was, I had no problem and saw right through her weak-assed scheme). Additionally, my sister's bunk plan was to have me pay three months' rent on an apartment in Cleveland without a job or steady source of income. Absolute insanity on her part. I would have become homeless in the dead of winter. When I refused, citing the same reasons why, she became furious, saying emphatically, "I think <u>something is</u> wrong with you," implying a lack in my mental capacity. I didn't have to beg to differ, I simply did, and continued on with the best choice, putting my furnishings in storage and going to stay with my uncle and his wife in Columbus where I knew my maternal grandmother was, further that I would not have to pay or contribute to any bills as I got better. Also, there'd be people around who could assist me and who loved me, especially my uncle.

I paid for an airplane ticket for one of my non-working female cousins to fly to California for the purpose of helping me pack my things. On the way from the airport, I treated Linda to a pizza dinner and a movie, *Munich.* In the parking lot on our return to my home she, as part of a 12- step drug program informs me that she'd stolen money from my purse during one of my past visits to Ohio. A hell of a thing to tell someone. And here I am about to take you into my home to help me. I wish I could have zapped her ass back to Ohio, but I had no choice but to avail myself of her assistance. Pam had gotten sick and couldn't help me. Thus began our strained time together. Linda was a newly licensed driver, or so she claimed, making many errors and with that came discomfort on my part. I later found out that Linda was in fact unlicensed at that time.

Actually, I only trust two people's driving and this is in primary part because of my work as an investigator of accidents for more than 20 years. We made it. It was difficult but moving day finally arrived. I'd arranged to have three Mexican males move my things to storage. Linda bitched about everything and even wanted me to pay the men before the job was done. Granted, they'd worked longer than estimated, but I had bought them breakfast and lunch. Finally, and gratefully, all my things were stored. Only 2 days to wait until our flight to Ohio. I had spent nearly $800.00 since my cousin's arrival. My sister had told me another lie that I had to spend all of my money, that I could have no money in the bank and get my disability check. A damn lie! After I'd been in Ohio for about a month, something struck me one day, and I called Social Security and was told that I could have as much money in the bank as I wanted and still get my check.

In short order I was flat broke. My storage was being paid and I was afforded toiletries through my most dear friend, Henry.

After my grandmother died (read "Thirteen Days") I endured a mini-nightmare of hell for one year, all of 2006, until January 2007. I extolled acknowledgment upon my uncle and aunt on January 12, 2007, the day I put my wings in flight (driven by Homer Gooden, my "first love" and life-long friend) and ironically moved to a beautiful 8-room apartment in a suburb of Cleveland, in which my female sibling once resided. I did this only with necessities, an air mattress, microwave, paper plates, a TV (purchased the night of my arrival), etc. My disability check would not start for another month, after which I could retrieve my belongings from California's storage. In all fairness, I must say that my female sibling gave me some small housewarming gifts and ironed my shower curtain. She was thanked for this kindness.

I had a rough go of a time in Columbus, trying to regain my footing literally and figuratively. I'd been promised or rather told by my aunt that she was to have a therapist come in daily to help with my left hand. I've yet to meet the man. After a new family moved in across the street, I, when I had it, would pay the oldest daughter to stretch my arm and hand. Sometimes, I'd pay a friend of my aunt to stretch my hand/arm.

I had signed up for Paratransit so I could go to the doctor or wherever. My uncle was great in that he always picked up my prescriptions and took me to most of my doctor appointments.

During the summer in Columbus, I began walking to the bus stop in order to test myself and to go to a nail salon. No one helped me with any personal grooming. My aunt told me once that I did not have to shave under my arms because it was winter. I figured out how to do this part of my grooming by myself. Family members did assist me with buttons, which I still can't do. I'd started back smoking, nerves, I guess. My uncle or one of my cousins would always light my cigarettes. One day my uncle refused, not in a bad way but only to say, "If you want to smoke badly, you'll light your own cigarettes. The next day, I'd devised a way to hold the lighter between my knees and I haven't asked anyone to light a cigarette for me since. Although I no longer place a lighter between my knees, I do an awful lot with them, like hold jars or bottles. I also use my feet for gripping when needed. I also began to test myself and prepare for my exit. I did this by assisting with light cleaning and taking out the trash. I mastered (specific to me) techniques of balance, stooping, reaching, lifting, and bending. I even taught myself to write again.

Over the course of that spring and summer I gradually became physically stronger. I suffered primarily from three things: mal-treatment by purported family, the discovery of deceit by certain family members, longing for my personal things and privacy. Because I went out in public more I experienced a lot of discrimination on all levels. I still do, daily.

In 2007 and on my own, I spent the first 6 months by myself, no car, paying for transport when I could find it. One service charged $2.00 per mile. If I wanted to eat, I paid it. No one helped me, really. One niece, Nakkia went to the store for me a few times. My friends Linda or former teacher, Mr. Young, would take me grocery shopping.

I could endure it no longer, I was folding. I decided to get a car, hesitant though I was, because I hadn't driven in nearly two years. I began to earnestly look for a car in May 2007. I had my sights set on a Volkswagen Beetle but soon learned, the note was out of reach, and or rather the dealer was not willing to work with me.

I called a dealership in late May, spoke with a salesman, and explained my dilemma that I had no way to get to the dealership. My plea was heard by Jerome Lavender of Bedford Toyota who agreed to come to my home and take me to the dealership. The next day, he picked me up as promised; telling me it was something about my voice. Preliminaries and a nervous test-drive out of the way. I just knew my bankruptcy was going to be a disqualifier, but it had been dismissed in January 2006. Jerome let me know that I could rest easy, that the next day; I'd drive off the lot in the car I'd chosen. The next morning, June 2, 2007 Jerome was right on schedule. I drove my car home, pissing bullets all the way and I've been driving ever since. I celebrated my one year driving anniversary recently and drove by myself to Columbus in the time of a two-handed driver with one 10-minute rest over 137 miles.

I've endured a lot, more than many, not as much as some, even considered suicide in the face of having to ask complete strangers to assist in dressing or undressing me, having family steal from me, having "friends and family" become in your face non- existent. One thing I've had to remind myself of is that a title is just that, family and friends mean nothing in and of themselves. They are merely words, the meaning of which is in an action. Some family and friends are even, albeit of silent display, glad in their own warped minds that what has physically happened to me did. Their airs seemingly are now superior~ as if saying, "You aren't so much anymore." This also applies to several 'friends or associates' particularly those who envied me anything pre-surgery. I choose not to identify them by name; the list would be long and give credence to trash.

When I was in a police academy 12 years ago, my Training Officer, T. O. Shabatura, told me, "All it takes is courage, and you have that." My absolute best friend, confidante, and sustainer Henry, has, since I've known him preached "stamina and perseverance."

These three words ring with me daily: **courage** to face and deal with life's obstacles and hardships, **stamina** to shoulder or back-carry the load and **perseverance** to shuck the load and keep towards the questing of the goal.

Mama Rose and Al

It was the fourth medical facility to which I was transported on December 1, 2005.

I'd waited for a bed for nearly 2 months. This place in Vallejo had been touted as the place to be, where I **should have been taken** after that fateful October day in Redwood City; but instead, I was thereafter transferred to Richmond for a few days. I suppose the psychological impact of that, being that it was close to my residence, I was taken via ambulance by a couple. I felt that they were more than co-workers. I was feeling bad, but I talked with them and probably smiled for the first time in weeks. I was told that my transport had been approved in order for me to wait for my bed in Vallejo. I'd wanted to thank this couple by giving them a Roberta Flack CD, *Blue Lights in The Basement* that features a song titled 25th of Last December. I'd told them I would, but upon my ultimate release, I was faced with getting my basic life necessities in order. It was a mess, just bad. I had to recoup **my** money from my forever regretful and not to be repeated Power of Attorney.

The bottom line is that I really don't like not being able to keep my word of promises. That bothers me terribly and always has.

Upon arrival at Vallejo it was discovered that I'd not had a bowel movement for many days, seven to be exact. I have never been able to defecate in unfamiliar surroundings, I just can't do it. I was summarily introduced to Nurse Thelma who was in charge of *bowel programs.* I was later to discover that the staff kept a large binder at the nurse's station in which patient's bowel movements were recorded. Anyway, Nurse Thelma was/is Filipino, short and petite with a mop of raven hair, very pleasant and as I was soon to learn an expert in bowel movements. She was great, absolutely wonderful. Oh, what a relief it was to have a bowel movement. And move them I did. I had to give an accounting of the amount of waste that jet streamed from my rectum.

Nurse Thelma appeared with a grand smile and a metal pushcart on casters. After the cursory introduction was over. Nurse Thelma gave me her spiel, explaining that she had to perform a rectal exam. Thelma's explanation was most thorough and included the fact that she wore three pairs of gloves, one pair to be removed after each phase of the program.

The rectal exam was first with a detailed accounting of what and how. "Oh, I feel it, a little pebble. Well, we have to move that first, get it out of the way. I released and my held breath. "I'm going to give you an enema. I remove one pair of gloves, the enema is warm, and I warm it in water for a few minutes, first. Okay, ready?" I mumble, "Yes, fine" and ready myself. The enema nozzle is inserted. I wince and think, "Nurse, I'm going to need more than this." Thelma must have read my mind. She gave me further info about how many fluids to intake in order to insure a daily movement. Thelma left me with 2 pills and instructions to remember, the amount of daily excrement. A day or so later, I was back on track and verbally recording my movements as "enough for a cake" or some such comical description. I had the staff cracking up with laughter.

In this facility, there were many much worse than myself, definitely mentally and with no doubt physically. One man received his therapy in a suspended from the ceiling net. Another man could only stand while donning some kind of globe with steel neck rods fitted over his head.

On my first day, I was told that even though I was walking, that for liability reasons I had to be fitted for a wheelchair. I was fitted for a "small adult". The chair was brought to me the next day with my last name on it. I glanced at my name so taped and told myself, "Don't claim that chair as yours." I snatched the tag off. However, for three days, I was made to use the chair, so I said to myself, okay, if that's what you want. I would scoot in the chair to my therapy sessions along the blue colored tape towards the PT room. But on my way back, I'd purposely wheel myself into garbage cans or anything that could move or fall over. As I'd round the corner towards the nurse's station, I'd go into action. I had a ball. They were trying to play games. Not the nurses so much, but the "white privileged" psychiatrist/shrink who came into my shared quarters one day. I saw his polished shoes beneath my drawn curtain as I spoke on the phone, hinting of his presence. I suddenly drew back the curtain. He was surprised that I'd caught him eaves dropping. I blandly smiled and offered him a seat in the wheelchair at which he stiffened, backed slightly away and refused, deciding to stand. That doctor was a pompous son of a bitch. I couldn't stand him. Needless to say, the wheelchair to which I did not lay claim was taken from me in three days. I had told them... and as it turned out, I proved potentially more hazardous to other patients/staff, equipment, and myself in a wheelchair than walking solitaire.

Thank the Lord for Rose, who showed up on about my 4th or 5th day. Rose was an elderly Caucasian lady of about 88 or 89. She'd suffered a devastating stroke. I say devastating because it had left her with a severe memory loss. Many strokes are devastating in some form or another, but Rose was thrust back to 1958 and there she remained until I left.

Rose was a petite, frail short lady with snow hair and Al was the same in male opposition. They reminded me of Hume Cronyn and Jessica Tandy. I felt so bad for her and Al to whom she'd been married for more than 50 years. She and Al were retired and living in a ritzy section of San Francisco. Al had decided to stay in a nearby hotel in order to be at the hospital early in the mornings. Al would come like clockwork, eat breakfast with his beloved and then spend all day with her over the course of her therapy sessions, lunch and then dinner. In the evenings when Al had to leave, always exhausted, it would start. Rose cried a lot, all day. Al would begin to soothe Rose with a comforting voice. Each night he had to reassure her that he was only going back to his hotel, nearby. And that he'd be there in the morning. Rose was having none of that, spitting epitaphs at him, "I know where you're going. You're going to that woman's house." She'd yell and cry until poor Al was wiped out. When Al finally convinced her that he had to go, the cries for her beloved did not let up for a few hours. She'd moan and scream his name for hours in addition to commentary about Al's long ago adulterous ways.

Staff had told Rose she couldn't be released until she'd gotten some of her memory back. I helped Rose each morning by telling her the day, date and month. I'd have her repeat them for me several times and she did well, but by the time the nurse would ask her she had returned to 1958. It got so bad for the three of us other ladies that Mama Rose had to be removed to another wing of the hospital. I still saw her and Al in therapy but Rose never forgave Al for his transgression. I'm betting that Al's affair was in 1958.

Helping Mama Rose and a few other patients in my own way, helped me recover. I also helped another man get out of his wheelchair. I shared with him my plight and story and before I left he was walking through the parallel bars.

    Witnessing Mama Rose and Al reaffirmed what real love is all about. I think Al truly realized for the first time how negatively impacted Rose had been by his affair but apparently, she'd been mum about it and now at this late stage she was regurgitating all over the place. Al never denied it during their overheard conversations. Once or twice he did threaten to not return to the hospital if she kept it up, but he didn't keep his word. He always returned, a gentleman. I prayed that Rose would return to her Al just as he surely did pray for his Rose.

A THANK-YOU BLANKET

ALL PRAISES ARE DUE MY COMPASSIONATE AND MERCIFUL GOD WHO HAS GRACED ME WITH THE RENEWED ABILITY TO PREPARE THI S ALL ENCOMPASSING BLANKET OF THANKS AND APPRECIATION TO ALL WHO ASSISTED ME DURING MY RECENT JOURNEY TO MY NEW SELF.

BECAUSE I AM NOW, ONLY ABLE TO TYPE WITH MY RIGHT THUMB AND THERE ARE SO MANY I'D LIKE TO MENTION UNDER THIS BLANKET, I AM OPTING TO IDENTIFY MANY PERSONS OR GROUPS BY INITIALS ONLY.

I AM GRATEFUL FOR MY ROUTE OF PRAYERS BEGINNING WITH TIM. E. IN NORTH CAROLINA, FRIENDS AND FAMILY IN VIRGINIA AND W. VA., THE COLLINS' OF DELAWARE. DEAR SISTER-FRIEND, Y.B. OF THE BRONX, N.Y... MY NEW-FOUND <u>FMD SUPPORT GROUP ESTABLISHED IN HUDSON, OH, MIMI PETERSONOF SEBASTOPOL, CA., MIMI, WE HAVE TO HAVE THAT VICTORY LUNCH, YOU WERE A GODSEND.</u> MY DEAR FAMILY MEMBERS IN COLUMBUS, OH. I ADORE AND LOVE YOU ALL RIGHT BACK. FRIEND, LINDA J. AND FAMILY OF E. CLEVELAND, OH. THE TWINS, REGGIE AND ROGGIE LANIER AND THEIR CHURCH CONGREGATION IN SPRINGFIELD, ILL. THANKS GUYS. LOVE YOU MUCH. KLM AND FAMILY K. THANKS FOR CHAMPIONING FOR SO MANY AT THIS TIME.

MUCHAS GRACIAS PARA TODO ESPECIALMENTE LAS ALMOHADAS Y PARAEXISTENCIA UNA DE MI FAVORITA AMIGAS, MARGA BOUZAS DE ALBANY, CA. NAM-MYOHO - RENGE KYO. MUCHAS GRACIAS, MI AMIGA.

SPECIAL ACKNOWLEDGMENT AND LOVE TO STEPFATHER, OLIN FORD AND STEPBROTHER. AL. YOU ARE WARRIORS, I

LOVE YOU BOTH. YOUR LOVE AND CARE FOR ME CONTINUES TO SUPPORT MY SPIRIT.

A VERY SPECIAL THANK-YOU TO MY SURROGATE FAMILY, THE MCGHEES OF OAKLAND, CA YOU HAVE LOVED AND NURTURED ME FOR 20 YEARS. MAMA HATTIE. YOU ARE AN ANGEL. OK. GRANDMA MAGGIE IS ONE TOO. SHE'S A 97 YEAR YOUNG EARTH ANGEL WITH AN ATTITUDE THAT SHE HAS EVERY RIGHT TO POSSESS. SISTER DORIS HAS BEEN WONDERFUL TO ME, THANKS DORIS FOR THE CURBSIDE SERVICE AND YOUR NEVER-ENDING WORDS OF ENCOURAGEMENT. ALSO, THANKS FOR CARING FOR MY BIRD. MARK, SPECIAL GREATFULNESS IS EXTENDED. SISTER-FRIEND. PAM WHO SPENT COUNTLESS HOURS ASSISTING ME IN MY SURGERY PREPATORY STAGE. IKNOW I TRIED YOUR PATIENCE AND OUR FRIENDSHIP. FORGIVE ME? IKNOW YOU ALREADY HAVE. GOT TO KEEP IT MOVIN'. LOVE YOU GIRL I'LL MISS YOU. TO MY GODDAUGHTER. MAYA. I APPRECIATE YOU FOR ALL OF YOUR GOOD DEEDS. THANKS PAM, FOR SHARING YOUR CHILD WITH ME. ALL OF YOUR CHILDREN'S PRESENCE WILL REMAIN WITH ME,

TO MY KING, ZUBERI (NOONIE) PETE. YOU ARE A BEAUTIFUL SPIRIT. AN ANGEL FLYING TOO CLOSE TO EARTH. GLAD YOU TOUCHED DOWN IN MY PATH. I'LL REMAIN YOUR QUEEN. MANY THANKS TO YOU AND YOUR CONGREGATION FOR YOUR PRAYERS. BOTH HAIRCUTS. MINE AND YOURS WERE MOST APPRRECIATED.

TO MY SIBLINGS, TONA: THANKS AGAIN FOR TAKING CARE OF MY BUSINESS INTERESTS AND FOR BRINGING MELVIN((MICKEY) TO ME. THANKS ALSO. FOR YOUR NOVEMBER GIFT

BROTHER KEITH, THANK YOU FOR YOUR DECEMBER GIFT. MICKEY, YOUR UNFALTERING LOVE AND CONCERN SHALL REMAIN WITH ME ALWAYS. <u>THE DOGPOUND LIVES ON RUFF RUFF. RUFF.</u>

IAM MOST APPRECIATIVE OF THE SUPPORT RECEIVED FROM O.U.S.D. EMPLOYEES, CURRENT OR NOT, ESPECIALLY L. EPPS, MISS DEE, J, WOODS, A. LAYTON AND THE MANY SITE PRINCIPALS, SPECIFICALLY THOSE AT CARTER MIDDLE SCHOOL AND CASTLEMONT HIGH SCHOOL OF BUSINESS AND TECHNOLOGY

SPECIAL THANKS, TO MISS J. KENT, MY LONGTIME FRIEND OF LAS VEGAS. IT WAS GOOD TO SEE YOU. THANKS FOR YOUR TRUE CONCERN.

SISTER, CLEONA OF CLEVELAND, OH. THANK YOU FOR YOUR INSTRUCTION AND PRAYERS. MY MOTHER IS WATCHING YOU TOO.

A. FONTAIN OF OAKLAND WHO, IF THERE HAD BEEN ONE, WOULD HAVE WON THECONTEST FOR MOST HOSPITAL VISITS. QUITE A FEAT CONSIDERING THAT I RECEIVED CARE AT 3 FACILITIES OVER A 2-MONTH PERIOD.THANK YOU FOR LOVING AND CARING ABOUT ME, THE LEFT ARM THERAPIES WERE GREAT. I NEED A FEW MORE (SMILE)

GRATITUDE IS EXTENDED TO THE JACKSON FAMILY OF VALLEJO. CA, FOR ALL THEY'VE DONE FOR ME DURING THIS TIME.

I WILL ALWAYS BE GRATEFUL TO DR. L RICHMOND WHO HAS ON SEVERAL OCCASSIONS AIDED ME IN TIMES OF NEED. YOU ARE A GODSEND.THANK YOU FOR BEING MY FRIEND

TO H.A.P, MY DEAREST FRIEND, CONFIDANT, ANDBIGGEST SUPPORTER. MY LOVE FOR YOU REMAINS UNDIMINISHED. THANKS FOR STICKING BY ME. SOMEONE. NOT IN THE MEDICAL PROFESSION. RECENTLY SUGGESTED TO ME THAT I MAY NEVER BE 100% OF THE WAY I USED TO BE. THAT WAS PRESUMPTIVE OF THAT PERSON. MY RESPONSE IS THIS, WITH MY GOD'S CONTINUED GOOD GRACE AND ALL OF THE STAMINA AND PERSEVERANCE I CAN MUSTER. I WHOLLY INTEND TO BE 500% OF THE ME THAT IS TO BE.

HIGH RECOGNITION TO MY PRIMARY CARE PHYSICIAN, DOCTOR LAURA MORGAN WHO DISCOVERED THE BRUIT IN MY CAROTID ARTERY. I'LL NEVER FORGET THE LOOK ON HER FACE AS SHE LISTENEDTHROUGH HER STETHOSCOPE, GIVING A SHORT NOD COUPLED WITH A REASSURING PROFESSIONAL SMILE. MY HEART SKIPPED A BEAT BUT THE ALL-TELLING IINSTRUMENT WAS ABOUT 6 INCHES AWAY.I GRACIOUSLY THANK DR. MORGAN FOR HER SINCERE CONCERN FOR MYSELF. I AM MOST APPRECIATIVE OF THE GIFTS SHE AND DONNA HAVE SHARED WITH ME. - 01-11-06

Author Note: I have intentionally, left this "Thank You Blanket" in its original form, uncorrected and representative of the 'fog' I was still in three months post my 'diagnosis and surgery aftermath. I clarify now that the respective November and December gifts of Tona and Keith were COBRA payments for my Kaiser premiums. The fog I was in then represented more clarity than any of you will ever know. Today, March 26, 2014, I completed my memoir and print this blanket as my final documented entry of Act III of (my) Life's Opera.

Lee Malik
(Mine King)

In Honor of
Zuberi Mwunathaura

Anticipation built. The moments pulsated his arrival. Stars danced in the blue night skies as he spawned, arched, twisted and sweet shea buttered his way through his mother's birth canal. There, now! A new Malik. Not enough hands to hold the gold, to bestow as welcome and gratitude for this special benevolence. His mother knew she'd have to give him to and share him with the earth. She loved, shielded, guided, fought, instructed as only she could and must. His father a panther warrior did the same but in the manliest of ways and as only a man could and should do for the offspring of his loins, his son- prince- to- be- king.

By the time I was pleasured with the presence of Lee Malik he'd been anointed "*GQ Noonie*" of Oakland, California. Once again, a woman, I, stood in anticipation of his arrival. At near the instant of his entrance, I beamed towards his face through a crowd of onlookers. No, he didn't recognize me, wasn't supposed to. I was only meant to observe him; to see what all the excitement was about.

My eyes told me, "Yes, he's fine as hell, young, all the young girl-ladies are going gaga over him and his tailored dress". But my heart and my God told me something a lot more, "Aesthetics aside, this man is kind, gentle, intelligent, God-fearing, loving and giving towards his fellow man and that's what I like and am attracted towards.

Some time passed. I'd only see this beautiful specimen once in a while, on special occasions where I worked part-time. But on each of those occasions I was reminded of and gently pierced by my newfound angel's emanating aura. Just something very extra special. I don't even know if he knew my name. Certainly, he didn't know how I felt about him.

As it was told to me afterwards. One evening Noonie was being driven home by a male associate. Noonie was a front seat passenger. A gun shot, believed to be meant for the driver, rang out and flashed through the darkness, through the vehicle and pierced the flesh of Lee Malik. When the events were recanted to me as I stood transfixed in my living room, I was absolutely dumbfounded, angry, aghast, wanted to strike back. The whole community was in overdrive. Lee Malik was ultimately rendered a wheelchair bound paraplegic after intensive rehabilitation and he still didn't know how I felt about him. So, when his uncle, Geoffrey Peete, owner of Oakland's *Geoffrey's* night club put out the word that Noonie, now Zuberi was returning home from hiatus in Atlanta where Noonie had attained his Undergraduate degree and that a celebration was to be given in his honor, I figured it was time to let Noonie know what and how I thought of him.

I remember the night well. Everyone clamored for Noonie's attention and pictures with him. I believe I lucked out on a picture. Noonie was as handsome and dapper as ever he had been with his pearly smile spilling over his beautiful lips. I still didn't get a chance to talk with him one- on- one. I was dressed in all black, (not to be somber but it was one of the best I had and I wanted to look nice for Noonie) an outfit purchased in part from I Magnin.

A few more years passed and in 2001 my best friend Pam and I visited *Friday's* in Jack London Square. On route there, down Broadway Avenue, I played over and over *Brandy's* "Have You Ever Loved Somebody?" In my excitement about being out, as I exited my car, I closed the door, locking the keys in the ignition with the engine running. By the time AAA had arrived and retrieved my keys, I just knew that the happy hour was going to be over, but it was only just about to begin.

Pam and I finally entered the establishment and sat in the bar area at the far right-side. We sat at a table so we could see patrons entering, even though we were only there to eat.

Before Pam could say it, I saw, my angel, my Lee Malik. I leapt from my stool and strode to him, reached for him and nearly pulled him from his seat. Finally, there he was, by himself, no clamoring girl ladies, no cameras, just him and me. My heart said, I've got you. I'm here now. I'll help you, do all I can for you. My lips spilled questions, lots. We gave brief updates. I kept my promise to visit him that 4th of July holiday time. We shared lots. Kept some things to ourselves, I'm sure.

We traversed from there, our hearts and spirits never far. Thinking of his recently earthly deceased mother, Noonie called me today, September 26, 2008, my own deceased mother's birthday. We are kindred like that and, too, in other ways, many.

A few years ago, when I was ill, it was Noonie, his strength and fortitude, unrelenting love, exhibition of grace under insurmountable odds that enabled me on many levels to be in a place to pay homage to him, even if my hug and more are, for the time being, whispers on the wind. I have and always will love this angel flying too close to earth, Mine King, Lee Malik,

Zuberi aka *GQ Noonie*. He once told me, "Don't give up the fight." I won't, as my own rekindled anticipation builds towards the time I see you again.

Sincerely,

Your Queen, Adrea

The Transition that got Away

Fear or trepidation about death has never really given me pause. In fact, I did die in nearly every conceivable way on October 18, 2005.

A few minutes more and it would have been irretrievably too late to have breath sustained in my lungs. My brain flooded purplish blood and my arterial system implored relief. My heart and other organs trudged on reserved power, nearly imploding. BUT, after a bevy of intranational phone calls, it was decided that my Power of Attorney (PA) should grant authorization to prolong my final transition and that I should remain in disabled physical capacity upon this planet. My limbs had already begun shutting down, and returning to a fetal state, balled fists as with a newborn, weakened lower limbs, muted to minimally babbling speech, unfocused ocular movement, etc. I was rapidly wheeled into an operating room, where another surgeon waited. On route to this destination, I heard everything, all of the overlapping verbal commands of medical staff, directing the gurney and its attendants. I remember wanting to simply die, was there in the warmth of the light that beckoned me. Ah, the warmth. There was no face of God. God has no face. No images abounded, only the most simplistic of the deepest, purest feeling I know any human has ever experienced. I wanted to go to that lighted overwhelmingly wonderful charged feeling; just be absorbed within and by it. I had died, pleased to have left this earth, but then 'man' interfered and brought me back to this shit hole. (No, Karla, (my niece), I was not 'happy to be alive' as you say my PA thought I would be when she, with your input (ultimately and medically too late, decided to have me "alive" but sans my former physical self).

I sarcastically ask you Miss Karla, "If you went to sleep one evening and awoke without the use of your hands to perform the most basic of tasks for yourself, like eating or dressing, would you be happy!? Then, Miss Karla, imagine you could not perform any of your profession's duties, would you be happy!? Particularly if you, Karla had instructed your PA to not have you left alive in such a physical state. <u>Perhaps you, Karla would be happy, but I doubt it sincerely.</u> I was happy where I was before the incorrect and late decision was made, I had transitioned as none of you have, but you all took the transition away from me. It was my time and you all stole it from me. Not one of you considered how my living would be as a disabled person, alone. NOT ONE OF YOU GAVE A DAMN ABOUT ME, except Uncle Harry and Aunt Sadie. You all wanted me alive for yourselves and then you essentially abandoned me, and when many of the family came around, it was just to gawk, and appraise how I looked or assess how I was managing on my own. The PA took my money, (although I recovered it, but the damage had been done) and your father demanded of me "open your hand." as if I wanted it closed. In the entire two years I lived in Twinsburg, you, Karla, only visited me once for driving me to a business appointment and for which I thanked you albeit you said I didn't have to. And I had to endure your insensitive prattle about how in previous years, I would come home, cute, walking fast, dressed in fur and jewelry. Well, for your information, I still owned furs and jewels when you said those stupid words, and my "cuteness" is in the eye of the beholder. My gait is irrelevant as is yours. The important thing is that we still have one. Females cease being 'cute' after 29, an observation you should have made by then (2008) in your own person."

As I've said before, but will reiterate again, supposed family stole from me, particularly two of Aunt Hannah's kids, Linda and Marcella (Ludi). Linda stole money from me. Ludi stole jewelry from me. The PA stole my self-saved pension contribution and tried to have me declared incompetent to handle my own affairs, and then you, Karla, and she, the former PA, had the unmitigated gall to send me insultingly vulgar E-mails, subjected: **"SLAP IN THE FACE"**, I know you remember that, I do. And the PA, while stating, again, that she did not inform medical personnel of beeping machines; left me and went home because she was tired, had the weak audacity to integrate diluted psychology by suggesting to me that I kill myself. (Forensic technology, i.e. E-mails with server identification inclusive of dates and times do not tell untruths or half-truths or "perceptions", but rather support fact of my very much intact memory). Don't make me produce the E-mails I reference. None of you will ever have any kind of controlling say so over me again, not in this realm, most assuredly, and Allah will not allow you to impinge on me in the hereafter.

Afore comments should not be construed that I am unhappy. Happiness for anyone is a pursuit, possibly never to be attained by any human. I do not hate, never have. What I do is rightfully and justifiably dislike, and thus extricate myself from the orbits of persons unlikable or displeasing, including atmospheric situations similarly afflicted.

What I am is content. I am self-contained and all five of my dimensions of health (social, spiritual, emotional, intellectual, and physical) are aligned for prosperity via a hierarchy of pre-potency. Can you dig it?

My transition got away, once, but my rise will come! Amin.

THIRTEEN DAYS

Jan thirty-one, Tues Eve: I'd been asked not to tell her I was coming, so I didn't but I knew the moment after I'd ascended the stairs to her dimly lit but warm and inviting room that she'd been told I was coming; I saw her from the hall reclining in her armchair. I smiled, as broadly as I could, wishing she did not have to see me like this, my God, but she's my grandmother, my Mama Ada. "<u>She</u> loves me", my heart raced. I could tell she'd been told of my impending extended visit; the extenuating reason behind which I'd been asked not to reveal and I had not. I stepped into her room as she came to her tiny feet. With outstretched arms and arched necks, planed cheeks and lips we lovingly greeted each other with the inherent understanding as only a maternal grandmother and the grandmother's namesake could.

I felt safe. I was with her in her son's home (Uncle Harry's and Aunt Sadie's home). After I rinsed myself of too long of a travel day from west to east coast, I lay and chatted with Mama Ada; nothing too heavy, just chatter and light laughter soft heaves and sighs in the darkness of our now shared room for 12 more days but I wasn't counting. I was paying attention. I may not speak up a lot but I do pay attention and the true story will be told.

Feb One, Wed: A pretty good day. We're soaking each other in; doing a lot more talking. I'm getting directives. I'm used to being my own dictator. Minor adjustments. It's OK. We're served our breakfast/lunch on white pull-up tray tables. Kind of cute. I'm not used to being waited on or … I'm continually searching to follow Mama's lead. She's a good leader. OK, she's had a longer time to do so. The Lesson learned today: Small space, pace self, grace, prayer. She's my kind of lady and I'm her red bird again.

Once when I was 9 years old and visiting during the summer in Williamson, I dressed all in red one morning, walked into the kitchen and greeted her as she stood at the sink. She pivoted, smiled and called me her red bird. I never forgot that. And that's how she made me feel again on day two of Thirteen Days.

Feb Two, Thurs.: I think we're getting more used to the other. Mama knows I do not have this kind of routine down yet. But instinctively, I know what I must and have to do for myself. No big deal really. "But really Mama it's a deal bigger than you know." I want to scream, cry, holler out, but of course I do not do any of these things. I'm missing my home. Mama reminds me that she misses hers too. She hugs me, a lot. What else can she do? I hug her right back. We don't cry; we're strong; it's only for a short spell. I believe we tell ourselves. At least I tell myself.

I think it's been a few months since she's been to Williamson.

This must be the day or maybe it was yesterday that she helps me with my bra. Anyway, I step into my bras, which means they have to be pre-hooked before being put on. Mama hooked a particular one for me. (To this day, Oct 9, 2007 it has not been unhooked, albeit washed)

The beginning of our third full day. We're still being served breakfast after Mama has returned from her bathing. Each morning she carries with her a small green plastic rectangular-shaped tub filled with various toiletries as if for a doll. Toiletries consisted of soap, Vaseline. Body creams. She used 2 different kinds by Delon, Aloe Vera or Coca Butter, Lanolin hairdressing, I don't recall seeing deodorant, maybe she kept that in the bathroom. But, then again dolls don't need deodorant, and Topaze perfume by Avon.

Anyway, I've been instructed by Melanie to not perform my bathing until after 11:00 a.m. So, fine, that gives me a chance to chill with Mama Ada. While the balance of the household gets in swing and it seems to always swing and I guess that's a good thing. I'm still catching my bearings, teetering this first week not quite come and gone.

We talk, talk, listen, watch TV, read, talk of our shared love for poetry (the poems I'd copyrighted and given her with a Mahalia Jackson gospel tape. During this day, Mama reveals that she keeps poetry books tucked away in the pockets of the La-Z-Boy recliner. I smile at this revelation. I like books too and among my possessions I longed for them most. I primarily keep mine in my bedroom. Because they bring me a certain peace and comfort which nothing else can.

After my bath, I suppose I express concern over my hair. At any rate, Mama sends me to the bathroom for a brush and lovingly tells me to come back and sit down. I happily oblige her. She oils my scalp and brushes my hair as I sit on the floor between her outstretched legs, while she sat upright in the La-Z boy. I was her red bird for a second time in as many days. I was loving being the granddaughter of Mama Ada.

We're taking all meals, pills, most guests in our room, but I'm beginning to move about the house a bit more. I continue with my nightly bed exercises.

About 10:00 p.m. or so; it might be slightly later, Little Harry comes and asks me to go make a run with him. Mama is asleep, but stirs. I jump at the chance to get out of the house with my fun cousin who I've missed. I hurry into some pants and a sweater. Shoes, black leather jacket and down the stairs and out the back door. We don't stay out long, about 20 minutes, back in a flash, can't really remember where we went, nowhere really, but it felt good to just be out.

Feb Three, Fri: Basic repeat of yesterday. But I'm tiring of the room. Mama Ada has her routine. She comes out, moves about more after lunch. She'll visit with Granny, Aunt Sadie's mother whose room is next to ours. Granny is a kick, sassy. She loves to watch Walker, Texas Ranger. It comes on at 7:00 p.m. They enjoy that while I go to our room for Jeopardy. // I shipped my DVD's but they haven't arrived yet. The day wears on. Mama Ada is tired today and lies down early. It is early evening, but dark when a pastor, unknown to me, and his wife arrive at the kitchen door. I am seated at the kitchen table near the corner by the fridge. I am introduced by this order (1) name, then (2) <u>private medical status (a person's medical status or for that matter any status is always private unless that person reveals it.</u> Needless to say, this manner of being introduced to an absolute stranger ticked me off. I abruptly left the kitchen and went to the room I shared with Mama Ada who was awake but in her bed. In tears, I flopped on my bed. Almost immediately thereafter, Aunt Sadie, the pastor and his wife, entered our room. An announcement was made that the pastor was there to pray for us, Mama Ada and me. Well, we can welcome that kind of news and we did too. We both brightened up. What a difference the mentioning of the Lord or prayer can make. So, the pastor began his laying on of hands with his pretty and dutiful wife serving as assisting witness. First Mama Ada, then myself, receiving the Lord's grace and favor through his anointing oil. I am certain we, all in that room were blessed with the holy presence of the Lord, God. I'll never forget the moment. And I'm sure Mama Ada was so embraced. We didn't talk much more that night, just let the anointing steep us to sleep. Thanks Aunt Sadie. All's well that ends well.

Feb Four, Sat: Uncle Harry hasn't been mentioned too much thus far, however, he's ever present, here, there, in and out, running errands for everyone, checking on us one and all. Mama Ada is more energetic today, more pep in her tiny feet. Smiling. She wants to see Keitha and her kids and so do I, wonder where they are and why they have not been down to see her, Mama's walls are pasted with photos of her grands and her newest great grand, "G's daughter, who has a mop of raven black hair atop pale ivory skin. Mama just loves babies (children). She also has a strong fondness for porcelain dolls of all sizes and designs. I don't know it yet, but, the bedroom closet floor space is stacked with boxes of dolls, as well as some of her other personal affects. I' don't have an affinity towards dolls. Lost my affinity for them with the 5th grade Christmas season. I may still pick one up, but I'm not a lingerer.

I'm becoming a bit lethargic, feel the need to move more. Anyway. I decide I'm not taking any more meals in the bedroom.

The day seems to drag. It's my first Saturday, weekend day. Melanie is off. No one my age to kick it with today. During the weekdays, I shared Melanie's breaks. Aunt Sadie is busy with household things and Granny. Uncle is out and about.

I've kept my California cell phone number. I get calls sometimes for which I am most grateful. When the house phone rings which it often does, I continually have to remind myself that "this is not your house/home, so the caller is not seeking you."

The Saturday schedule is a lot different from the weekdays. We see more of Paul and Allen. Paul is filled with sweet hugs. And Allen with endless teen wit and energy. Paul helps me with my earrings, anything I ask of him that he's able to assist me with. Likewise, with Allen. I also do what I'm able to do. I assist Mama Ada. Actually, we are helping each other as we can. Nothing major. Mama Ada stays upstairs most of the time, so, I'm with her and Granny there. When Aunt Sadie goes to the kitchen or basement I want to go with her, to watch her cook, 'cause I'm still learning some of her secrets. I don't want to leave Mama or Granny alone for too long, but they are OK, I am assured. It's just that I haven't seen them in such a long time. I just do not want to miss anything if I can help it. No, I do not mind to just simply sit with Granny for hours. I was asked to do this once and I guess it was forgotten about and then when it was remembered, I suppose it was somehow not truly believed that I was still sitting with Granny after a few hours, but it was my pleasure, not a problem.

Finally, and without much fanfare, Saturday bedtime arrives and I am thankful the night has come.

Mama Ada readies herself for bed, as do I. We say our prayers, talk ourselves to sleep under our respective snug blankets and look forward to First Sunday Communion.

Feb Five, Sun: The 3 of us convalescing women awake to a bright morning. We have to present ourselves and our rooms before noon to the visiting pastor and his church members who are to give us and Aunt Sadie Communion. I believe the pastor is from Aunt Sadie's church, Mt. Zion A.M.E. We gather in Granny's room where we receive prayer and Communion. The room is brimming with many people. The pastor, we 4 women, about 4 other women to assist with Communion. It is as grand of an affair as it can be considering the tight quarters. I'm impressed. Mama Ada is pleased. Granny likes the attention and is behaving.

Food odors are wafting throughout the house. It's Sunday dinner we're sniff-tasting through our olfactory systems. I'm wondering if there'll be many guests today. Mama Ada seems to be up to some company. I'm feeling hesitant, insecure. I still haven't seen all of my family members since I've been here, so I'm not at all anxious or excited to meet or greet strangers, but, I shield my anxiety. I shield a lot.

To be honest, I do not recall who most of the dinner guests were, other than cousin Terri-Jo and her 3 rambunctious boys, members of the immediate household and perhaps 2-3 other people. Aunt Sadie did prepare some of my favorite dishes, Macaroni and cheese, "your Uncle wouldn't know it was Sunday if we didn't have these sweet potatoes, sweet potatoes" dressing, green beans, turkey, pound cake. There probably was another meat, roast beef perhaps, choice of beverages. Grace as always led by Uncle, followed by our individual bible verses that in our family have always been mandatory and from one's memory since speaking age. Dinner was good.

Mama Ada and I retire early this Sunday. I've had a full 5 plus days and am feeling somewhat overwhelmed; not being used to so much movement in my home environment, is exhausting and draining. I had to remember to keep ahold of me while I continued to redevelop and know my new me; all while displaced from my home 3,000 miles away, not easy. But I knew it could be done for I had been out west for most of my life, away from all blood ties. So, I've got the key skills for survival down pat. And so, I silently hummed my freedom song, the tune the civil rights marchers chanted in the 60's or

I'd silently recite a Buddhist chant for calming effect; multiplicity. Whatever it takes, but we're making it. I miss my friends and family in California, especially Henry, but I'm glad for the safe feeling Mama Ada gives me.

And so, we nestle in once more. I do some leg exercises. But I drift off before I'm aware that I'm more tired than Mama Ada. Good Night.

Feb, Six, Mon. I awake seemingly, longingly exhausted. I'm longing for my true and real home. I'm not going to get used to being here under these circumstances. Nothing is mine, except what I brought in my three cases on the plane. Mama Ada bathes, dresses, smooths her straight thin as fine silk hair back from her slight oval face into a tiny knot at the back of her head, which seems so small now. Her facial features have always been small and purposeful. Just pretty and intentional. She is wearing a sweat suit, not one of her 2 new ones, a pale whisper of pink or the white one. They hung in our now shared closet at the right end.

I stir around a while, passing time, waiting for Melanie to come and get Granny's bathing done so I can start my own. Melanie comes at 10: 00. So, I have to be in and out before she gets there or wait until she finishes Granny. With all of the people in the house and since I'm the newcomer and to avoid confrontation on any level. I've decided before today, it's simply best to delay my bathing time until late morning/early afternoon. Anyway, when the time is right, I ready myself for the day. The day moves all too slowly. I'm still, of course, making small adjustments on all levels. Mama Ada and I skip back in time. We do a lot of talking, or she seems to want to do most of the talking. She seems more tired. Her appetite is not so good. She's sitting bundled in her La- Z-Boy wrapped in a blue and beige blanket that snaps along the edges, watching more TV, visiting with Granny in the next room.

The day wears on into nightfall. Time for Walker. The elder women gather in Granny's room for the show. I stay tonight, realizing that I can watch Jeopardy tomorrow.

Feb, Seven, Tues. I've made one week. It seems like a lifetime away from my home. I'm so sad inside. I know Mama Ada knows it. She doesn't ask many personal questions. Today is a basic repeat of yesterday. Mama Ada seems more tired and short of breath, little coughing, not hard. It's getting colder. Her doctor has been contacted. We've been told to increase pain/heart med if needed; Anyway. Uncle and Aunt know what that's about. She's being closely monitored to ensure her comfort and dietary intake.

The evening passes, rather drifts. I suppose I sleep. I keep my senses as much awake as possible, on guard for my Mama Ada.

Feb, Eight, Wed. Essentially a ditto of yesterday. Mama Ada performs her daily routine with a smile but not so much energy. Her appetite is not good.

Feb, Nine, Thurs. Ditto Wednesday, only Mama is becoming weaker with more complaint of pain, more coughing. Medicine is increased. Mama is mostly in her room today. She visits Granny for a short time.

Feb. Ten. Fri. Mama seems weaker, but does ready herself for the day. No real appetite. I think she has tea and toast in the morning. We all seem to meander through the day. It's cold and sunny, not a lot of snow, just brisk. Mama's meds are increased around 10:00 p.m. She's given a liquid by Uncle. I believe it may be for pain or her heart, but I know it's strong and serious stuff, I guess, because it was put away in another room. She goes to sleep.

Feb. Eleven, Sat. Mama awakes in better spirits, but with a very limited appetite. She seems more physically strong. In the early evening, I cajole her into eating some soup. I prepare it for her, bring it to her, and serve it on the white pull up tray-table. She smiles as she becomes my "mama-girl." I feed her, alternately dabbing her always tiny baby lips as her eyes dance smiles towards my face. All the while, I'm thinking, I love you dearest of women, my grandmother, my Mama Ada, I'm praying through one of her favorite songs, "Precious, Lord". After her meal is finished we ready ourselves for bed. It's been a long sort of day. Everyone seems tired and a bit on edge. But we're all adults so we're cool and collected and know how to keep our composure under stress and duress. Plus, we've got the Lord on our side. I know I do. Before Mama can get to sleep she has to be given some of that extra medicine again, just like she was last night.

Feb Twelve, Sun. We awake to another bright Sunday. Bathing and room readiness seems to rush by today. It's cold today. By early to midafternoon, my female sibling arrives, seemingly out of the blue, I don't recall anyone saying she was due to visit. Nonetheless, I'm somewhat surprised to see her. We exchange a civil "Hi". Within minutes she asks me if I want to go shopping, perhaps, to get me out. Anyway, I agree to go. She takes me to a strip-type mall where she pays to have some records copied for me and buys us a look-alike sweat suit. While we're in the clothing store, I remember getting this urge to go home. We're gone maybe two hours. When we get back, I take my bags upstairs, go back downstairs, leaving her with Mama Ada. I'm sitting at the dining room table with my back to the window as dusk is peeking behind me when my sister appears across from me to announce that Mama Ada has passed away. I am stunned and want to swipe the words from the air, over her lips and through her teeth and back down her throat. How dare she come to town and be the one to be the bearer of such news and with such a blank unemotional face. I didn't and will not discuss with her what occurred during her visit with Mama Ada. All I know is an angel named Ada Mae Rumley Cox Gregory is no longer fluttering and strutting among us and I miss her an awful lot. May our Lord keep her warm in his bosom, until it's her redbird's time to light therein.

~Shahada of Adrea Adams~

As-Salaam-Alaikum

My awakening or awareness predated my actual public declaration by about 45 years.

I first became exceptionally, vividly, and acutely aware of cultures other than American in Columbus, Ohio's Hamilton Elementary School's sixth grade. Acute awareness migrated to chronic investigation, recognition, and physical and spiritual embracing of Middle Eastern lifestyles and habits beyond textbook and film introduction. Specifically, I was drawn to Egyptian everything to the point of desiring to become a paleontologist or some kind of expert of that region of Africa. No one was listening to me; I doubt I let it be known much above a whisper, but once I had accumulated enough knowledge, members of that region somehow sensed it and began flocking to me in my early college days. In fact, I sought out local college campuses including Case Western Reserve University harboring students from as far away as Saudi Arabia. There and among other inlets I interacted on a global level, learning all I could about far off lands like Senegal, Libya, Greece, Pakistan, Persia, India, and the Philippines. I made friends or close acquaintances from every inhabited continent. In fact, I have dated men from all over the globe, except China. Vietnamese men were attracted to me, later in the Bay Area, but by then I had married. And when I say 'dated' I mean it from the strict clean sense of the word. During these travails and interactions with African Muslims on my own college campus, I was formally introduced to Islam. In those times, it was an "in thing" to frequent Muslim eateries, partake of whiting fish dinners and bean pies served by Fruit of Islam (FOI) members. I would purchase boxes of whiting fish from my fellow Muslim classmates at the same time making inquiries about their culture/religion or invite them to my family's home to ask more detailed questions and to observe on a more personal level. These students were educating themselves and so I did.

Blessed decision of my youth led me to a new birth of sorts; certainly, new horizons. On March 2, 1979, I floated in love, unafraid of a thing or person to California's San Francisco –Bay Area, braced for whatever my college degree, 18 months of insurance executive experience, $600.00, and the bold unflinching raw nerve of a 23-year-old lady –blossoming –to - woman could behold and absorb in her being.

My husband, Rahim and I did not discuss religion a lot, but I learned from him three of many very important beliefs held within Islam: No one is born a sinner, therefore baptizing is not warranted or required for the washing away of sins of an infant child or anyone at any age. Second, Jesus is recognized as a messenger of Allah (God) of which there is only one or Him, and thus thirdly, Jesus is not God or His son, cannot be, for to say so makes Allah human, that which He is not. Embracing these three beliefs (to me) is sufficient support. I still have the Qur'an used in our wedding ceremony. Actually, I own three Qur'ans the second is a paperback English translation and the third was gifted me on the day of my Shahada or public declaration on June 6, 2010 at Masjid An-Noor in Santa Clara, California.

When marrying Rahim, I was not required to convert to Islam, but I did conduct a Muslim household which I never ceased practicing even after we divorced. One of my favorite pictures I have is of Rahim performing salaat or prayer.

The revelation leading to my declaration occurred a week prior during a mini vacation return trip from the Sacramento area to Oakland. I met an Afghanistan Muslim sister on the train and we sat at the same train car table and talked until we arrived. It was during that time, we connected. I shared with her my desire to convert to Islam, just like that. It had been a long time coming, but at that precise moment, Allah revealed Himself fully to me and I felt ready. The next weekend, I met my new Muslim sister at a masjid in Hayward. I was introduced to the Imam and other Afghan women who were impressed that I spoke their language, not fluently, but enough. I was immediately embraced and accepted. I began my transforming preparation. Because of scheduling conflicts my Shahada had to be held in Santa Clara County and my newfound sister, Nazifa, would be unable to attend. However, she made arrangements for me to meet with a mother and son, Edris Amin who would assist me.

I purchased a pale gray hijab for covering my head and a traditionally sewn and an adorned black with gray stitching outer garment. The retailer gifted me rose oil. Likewise, at the masjid I was given two beautiful head scarves and another exquisitely made and adorned outer garment worn on pilgrimage or hajj to Mecca by the bearer (very special indeed). I have, since been photographed professionally in high appreciation and recognition of this most dear gift, my most treasured clothing. I was also given a prayer rug by the mother and son who assisted me.

My journey to Allah is continuous until I return to Him. I am not a perfect Muslim and do not seek perfection. I seek that which is earthly possible, to be the best Muslim I can and with all earnest effort it is my desire to return to Allah rid of as much of this world's gross impurities as He wills. Peace and blessings be upon Muhammad, His (final) messenger.

Kahlimah Shahada:

I bear witness that there is none worthy of worship except Allah, the One alone, without partner, and I bear witness that Muhammad is His servant and Messenger.

Adrea Adams

Coming Out of the Dark

Expressly for 12-12-10

It is all right. There is a pulse of light to lead the way. You will see it is beautiful with rhythmic rhymes to secure your stepping up, out, and toward yourself. Look for the beauty within yourself and others. Reclaim and regain your footholds.

Life happens to us all, while some life ebbs are short windows of time and others long ago, I learned to not attach or cast the rained upon pain meted by others to the exonerated being of another. Let it go, so, you can, you can, come out of that aged and past dark.

There is so much- in between- the chasm of the black and the white, the dark and the light.

So much, do not compartmentalize, 'les you position yourself to block your blessing

Let it go, go with the wind that blows. Then, soon, you will be

Coming out of the dark

Just so, you know, women of white might as you have said feel some sort of entitlement. You have deduced that women of black are more humbled. Sorry to say, but that is not the right. What, precisely, does that mean that white deems itself more deserving and black does not? I am black and humble myself before no man black or white.

I have told you, I honor you. I further explain. Honoring you means only following a law of adaptation, as proof of that honor, not a placing of you in a higher or superior compartment. I will not adapt to any disadvantage or degradation.

Come out of the dark.

For My Mother
A Song Unsung

My dear mother, as I write these words, taking but 2 or 3 of my right-hand fingers to type them out, many issues confront and are entangled within my mind. A sense of urgency oversees me now. I don't know the duration of the number of days, weeks or months standing before me now. But I have some things to say, to report, to share with you. I'll not seek your counsel or that of anyone else, for that matter. In a sense, I'm sort of lying in wait; I feel time upon me now.

If from where you are you can see me or feel what I am experiencing, then good, that's a really good thing. As you may know, in another of my recent stories, I questioned the period of time for which one is to follow the command of "Honor thy Mother and Thy Father".

Until, and for years past the time of your death, I did in fact honor you, you having been on this earth. In my 17th year, I wrote you an acknowledgment of appreciation and promise on the inside of the frame that held my high school graduation picture. I still have the frame, but the picture must have been taken from you without your knowing it. I don't believe you gave that picture to anyone. People stole a lot of things from you over the years. They took advantage of the fact that you were blind. And now, I'm faced with a similar scenario. I, too, am being taken advantage of. Because of my recent problems, and if you're watching, you know who is greatly responsible… People have stolen things from me too, some tangible. But the most important and crucial of things stolen from me were parts of my physical attributes. And now I am feeling more of an urgency to get the truth down. To my mind comes the Sly and

Family Stone song, 'It's a Family Affair' that you liked and from which you quipped to me one day one of the lines: "One child, loves to learn" ... "that's you Nicie" ...other child you'd just love to burn" ... "now, that's T---."

Now, if you quipped to me this analogy of burning your own child with the lyric of a song, I certainly know that all you've said about me was not glowing, and you probably said it to the one you would have loved to burn.

Mama, I came to Ohio for only one reason, because I had to. No reason theretofore was sufficient. I chose to reside in the Cleveland area, in large part so as not to be reminded of you and your youth, transgressions withstanding. I hated being compared to you by the people in Columbus. They didn't understand, and it's not for them to understand. The people who knew you as a very young person also knew of the good and perhaps not so good. That's cool, but I was sick and tired of being compared to you. **I am not you. I only happen to be of you, and that's too bad**.

I've also learned since coming here, of your absolute and unforgivable betrayal of me. Matters that involve my early childhood and even beyond. I can say with all certainty that just as I kept my promise to always be there for you (during your life) that if I had it to do over again, one thing I would not do is damn near go broke caring for you. No one else did it, no one. None of your other children gave me a dollar towards your care. Your own mother only gave me one twenty-dollar bill, near to the time of your passing and this was after she had us all stand in a circle, pray, and tell me, "You should be thankful, it could be worse, she (meaning you) could be ranting and screaming out all of the time, all times of day and night."

I know you did your best, sometimes doing things you didn't want to, to feed or clothe us but you chose to have us. It was your duty to take care of us. I did something once, with your knowledge and prodding to assist you and myself when we lived together in my last days of college. It was so demeaning. Shame for shame on you and the myriad of other things you nearly brought me to. But I persevered, and will still be damned if I visit there again.

There's a line in a poem by one of my favorite poets, Nikki Giovanni, "When I die, I hope no one, whoever hurt me cries and if they cry I hope their eyes fall out." These are my sentiments exactly.

Bye mama, if I see you again, we'll have to have a long, long chat.

Reclaiming my Identity

My life's journey continues and will not be complete until my last breath. The question of Why was I left here after October 18, 2005? is answered by the presentation of my memoir. The answer can be nothing else. Hopefully this harvested crop will have quenched a thirst or quieted mild pangs of hunger for understanding.

I was stripped of most of my Adrea (ness) with the exception of my innate abilities of esoteric spiritual awareness, to remain inwardly calm in the face of extreme opposite, to summon resiliency, coupling abiding guiding faith. How else could I have mastered a plan to reclaim my identity, all the while staring down and defying my enemies, past and present? Enmity crept from crevices of all descriptions, while a few armed allies waited for instructions from their tattered, exhausted, and worn, but still standing warrior.

There was no questioning, no time for wistful pondering, no negotiating of anything; only a reaching to, a tapping on, a knowing and trusting of me, me. And so, I reached to my very center, my core, of which I know and trust most. I extracted the truest obliging elements and armed myself with assured determination, delineated myself from all negative energies and persons in my immediate environment, stood erect, squared my shoulders and prepared to defeat the onslaught of some familial, supposed 'friends' new self-styled worthy associates (in their warped minds), and medical practitioners' vermin. I was very grateful that I had made a purposeful and conscientious effort to broaden my physical and mental dexterity in the early 1980s - I was right hand major, so I reversed my watch wearing to my right wrist, vicariously training my left side to look right for the time. I also taught myself to feed myself with my left hand and to write with it as well, so my brain was (thankfully) just about equal in processing ability at the time of my misfortune. I was a former athlete with tremendous physical flexibility, so my brain and body were able to extend in directions untried or untapped by most. "The will to survive" had been hammered in me during my police academy training. Thus, so armed, I began the reclamation of my identity.

****

In the dreaded wintry stillness of my solitaire room, after my grandmother's funeral, I began further strengthening my body as best I could, unaided. Initially, Allen, my uncle and aunt's adopted son, helped me with nightly bed leg raises. I exercised my pelvis and stomach under the covers. I had been prescribed a plethora of presumptive prophylactic medications, including unwarranted anti-seizure medication Dilantin and gabapentin Neurontin, for nerve pain. At one juncture, I was placed on another awful medication, Depakote, (the worst medication I've ever experienced). This medication is designed to keep a person in a non-lucid state, like a frigging zombie. These medications were prescribed, not because of symptoms exhibited by me, but because the medications were widely used in the practice of medicine. I took a cocktail of meds twice a day. The cocktail also included anti-hypertensive (s) and a pill for recently diagnosed Graves' disease (genetically predisposed overactive thyroid). I was a mess; felt myself declining, from lack of focused mental energy. It was becoming all too apparent that I had to take the reins and gain control over my destiny if I was to have a half way independent healthy life post the botched aftermath of my surgery. Added to the onslaught of drugs was my aunt's insistence on regulating and increasing my dietary intake. I do not eat, have never done so, when I take medications. I had and still do maintain excellent gastrointestinal function. Only now, these meds caused habitual constipation. This increase in food without consistent physical ability to exercise caused my weight to increase to my disliking. Pre-surgery I was a size 'petite four', 128 pounds. Now I could almost literally feel myself expanding. That added to my sadness. I obliged my aunt, but slowly began to refuse her late-night snacks of cake wedges or sandwiches with butter pickles.

I became firm with my refusals of almost forced food, (aunt truly meant no harm; just the mother in her) and began to wean myself from those awful meds. My goal was to take only those class of medications I was taking pre-surgery (anti-hypertensive and thyroid). I accomplished this on my own, with greater impetus impaled by response to my observational inquiry of a Social Security psychiatrist to whom I had mentioned, "I don't want that glassy-eyed- far off look," (because of the meds) and she remarked, "Well, you already have it." That did it. Within four weeks, I was off those medications, totally! I did not abruptly cease, just continued weaning according to specifications on the packaging. It worked. I began to taste my freedom, almost literally. I never had any of those awful meds in my system again. Now, I controlled the ingestion of my meds by myself and I ceased food intake with them. My weight readjusted to around 135. I began to think more clearly and set forth a plan to leave my uncle's home. I must note here that as part of proving my ability to live independently, I had to exhibit my capability to Social Security via their psychiatrist or one at Ohio State University where I received primary care. My disability checks had not begun, but when they did I wanted them deposited in my own bank account, not issued to any "Third Party for Me" (to dole out or not as <u>they</u> determined best). Oh, heck no to the nth degree! I drew many clocks for the doctors, to show sequencing ability. Sequencing ability spills over into planning for desired result and even has a mathematical component, in which I'd shown proficient ability in Kaiser in San Leandro rehab. Sequencing and math abilities were the primary ingredients for independency. If I could sequence, I could cook, groom and dress myself, etc. I could add and subtract sufficiently before I arrived in Ohio. My deductive reasoning was another area I was pretty strong in, in my initial scary stages of recovery in California.

With fog lifted from my life source, I set in motion further strengthening of my body and mind. The days were set aside for upper body (hands, fingers, light up and down staircase walking (balance and posture, brain exercises, and dreaded social interactions). Nights were reserved for lower limbs, continued brain strengthening that included reconfiguration of "how to do" with one hand, which I had to do in the day, also). Self-initiated and designed brain exercises included reading poems and books on philosophy and engaging in alphabet and numerical games I had created on my own as a child.

My day strengthening began with my bath. I was a shower person, but there was no free shower in the upper bath. My balance was insufficient to accommodate the installed manual shower nozzle, so I had to take a bath. During the bathing time, I practiced getting in and out with one hand, pulling myself up from a seated position, while ensuring steadiness before grasping the right edge of the tub (sometimes I had to get on my knees first before hoisting) to wash my private areas and then gingerly returning to a seated position. When I became comfortable enough, I would save the private until last, and simply balance on my feet in a squat position and let free-running water rinse me. Then, I'd stand, alternately bend to get cloths full of water to squeeze over my entire body.

Stepping out was easy. Bathing and dressing remains one of my most strenuous activities to the point of near exhaustion, but I only shower now, took my first one in my own home in January, 2007. My shower balancing has returned to pre- incident status, as I can now pick up my cloth, should I drop it, with my curled toes of either foot. One of the best ways to help and test balance is within a staircase; you can walk backwards, down or up; do knee bends while holding the rail. It took me a long time to lead with my left foot, descending steps. Now, I can do it without thinking about it, but that came from months and months of practice, which I still do consciously on occasion. I also practiced walking on my toes, walking heel to toe, front and backwards with eyes closed in my larger living space. I can no longer sprint since I lost left arm swing. However, I am able to lightly jog, only, primarily on a moving treadmill. Something about the belt's movement connects with my brain and I can lift my legs in time with belt speed. God, I miss running almost more than anything I lost, but I am grateful that I could run 50 yards in timed 5.8 seconds and nothing can take that knowing away. I worked on my legs on my bed at night which I still do, but admittedly, not with the vigor I would prefer or had eight years ago. Give a girl a break.

Hand strength and dexterity was accomplished in part with a deck of cards, dice, an ergo ink pen, and regular No. 2 pencil, and because no one really helped me dress, I was compelled to master methodologies to do it by myself, ultimately and gratefully. Picking up cards transferred to grasping small flat items, like coins etc. I had to retrain myself to print. I lost the ability to legibly cursive write. I was ambidextrous and could perform American Sign Language (ASL) before incident. I also am unable to perform ASL. Picking up or maneuvering large articles like a jug of bleach (no problem with a good grip and jerk); a heavy box requires a specifically designed set of movements, aligned the object. This is basic eye-hand coordination or enhanced ability to engage knees, buttocks, legs, and feet for sliding large items across a room. I only maneuver this way in the privacy of my home if I have to scoot while moving a large item or cloth while washing my floors. Fortunately, now, if I have major tasks, I engage another's service for which I sometimes have to pay. I am also unable to style my hair in other than a straight style; cannot roll my hair; neither can I give my own manicures and pedicures as before, so I have to pay to have these done professionally. People have remarked about the mani-pedi, "Just treat yourself". That's not the point. The point is two-fold, an added expense on a fixed income, a cost not incurred before incident because I had expertly done them myself. Add the hair and nails up for a year and it amounts to several thousand dollars, a lot of money when you **have to** spend it, or else it's not done. Believe me, people (purported friends like to see me coming) guaranteed money, 'cause they aren't doing anything for me and certainly not for free. <u>Don't (anyone) ask me how I do anything,</u> (Karen), especially if you have not asked me whether I need help or if you can assist me in any way.

In early to mid-summer, my shorn hair had grown back. I had no summer clothes and Aunt Sadie took me shopping for a few dresses to wear to church. The dresses were cute, very feminine, but for my tastes, too revealing in the breast area, but they looked good on me. I began to wear a little face powder and mascara and one Sunday, after I received all my shoes from friend Karen in California, I put on the lilac with yellow flowers dress and a pair of muted brushed satin purple pumps and went to church as usual. A few male members of the congregation seemed to notice me for the first time, but I'll always be grateful to Brother Bates for truly seeing me beyond that outfit; he saw deep inside my wounded heart and his eyes told me, you're still attractive, you're pretty (again), and physically desirable. Many of the congregation recognized this from Brother Bates, especially in a few Sundays when he, extraordinarily sang a beautiful song, while looking at me. He meant it from his soul and I thank him, again with wet eyes and affectionate appreciation. And then Lady Janice sang her heart out. I was embraced with a whole lot of love that day.

While at Uncle's, I began to ask to do small household things like take out the trash. This activity helped me balance while walking and carrying something while engaging my left side. I would, and still do loop the bag over my left wrist/arm, walk across the yard and back alley, set the bag down. Use my right forearm to push the can lid up and let it fall back on my arm, then flip the lid up with my hand, grab bag and toss it in. I still do this. I also carry groceries on my left arm 2-3 bags at a time simultaneously on left and right while walking up 12 steps to the landing of my apartment home. This activity helps to maintain arm, back, and buttock, and knee, and leg strength, balance, lungs/heart all at the same time.

Essentially every daily activity I perform has been perfected, enhanced, and improved upon over the last eight years. My driving still amazes me because I have been able to successfully integrate interior activities while keeping the car on course with one hand. I'll leave it at that.

Near the end of my stay at Uncle's a small series of events occurred, involving false accusatory statements against me. I will not mention the events or name the persons here, but suffice it to say they were all traumatic enough for me to tell my sister who came and got me for a respite. While gone, my things were searched. I never said a word, just bided my time and laid my plan to exit. I prayed to Allah, my sustainer, nearly constantly. I never became outwardly angry; keeping my calm, while righting my life's course. I was redeemed for continuance of my journey of reclamation.

When I wrote *Thirteen Days* completely from memory (my first story, in 2007), I knew I had been compassionately blessed and favored by Allah. To show my deep appreciation, I continued to reach back into my preserved memory banks and recapture for my earthly audience reels of my existence. Further and on a very personal level, to prove I could compete academically, (just for me), I enrolled in a Bachelor of Science Criminal Justice Administration degree program (graduating in July, 2011 with honors and the highest GPA of all program participants at my university site); my final reclamation activity, after I returned home to California in February, 2009.

I was able to return to California with my identity intact because I had maintained my post office box, a bank account, my California driver license, and California private investigator license, but importantly my best and most trusted allies bade me an unfailing supportive farewell from Ohio as others awaited me, Adrea Anise, all the time I was away.

My trusted allies were and/or remain:

Henry Paige, Pamela McGhee(d.2016), Brenda Lee, Zuberi Mwanathaura (GQ Noonie), Homer Gooden, Uncle Harry and Aunt Sadie Cox, Linda G. Jackson, Cleona Blakely, Karen Lebeau-Montalvan, Austin Lanier (d. 2013), Antoinette Jefferson, Olin Jules Ford (d. 2012), Alvis K. Ford, Mr. Eugene Young, Doris McGhee, Terri Branch, Dianne Derouen-Robinson, Creola Huston, (Pastor Johnny Griffin and Lady Janice Griffin and Serena Wilson, for helping maintain my spiritual equilibrium), Dr. Lawrence Yabroff, and Allah.

Acknowledgement is hereby bestowed upon two stalwart pillars, my uncle, Harry T. Cox and aunt, Sadie L. Cox. Eternal gratitude is submitted to you for opening your home to me during the year of 2006, in order that I regain strength for the promise of my new birth.

Dearest uncle, Harry and aunt, Sadie you not only ensconced me in your love, but you caused me to reaffirm the gifts of joy, peace, faith, and hope.

A year ago I was a wounded bird, but now in large part, because of your nurturing love and support my wings are now strong enough for flight. My nest and perch will not be far away.

May God continue to bless your household.

Your loving niece,
Adrea (Nete)

January 12, 2007

Mr. and Mrs. Cox
Harry T. and Sadie L. (Whitlow) Cox have celebrated their 50th Wedding Anniversary. They were married August 2, 1954 in Williamson, West Virginia. They are the proud parents of five children, tons of great-grandchildren, great-nieces and great-nephews. Mr. Cox is retired from Columbus Board of Education and Mrs. Cox is retired from Crittenton Family Services.

In Memoriam

My life has been touched, impacted, or graced by persons incalculable. However, I acknowledge many of those who have transitioned since my October 18, 2005 incident.

One of the first to leave was a former neighbor, Pam Davis, who responded to assist me in my prelude hours and then upon my brief return after my hospital stays. It wasn't until I was in my own space in Ohio that I learned that she had succumbed to illness she'd shielded from her spouse and me. Other friends transitioning were all very dear to me and included Sterling Boxley, as perfect a physical specimen of man you'd want to lay eyes upon. I say this because his body was exquisitely proportioned; so much so that he was an in-demand nude model for art teachers and students. I was never privy to that kind of viewing, however. Sterling was also an evolved intellectual. Jacqueline (Jackie) Kent, and Andre Jackson. These latter three had at one time period resided in the same building with me during the 1990s. All of them were special spirits and I have included, separately, the remembrances I gave the families of Jackie and Andre. I learned of Sterling's passing while in Ohio as I did Jackie's. Andre and I saw each other within two months of his passing.

My dear friend Joyce Schimizu-Stone's transitioning occurred after my return to Oakland in 2009. Joyce's spirit was one of the grandest I have ever been graced to know. Joyce, too, shielded her illness, pancreatic cancer, from me, politely refusing my requests to visit or have lunch with her. I understood, later, when I received my computer from Ohio and discovered that I had been invited to attend her celebration of life, but it was too late. I spoke with a few attendees and was told, the experience was the most poignantly beautiful they had ever partaken of. Joyce was truly selflessly generous and I miss her. She was one of the first to come to my aid during my time of need (2004), never seeking anything; only that the blows of my condition be softened by a cushion of sanguine optimism. Joyce left two beautiful and scholastically endowed children, Sarah and Alex, among the many who loved and cherished her.

Longtime and special friend Renee McDowell-Jackson. Renee is mentioned in several preceding passages and I add the remembrance submitted to her daughter Rayshawn, and sons Donte and Hasani. She'd be so proud; in fact, she was; but Hasani now has a child. (Rayshawn had two children before Renee's homegoing in 2010).

Three colleague teachers, Mr. Reeder, Mr. Parker, and Mr. Joseph Coy Shields, my mentor for whom I include my remembrance submitted to his earth family.

Four former high school classmates, Shelton Elkins, an author (we shared homeroom from ninth through twelfth grade); Plummer Richardson (we shared birth dates and love of Jimi Hendrix); Herbert Baker (we also shared homeroom for four years and English classes. I allowed Herbert to look on my paper for test answers in 12th grade English; he appreciated that and I was glad to share); and Robert Seats, a successful business and family man. Robert and his wife hosted a marvelously entertaining gathering in their grand Macedonia, Ohio home during our 20th high school reunion weekend. I was honored as a specially invited guest.

Sweet Frances Butler from my childhood days on 123rd in Cleveland. Frances bore four sons, Nelvin, Richard (Tootie), Clarence (Pippi), and Terrance (all friends and playmates). Frances was the aunt of my eldest brother's verifiable first girlfriend, Karen Patterson, daughter of Gerry, Frances' sister. I never not saw Frances when I visited Cleveland. In fact, I visited her right before I returned to California in early 2009. Frances passed away on December 21, 2009, her coincidental birth date. Pippi notified me immediately.

Austin Lanier, my mother's 'boyfriend' in the 1960s who remained my friend until his departure. Austin was like a father figure to me. I have inserted a copy of the letter I wrote his son, Paul, at news of Austin's transition. Nothing to say but a beautiful, caring, patient, and unrelenting giving spirit. He knew what he meant to me as does his family.

My (former) stepfather, Olin Jules Ford. I am compelled to confess that I was mildly disappointed by the fact that I was not acknowledged in his obituary, especially when I acted in synonymous capacity; while still living in Ohio, 2007- early 2009 visiting him a minimum of three times a week during his nursing home stay for his advanced dementia and two days during my 4-day return in 2012. But, I did and do recognize (presumptively) that I was most probably not considered his stepdaughter since he and my mother were divorced. That aside, I nonetheless, respected, loved, and cared about him in the experience in which I kept him. He was my stepfather, memorialized in 2008 in a poem appearing near the beginning of (my) Life's Opera. As he would have said, "I'm off that soapbox."

Annette Poindexter-Ailer, a brilliant woman stricken by blindness and congenital Muscular Dystrophy; she was one of the bravest and undeterred persons I ever knew; teaching French at Cuyahoga Community College; resourceful beyond imagination. It was Annette who was responsible for identifying the government program that allowed my mother to purchase our house on Page Avenue and it was she who phoned in a request for me on WJMO's morning request line to dedicate a song to me and my very secret 9th grade crush, Romerio Moreno, who, thankfully did not hear it, especially since he was pursuing classmate Donna Wells.

My California surrogate family members include, relatives of my friend, Pamela McGhee: her father, Clarence; his mother Maggie (Grandma Maggie/ Miss Maggie) for whom I wrote a separate included remembrance. Grandma lived the longest of all those memorialized, 101 years.

Serena and Ret. Lt. Col. Dr. Howard Wilson (West Virginia and Columbus, Ohio). Serena was a longstanding friend of my mother. Serena, first, and then Howard passed away within months of each other, having been married in excess of 50 years. Posthumously, I came to know more fully the tenure and expansively transcending impact their lives had within their family and the communities they educated, and enhanced through unrelenting dedicated Christian service; exceptionally magnificent in definitively exquisite embodiment, they were and remain.

Mary Griffin (Granny), Aunt Sadie's mother. No one could be in her presence without smiling, giggling, or laughing; Granny was food for everyone's soul. Granny was cheerfully loved by me. Granny was a master at being Granny.

My maternal grandmother, Ada, with whom I spent her last *Thirteen Days*, recalled herein.

First cousins, Daniel Singleton (Skipper), and Laverne Lee, both children of my beloved maternal aunt, Ruth Singleton Maroudas. Fraternal cousins Bill Wright and Sterling Wright; the former, cousin Elaine's brother; the latter Elaine's husband.

A Remembrance for my Friend
Andre Jackson

We met nearly 20 years ago, through a smile and hello as tenants in the same building on Lester Avenue. What a smile it was~ a little hard to figure, a bit of devilment but sincere pleasure, despite ourselves. You possessed that rare quality of instant likability.

So many moments of pure fun, the kind kids have in summer sun, harnessed by serious adult content, You, Jackie, Sterling, and me.

I will always remember returning to California after my three-year exodus and hoping to still find you which I (thankfully) did. I rang your bell and was overjoyed to see you looking down at me and when you said "Stay there, I'm coming down," it was as if you had pelted me with a kiss of your gentlemanly ways. You had to personally escort me in. I was so grateful and although I had physically changed, you never treated me any differently and for that and much more, I will never dissever my soul from yours.

Andre, you were a rare combination: a fearless chicory warrior, defying odds put upon you by societal factions of your decades of service. You did not go unnoticed or unappreciated. I appreciated you.

You impressed me with your charm, wit, culinary skills, (your smothered chicken was my favorite) and ability to maneuver that gigantic caddy. Every time I see one like yours, of course, I think of you, dear sweet man.

I will miss your voicemail messages left on my phone: "This is Andre, please call me back at your earliest convenience." I always did.

There were four of us and now it is just me. I know you did not want to leave, but in full, you paid the price of the ticket, my dear friend. I know you will ride the tide well in all of your mahogany glory. I'll see you on the other side. Until my time to join up, I'll be strong and steady as you would want.

I know God in his grace has embraced you in his abundant arms.

Thank you, Andre for making me laugh, love, smile, and feel like there was no one else in our orbit when we were sharing special friend moments.

Lovingly and Longingly Submitted

With Sincere Condolences and Sympathy

Your Friend,

Adrea

P. S. You still owe me that cup of coffee (smile)

Adrea Adams

In Remembrance of
Jacqueline (Jackie) Kent

Jackie and I met almost 20 years ago, doesn't seem that long now.

It seems the instant we met, we hit it off on an emotional and spiritual level. I was a newcomer tenant in the building in which she resided. We soon became friends, sharing a lot. We talked about our respective careers, our travails through life, including our educational backgrounds, our loves, some unrequited. We shared everything, our commonalities were uncanny. Jackie and I even shared the same astrological birth sign, Capricorn. We enjoyed the same style of cooking, and to this day when I prepare certain foods I always think of Jackie.

Our paths in life took us in different directions, but wherever they led us, we never separated as friends. One of the things I loved about Jackie was her unyielding devotion, deep and abiding love for her family, especially her children, all of whom she was very proud. She spoke of them equally.

Jackie was a true Black woman warrior, always fighting the good fight, whether it was in pursuit of her college degrees at the University of California, Berkeley, while rearing her children, and working full time. Like an Oak, sturdy and erect, only bending in the wind to shield and comfort her children and family with her outstretched boughs.

Jackie also exhibited a fierce dedication to her undertaking with youths at her workplace. Sometimes, she'd be exhausted from her dealings, but she never failed to show up and give them her best. Some lessons I Learned from her and imported them in my classroom as an educator.

I'll remember Jackie as one of my mentors, heroines and good friends.

I'll remember her fondness for the vocals of Sam Cooke and her carrying on about my white beans with pig feet and fried green tomatoes, but they'll never taste the same again without my dear friend Jackie to share them with even if it was sometimes over the many miles of the telephone wire.

I love and miss you much my dear friend.

With all my heart,

Your fellow warrior

Adrea Adams

Adrea Adams

Remembrance for Renee

We met nearly 31 years ago, as budding executives at Hanover Insurance Company in San Francisco. There was something about her engaging smile and "realness." I could tell we were going to become friends. In a sense, she was, at that time, akin to a younger sister. Our relationship flowered into friendship. We were both beginning to step into ourselves as young women. This was a climate of businesses possessing political correctness with coffers spilling monetary reserves. Renee and I were among six or so African American females favored for advancement in Hanover's Claims Department. I recall Renee's interview date with manager Tom Jacobson for the position of Adjuster Trainee. Tom was very impressed with Renee's desire to advance in the health care industry; studying while holding a full-time job and caring for her beautiful children, Rayshawn and Donte. Renee received the promotion. Ultimately, Renee's heart and spirit drew her return to the health care industry and she prospered therein. I have many fond memories of Renee and her children. I will share one amusingly funny one about Renee and me.

Renee liked music, especially concerts. We frequently attended concerts "in the round" in San Carlos' Circle Star venue. One evening, we readied ourselves for Aretha Franklin. Now, anybody knowing Renee and me in those days knew we girls could throw back some beer. Renee decided to have one before we began our jaunt in my Monza across the San Mateo Bridge. I only had a few sips of my bottle but Renee drank most of hers. We were, of course, very cute that balmy autumn night. Renee had on a crisp pantsuit and heels. About midway of the bridge, Renee's bladder called. I gunned the engine and almost sprouted wings to the first Foster City exit. "Hold on girl", I kept saying, we're almost there." "Oh, Adrea, I'm trying but I don't think I can make it." Girl, you can't pee in my seat, you're gonna mess up your suit." "I can get it cleaned and wipe off this pleather seat." "Hold on Renee." These went back and forth until, screech; I landed in the curve of the exit. Part of Renee's smile was still there as I drove into the lot of a Denny's next to a row of bushes. "Adrea, I have to go." "Go girl, in the bushes, no one will see you squatted down." Go, from the car, she did. However, just as she swung the door open with pants ready for lowering, a couple happened by. They knowingly smiled and walked on by. Renee probably told this story several times and I hope I've done it justice. It was one of our comical moments as friends. We made it to the show on time and had a ball. Aretha appeared in all white and did not disappoint.

One of Renee's favorite singers and performers was Teddy Pendergrass. She also enjoyed Bobby Blue Bland and B. B. King. One of the last times she entertained me, we played bid whist. We could put a hurting on you in a bid whist game while smacking on some bar- b- cue. Renee could cook. One of my favorite things of hers was baked turkey wings and her boss gravy. She was fond of my lemon chicken, a recipe I stole from mutual friend and Hanover co-worker Charles Dudley.

We shared the date of -July 12-, her birth date and my wedding date which was chosen before we met and it made her feel extra special to have commonality with that date, so I guess you could say we were kindred spirits.

Thank you, Renee, for everything, all the memories, and joyous times with you and your family. Especially, I am grateful that you allowed me to be a part of your children's lives. We will be there for them, on that, you can be sure.

May God ensconce you, in His abundant arms. Rest well, dear Renee.

Your always loving friend,

Adrea

P. S. Teddy came on my station as I signed this remembrance so I am certain you are together.

February 15, 2012

Dearest Father Howard,

It is with tremendous sorrow and deepest condolence that I submit to you my remembrance of your Serena.

From sheer respect, and adoration I referred to your earth love as 'Mother Serena.'

For me she represented the ultimate best in humanity, transcending with unparalleled dignity and grace all boundaries and spatiality's of gender and ethnocentricities.

Mother Serena's quiet yet surged energies penetrated the lives and spirits of many and I shall always cherish and hold dear the very special love and care she exhibited for me in the absence of my own mother; especially during my time of physical and spiritual strengthening need. There she remained for me, unyielding in her tenaciousness. For that, I am forever grateful and indebted, but I am sure she knew.

I share with you a fond recollection Mother Serena relayed to me about a time in her and my mother's youthful exuberance and daring wonderment: As you know, my mom was blind, but nonetheless wanted to experience the thrill of driving a car. In accommodation of my mother's desire, Mother Serena acquiesced, drove her auto to an open field near Williamson, West Virginia, and permitted my mother to get behind the wheel and go for a spin. I can only imagine the excitement of that moment but knowing them both it was a moment in time occurring with heightened and giddy anticipation as only youth could bring two friends in the summer of their wondrous lives.

Now, it is not the winter of discontent, but a season for rejoicing as your Serena surely sings with the angels as God embraces her in his abundant arms.

Humbly Submitted with Rivers of Love,

Adrea Adams (Nicie)

July 8, 2013

Dear Paul,

It was very good to speak with you last week.

I will share with you my fondest remembrances of your dad, Austin.

My mother moved from Columbus to Cleveland in 1964 when I was seven. We lived on Kinsman across from A. J. Rickoff Elementary, where Arsenio Hall was also a student.

Somehow, and somewhere during my mom's introduction to Cleveland, she met Austin. It may have been at a 'cool' entertainment venue The Majestic Hotel, on 55th that featured local musician talent in the Negro community –or– it's most likely they were introduced at Children's Aid Society where Austin worked and my brother attended school.

I vividly recall the first time my mom brought Austin to meet us kids. We lived on 88th between Euclid and Carnegie. Mama was a single parent and rarely brought adult males to our home, so we knew Austin must be someone extra special. And…extra special he was indeed.

Austin was tall and slender and possessed the kindest and most reassuring voice. He seemed to 'take' to us immediately. I distinctly remember him asking for an ashtray to prepare his pipe for smoking. I eagerly placed an ashtray on the coffee table. I had never seen anyone pack and smoke a pipe, so I sat enthralled and consumed every move he made; the tapping of old tobacco from the pipe, his reaching inside the upper left front pocket of his powder blue short-sleeved shirt from which he drew a pipe and plastic bag. He tapped the hickory bowled pipe's contents into the ashtray, opened the folded clear plastic bag, removed a skinny, white, flat, flexible stick, and swirled that tiny stick inside the pipe's bowl. Next, Austin used his right index finger and thumb and removed some tobacco from the plastic bag. He then packed the bowl with his thumb. Boy, was I enthralled. I kept rushing him to finish and he did, finally. He lit the pipe as he crossed his legs at the knee, left over right, sat back and changed my world forever when he blew out the first puffs of one of the sweetest things I've ever smelled, cherry tobacco. I studied Austin, in a sense, from a little girl's perspective and determined after some years that Austin had the nicest fingers and nail beds I'd seen, (except perhaps my own father's). Austin's nails were always clean and trimmed.

Austin ultimately became much more to me than cherry tobacco and healthy hands.

Austin and my mom stopped dating in the late 60s or early 70s, but remained close friends throughout our (then) young lives. - Time passed, but over the years when my mom would get an itch to uproot us kids in either Cleveland, or from Columbus back to Cleveland, my mom would call Austin who seemed to appear as if a genie of sorts. The last time and from my grateful perspective, Austin moved us from Columbus to Cleveland. He had brought Reginald and Rogovan to help load the truck. It was a wintry or early spring day, cold as all get out- Gomer Pyle, USMC was playing on the TV as we finished packing and the twins tussled w/ me (that is another story).

My mother took ill in 1987-1988 but Austin remained in phone contact with her in Columbus where she'd finally returned. I cared for my mom in her latter days- she succumbed to breast cancer July 10, 1988. Austin visited during this time.

Austin and I remained friends and although I lived in California, I always visited him when I was in Cleveland - I remembered and was thankful for the many times Austin ensured we had food or a 'ride' somewhere, and all of his good Godly deeds.

As you know I suffered some health issues of my own and when in Twinsburg in 2009, Austin would occasionally come get me, take me to Cleveland Clinic for physical therapy and return me home. He also took me to food banks when I hit a rough spot. Additionally, I also visited his home frequently once I got a car. I was surprised to learn he was still serving as community 'jitney' cab, another way he earned funds in the 60s. He was a hustler, when the word meant something good, -bless his heart.

The last time I saw Austin was April 5, 2012. We went outside so he could smoke his pipe, but the wind was too strong, so I walked him back to his unit. I was a little disappointed because I wanted to smell cherry tobacco packed and smoked by my beloved and cherished friend Austin Lanier.

Nothing can ever dissever my spirit from the true gift of Austin, one of the best persons my mom ever introduced to my life.

Paul, may your God comfort you, as Austin is ensconced in the abundant arms of his Faithful Savior.

Sincere sympathy, condolences, and abiding love,

Nicie (Adrea) Adams

P. S. When you can, I'd very much appreciate you sending me the pictures we talked about. Thank you.

In Remembrance of
Joseph Shields

I can still see him on that bright sunshine morning in October 2001, walking and talking (or rather power brokering,) his way through the front office of Fremont High School. I knew something was up and that I had to make my acquaintance known. Within a few days my main task had been accomplished. It wasn't really a task, but maybe so, being that I was a bit intimidated. I was new at teaching and all that came along with it. Mr. Shields revealed in short order that he was a pro and could maneuver his way around. My eyes were on him and his great bundle of energy, which he propelled in all directions.

Not too long after our first meeting and my first observation of Mr. Shields' class' up on the hill at Fremont, I knew I wanted to follow in his footsteps and teach English as a Second Language to the *Newcomers* just as Mr. Shields did. At every opportunity, I would visit Mr. Shields' classroom and observe one of the masters at work. I had a ball, a grand churn of a time. Anytime Mr. Shields asked, not very often though, I would oblige him and fill in for him or assist with any project benefiting him, his students, or the fluidity of Fremont's advancement.

Circumstances presented themselves so that I was contracted by choice to return to Fremont for the school year of 2002-2003. Mr. Shields was placed in charge of the CAHSEE Testing which was all consuming. I offered to take over his classes and while I was not a fully credentialed teacher, Mr. Shields expressed to the principal his preference for me to assume his teaching duties that I was more than happy to undertake.

Near to the end of 2002, I was observed teaching Mr. Shields' class by Lee Denlinger of John F. Kennedy University. I was reciting from text, the lyrics of "Sail On," feeling very much in control as the engaged eyes and ears of the *Newcomers* advanced towards me. I was enjoying myself a lot, I was teaching and it felt good.

Ms. Denlinger and I spoke after class and she convinced me to consider enrolling in JFK's graduate program.

I entered JFK's master's program in January 2003 with a full schedule. I never missed a day, I'd rush to my car after the last bell at Fremont, zip to and through the Caldecott tunnel just in time for my 4:00 class. I was so giddy with excitement each day; I was living a childhood dream. Only this was a lot better than teaching my stuffed animals and writing on the wallpapered walls of my bedroom under the threat of a spanking by my mama.

Mr. Shields had become my mentor, one of the most appreciated enablers of my life. I'm sure he knew what he meant to me. Yes, I'm sure he knew. Mr. Shields was also the one, who, when I had to relocate to Ohio hosted my return party in 2006.

Thank you, Mr. Shields. Your smile and humor will always reside within my spirit. Your tireless and unrelenting giving was indeed recognized. I am certain the Lord God has anointed you with oil enough so that your golden cup surely overflows where thou art.

I miss and love you dear friend and unselfish mentor.

Lovingly Submitted,

Adrea Adams

3, March 2008

Remembrance for
Daniel "Skipper" Gregory
Beloved Cousin

My list of memories is lengthy. Skipper addressed me as Niec, an abbreviation of my nickname Niecy. Not much else that I know of was abbreviated by Skipper. He lived fully and shared whole heartedly of himself, - and seldom without a smile or words to cause you, the receiver of his smile, to laugh or giggle –

Skipper was a philosopher of sorts, a gregarious teacher. In my early (little girl days), Skipper instructed me in many "how-to's". I learned from Skipper to scramble eggs with just the right amount of oil and still I think of him whenever I prepare eggs.

In the middle room, separating Mama Ada's barbershop from the hall, I learned from Skipper the "proper" manner of ironing a shirt, "military-style." And I can share that I can crease a shirt like nobody's business (no wrinkles in my shirt sleeves) (always impressed the men I've loved with "Skipper inspired, permanent creased upper backs/beneath the collar and point-extenuating sleeve and squared cuff creases". Thanks, Skip.

Although he was seven years my senior, Skipper always treated me as his intellectual equal, and that endeared me to him even more.

We shared all kinds of tells and tales. Some tell-tales tall, some not so, at all. Mostly though, our bond was of a braided love. The love stemmed from his birth mother Ruth, and her sister, Carletha. Plaited, we were by this blood bond – and it was with the greatest of joy I spoke with him a little while ago.

Ensconced is Skipper, now, in the abundant arms of our Compassionate and Almighty. Yet, my heart mourns and bleeds.

Humbly and Sincerely Submitted are my deepest condolences and sympathies to those who loved Skipper best.

Bleeding heart of Cousin Niecy

02-23-2011

May 12, 2009

Dear Aunt Sadie,

I extend you and the rest of the family my very deepest condolences and sympathy at the passing to Glory of dear Granny.

You and your immediate family had Granny for a very long time. Thank you for sharing her. She will be remembered by me as one of my favorite personalities I've experienced and enjoyed. I loved her a great deal and shall carry with me a bit of her charm, sass and wit.

May you continue to be comforted by the knowing that Granny is resting with the Lord, now.

You're always in my prayers, Aunt.

All my love to you,

Nicie

Adrea Adams

In Remembrance of
Maggie McGhee "Grandma"

She wasn't my grandmother by blood lineage or marriage, but she was mine nonetheless. Grandma was a pistol, even owned one for a time, just in case. Quiet, proud, even regal in her own way.

Grandma always greeted me, "Hi, you looking' good or "Your hair sho' looks nice" The nice was drawn out slightly with a Louisiana accent. I always smiled, kissed her, held one of her soft mahogany hands and helped her with anything she needed and then, I'd sit and listen or ask for life advice. Grandma never failed to make me laugh and feel good, no matter what or who was taking place elsewhere. We talked about everything and I do mean everything. Now, hush, I'm not telling of our private moments.

One of my fondest memories is of the time I readied her for an after - 5 family affair. I dressed her all in white and instructed her not to spit any Cannonball "bacca" while I returned home to dress. When I returned to her upper floor flat, there she sat with slightly poked lips, as pretty as a baby in christening whites and without nary a stain. We had a good time that evening and I took lots of pictures. I gave her one of us together. That picture is one of my favorites.

Grandma could cook and one of her favorite things was "ghetties" as she called spaghetti. She also enjoyed chitterlings and I'd sometimes bring her a restaurant dinner of some with rice with gravy and cabbage. I could tell about the time Grandma received a "Special Delivery" coon but all who were around that day will remember. Mother Hattie dressed it with the prescribed sweet potatoes and Grandma's figurative, soft, Louisiana whine was quieted.

Babies, especially her grands or great grands, each carry a special nickname that only she could bestow.

Grandma had recently been honored by President and First Lady Obama, who'd acknowledged her 101st birthday by sending her written recognition of this earthly milestone. I read it to her. Grandma seemed somewhat un-phased, remarking with a smile, "That's nice, baby."

I'm sure you're in heaven Grandma, and having a groovy time. Thank you so very much, beautiful and gracious one. I've been enriched for the better.

Your loving granddaughter,

Adrenne (as you called me)

Adrea

I'll miss you but I have your voice on tape to hear any time I need a good honest hug.

May 7, 2014

Dear Reginald,

I write you with a heavy heart, but not nearly as heavy as yours at the transitioning of your cherished brother-twin.

You know, I have innumerable memories of fun and philosophically engaging moments. I remember so much and I am glad I never lost touch with you both over all these many, many years.

I looked up to you both, admired and respected you for all you were and contributed to your country and your close-knit family. You both are placed in the category of my brother Keith, albeit, I was closer to you and Rogovan since Keith left us as a teen.

I remember being one of very few in my age group able to distinguish you from Rogovon. I never lumped you by calling you or him "Twin." Rogovon had his own distinctive characteristics and I recognized in him his groundedness and innate ability to pull you in; not that you ever strayed too far. (Smile)

Proudly and with some relief, I recently completed my autobiographical memoir, titled (MY) Life's Opera. I am enclosing a few of the introductory pages and one sampling. As I mentioned in my Facebook post to you of today, you and Rogovon are mentioned in a few sections.

A few moments, I am unable to distinguish, like which one of you introduced me to Etta James' voice in your Terrace Rd. apartment. I bought that album and still have it: "Etta James", the back album cover notes stating:

> one bird in the midnight
> beat wings against the mist

> broke one cry out of darkness
> to color the air;
> long before morning was there
> one song spoke
> with hungry tenderness
> reaching to be heard-
> one bird at dawn.
> Catherine Williamson '73

Rogovon is the bird, having completed his earthly flight, and is now perched in the abundant arms of his almighty Savior and Lord.

Reginald, you knew him first and longest in our time, but he was God's creation. You will have comfort knowing this.

Humbly submitted with my deepest condolences and sympathy,

Your loving friend,

Nicie

I Fill Better

Been purged, been on a continuous life-long purge

Emptied my bowels and shed those funky garments, the sometimes burdensome cloaks of others, just life stuffs.

Once and absolutely suddenly I was tommy-gunned nearly to my death. It stung, yes, they, those yawning caverns, but I kept my cool, always kept my cool. Good thing.

I caught my breath, held on and kept my sight force in high gear.

Dedications to not repeat, only to fill better.

I fill better

I fill with better love, better voices from within and without

I fill with different, better trust

My amniotic fluid has been extracted from my uterine spirit with all diseased beings I know or knew drained and cleansed away, whether supposed friend or family

Simply, I fill better

Not for what I have lost

But for what I have done

Adrea's favorite picture of herself (in a tree, Lake Merritt, Oakland, CA). She's still climbing.

About the Author

The author was born to a legally blind and partially deaf father and a totally blind mother.

It is suspected that her parents' disabilities were instrumental factors in the author reading and writing at three years of age. The printed word has always brought the author a sense of joy, freedom, enlightenment, and calm. Writers who have influenced the author have been Nikki Giovanni, Paul Laurence Dunbar, James Baldwin, Edgar Allen Poe, and Richard Bach.

The author's first book of poetry, "I'm so angry with myself, but I Smell Good" received copyright in 1991. That book will be retitled "Dripping Sweetness." Although the author began her autobiography in 2005, she became ill, underwent surgery after which she suffered two strokes leaving her hemiplegic and with the use of only one hand. Unable to type as rapidly as before, the author undertook the writing of her *Life's Opera* in the form of short stories and poems exclusively with her right hand. This was done in an effort to share her personal account of overcoming major obstacles through abiding faith, stamina, and perseverance.

Adrea has Bachelor of Science Degrees in Management and Criminal Justice Administration, in addition to a State of California Private Investigator License, which Adrea considers a Master degree, essentially.

I am a cosmic being, schematically designed for exploration, utilizing 'higher-order' critical thinking. I engage a complex network of creative action within my community (a fraternalized composite of hyper-individualism) re-imagined and re-routed for charity and equality of theologies predicated upon the thesis of the integration of immense creativity, thus my role as a human.

~Adrea Adams~
05-25-13

www.ingramcontent.com/pod-product-compliance
Lightning Source LLC
Chambersburg PA
CBHW071856290426
44110CB00013B/1162